The Birhors of Chotanagpur Region

(A Study in Tribal Geography)

Dedicated
to
my Parents

The Birhors of Chotanagpur Region

(A Study in Tribal Geography)

Sudhir Kumar

RAJESH PUBLICATIONS

New Delhi - 110 002

ISBN : 81-85891-40-0

Published by :
M.L. Gupta
Rajesh Publications
1, Ansari Road, Darya Ganj,
New Delhi - 110002

Typesetting by :
Sanjay Gupta
Sanjay Enterprises
New Delhi- 110002

Printed in India at :
A.P. Offset Printing Press, Delhi -2

Ist Published in India : 2004

RAJESH PUBLICATIONS
Rs. 500.00

Contents

Preface

Sociologists and Anthropologists have done extensive works on tribal conditions, habitation and social organization. Most of their works basically concentrate on the institution and genetic aspects of the tribes. Even their works on tribal culture hardly touch the basic aspects of the tribal culture, particularly those which concern land and people. Most of the works by them lack empiricism and are necessarily based on pre-conceived notion . Their works hardly touch upon genre de vie of the tribes and their works are peripheral in nature. It was due to these shortcomings that in most of the tribal works of sociologist and anthropologist, it became a necessity for geographers particularly those geographers who see 'human aspect' in geography, and necessarily feel to take up tribal studies in spatial perspectives. It is with this notion in the mind that an in depth study has been done with regard to life-style of the Birhor population in geographical context. The Birhors are a little known forest tribe with small population inhabiting in mountain and forest areas of Chotanagpur region, particularly in Hazaribagh ,Ranchi and Gumla district. Before being colonized under Government Welfare Schemes, the Birhors had been practicing nomadism and their population declined rapidly. However, with the Government efforts their mortality was checked and fear of being vanished, disappeared. Geographical study of the Birhor is important in two senses, firstly, to identify their habitation in the region, and secondly their social organization in spatial perspective. Since the work is positivist in nature, it seeks to develop hypothesis with the view to empirically develop theoretical structure about their life style. This aspect of human geography is not much developed in the country and there is a need for such work. Geographical works of any nature are empirical in character as a result such works carry more realistic explanation than other works done in other social sciences. The work is divided in Eight Chapters - The First Chapter deals with the conceptual aspects which includes aims and objectives, overview of Literature and Hypothesis. The Second Chapter concentrates on geographical background of Chotanagpur region. The Third Chapter is concerned with the Birhor economy while the Fourth Chapter deals with the Birhors settlement geography. The Fifth Chapter studies the demographic aspects of Birhors and Sixth

Chapter , studies the Birhor's cultural aspects and pattern. The Seventh Chapter is empirical study of seven Birhors villages and Last Chapter being the conclusion about the Birhors.The author welcomes critical comments and suggestions on the book.

Sudhir Kumar

Acknowledgement

I express my sincere gratitude to Prof. L.N. Ram, Prof. G.P. Jha, Prof. V.N.P. Sinha and Prof. R.B.P. Singh of Geography Department of Patna University, Patna for their advice and support.

I want to express my deepest sense of gratitude to Prof. S. Adhikari, Head of the Department of Geography, B.N. College, Patna University for his valuable suggestion and continuous encouragement.

I am also thankful to Dr. K.K.Maltiar, Reader in Geography, Mr. Ratan Kumar, Lecturer in Geography, Dr. A.R.K. Sinha, B.N. College, Patna University and Dr. Alok Kumar, Reader in Geography, Maharaja College, Veer Kuer Singh University, Ara, for their advice.

I am also thankful to Dr. Md. Ataullah, Univeristy Professor and Head of the Department, P.G. Deptt. of Geography, Nalanda College, Bihar Sarif for his support.

I am grateful to Mr. Ranendra Kumar (B.A.S.) , Block Development Officer of Bishunpur Block, Gumla, Mr. Sunil Kumar (B.A.S.), Block Development Officer, Angara, Ranchi and Mr. Anil Kumar Yadav, Block Agriculture Officer, Sadar Block, Hazaribagh, for their co-operation during my field work.

I am deeply indebted to my parents Mr. R.S. Roy and Ms. Radhika Roy, brothers Dr. Sunil Kumar, Dr. Abhay Kumar, Mr. Anand Prakash and Mr. Om Prakash, my sister -in-laws Ms. Seema Roy, Ms. Sunita, Ms. Rajni and Ms. Prabha, my sister Ms. Premlata, my brother-in-law Dr. Nand Gopal, my wife Poonam, my daughter Richa and other close relatives for their valuable emotional support and encouragement without which this work was just not possible.

I am grateful to my friends Mr. Raj Kumar Sinha, Mr. Prem Kumar Mishra, Dr. Rajiv Kumar, Mr. Jetendra Singh Deo, Mr. Rajesh Kumar Singh, Mr. Sanjay Kumar, Ms. Sunita Verma, Mr. Vikash Kumar Yadav and Mr. Arun Kumar.

I am grateful to Mr. Lakhan Prasad of the Department of Geography, P.U., for help in the cartographic work. I am also grateful to librarians of P.U. Central Library, Seminar Library, Department of Geography, P.U., A.N. Sinha Institute of Social Studies, Patna, Sinha Library Patna, and Bihar Tribal Research Welfare Institute Library, Ranchi.

Sudhir Kumar

List of Figures

List of Tables

1

Introduction

"Geography" is concerned with the description and explanation of the areal differentiation of the earth's surface.[1] In geography, exists mutually 'exclusive' and sometimes mutually 'inclusive' parallel thinking which intrinsically leads to 'dualism' in the discipline. These parallel thinking, sometimes contradictory in nature, one basically concerned with the 'raison d'etre' of geography - whether it should emphasize the study of physical phenomena or human phenomena ? The above definition is vague in the sense that it does not specify as to what 'areal differentiation' requires to be described and explained-physical or human ? Not with standing its synthetic character, the discipline of geography on account of its dualistic character appears to be divisible into physical geography and human geography.

Physical geography deals with the natural features of the earth's surface or in other words, physical geography is concerned with the areal differences in physical phenomena on the earth's surface. Human geography, on the other hand, is concerned with the relationships between man's activities and the physical environment. It is the synthetic study of the relationship between human societies and the earth's surface. 'Human beings arrange their lives in geographical space. They exist and perform their activities of specific location, and they move or distribute things in certain direction. They, thus, give character to places or areas, differentiating and connecting them with respect to various aspect of human conditions. Human differentiation in geographical space, forms system of region, or areas distinguished by some particular characteristic bestowing homogeneity or functional cohesion. The man made landscape is a college of these roads, networks and region.'[2]

In parallel with geography as a whole, human geography is made up of three closely linked components: the spatial analysis of the human population; the human-biospheric system and the regional synthesis which combines the first two components, there is an Areal Differentiation of the earth's surface.

All three themes are pursued at various spatial scales leading down from the macro- level to the micro-level.[3] With the passage of time, and particularly with the methodological and philosophical changes in the nature of geography is in the post -war period, human geography experienced systematisation, that 'idiographic concern with areal differentiation in human phenomena' was replaced by a 'nomothetic search for models of spatial structure ; and the sub-discipline tended to become a 'law-seeking discipline'. It has an obvious impact on the fundamental structure of human geography that distinct human phenomena is be studied individually within the framework of systematic paradigm. A number of distinct branches of human geography, concerning with various phenomena of areal association came to be developed, such as: population geography social geography, tribal geography, cultural geography, economic geography, urban geography, rural geography, agricultural geography, industrial geography and political geography. All these branches require to be model-based and law-seeking, and they successively experienced paradigmatic shifts.

Tribal geography is an emergent branch of human geography as it intrinsically deals with tribal phenomena in areal context. A tribe is a group of people with a 'Subsistence primitive genre de vie; ' inhabiting distant, inaccessible forested, and mountainous tracts, particularly in the frontier zones of the ekumenes. A tribe is distinguished by its territorial-specification and territoriality, and is equally held together by a common iconography or system of belief. A tribe is distinguished by its rudimentary social organisation.

Till recently, the study of tribes was confined to Anthropology-the discipline, however, specifically concerns itself with the institutional aspects of racial structure and genetics of various tribes but, is little concerned with the spatial attributes and areal differences of tribal phenomena, particularly the 'genre de vie' of various tribal people. The necessity of geographical study of the tribes was felt in the 50's when attempts, in USA were made to start a new Sub-branch of human geography. Population Geography that inhabitants who were pushed into the frontier and beyond the stipulated frontier as a result of innovation, diffusion in the Christian World, required to be studied in areal and regional perspective. Nevertheless, the geographical study of the tribes, had an intermittent beginning.

In India, too, the necessity of the geographical study of the tribes was felt in the mid - 50's when the new republic was undergoing sustained political- territorial changes regardless of the geographical pattern of the tribals genre de vie in different regions of the Republic. Tribal geographical patterns in the non-ekumene area were not taken into consideration at the time of the territorial restructuring of the federation. The tribes remained the most neglected lots and they had to contend with their Primitive subsistence genre de vie. The Tribal insurgency in the federation, particularly in the Northeast led to the beginning of intensive tribal studies in various disciplines and in geography, it started in the 70's and specific targeted areas in geographic research included were; demographic and population aspects, economic and cultural aspects with emphasis on variable nature of tribal genre de vie, and political aspects.

Indian geographers seek to identify the nature and scope of tribal geography in ten broad categories; (i) The study of the distribution of tribal social phenomena; (2) Study of the tribal concept of the natural area, and cultural area (3) Study of the adaptation of area; (4) The study of the geographical basis of tribal society, (5) The Study of the differentiation in term of tribal Characteristics (6) The Study of the tribal/ cultural landscape morphology, (7) Impact of innovation diffusion on tribal genre de vie, (8) The Study of the dynamics of tribal population (including distribution, density, growth and migration); (9) The Study of regionalisation of tribal groups societies, and (10) the study of tribal cultural ecology.

Tribal geography is sometimes defined as the identification of different tribal region of the earth's surface according to association of tribal phenomena related to the total environment. To Maheswari,[4] tribal geography is that branch of geography which studies tribal society, both tribes and their environment, and interaction with different non-tribal societies. Tribal geography, remarks Alok[5], consists of systematic analysis of tribes, in spatial and temporal perspective.

However, the above definitions suffer from philosophical and methodological weaknesses, therefore, an attempted definition is given. Tribal Geography is the study of ways in which spatial variations in the distribution, composition, migration, growth of tribal population are related to the nature of plans, and demonstrates how spatial variations are related to the spatial variation in the nature of places. It is indeed a systematic spatial analysis of tribal genre de vie. The understanding of tribal phenomena, within the systematic paradigm, operating in an area, helps in identifying the wide variety of causal connection between tribal people and total Physical, biotic and cultural environment. Tribal geography is a part of a whole that manifests human geography.

Tribal geography seems to have positive relationships with anthropology, sociology, demography, economic and history. Since anthropology's main concern lies in three major problems of man; the evolution of man; the auto-genetic development and the classification of human races, but when the spatial attributes of these 'concerns' are taken into consideration, the study comes well within the domain of tribal geography. Hence anthropology and tribal geography are inseparable from each other.

Similarly the study of tribal Social Phenomena and their attributes in areal context, is to bring together sociology and tribal geography at a common integrated place. Tribal geography's relationship with demography requires to be visualized in term of the statistical analysis of vital statistic of tribal population. The study of tribal population change intrinsically relies on the techniques of demography. Similarly, tribal geography's proximity to economics can be viewed in term of the later 's paradigm being applied to analyze the tribal economy. Historical techniques are a necessity in tribal geography but particularly when the tribal landscape morphology is studied. Nevertheless, tribal geography is rapidly becoming a law-seeking sub unit or branch of human geography, hence, it is model-based.

The present work attempts to make a geographical study of a tribe, the Birhors, which were till recently not much known to geographers though the tribe was known to the anthropologists and sociologists. But they were not much clear about their habitat and genre de vie.

The Birhors may be rightly called the 'forest mountain' tribe as they dwell in the jungle as well as in the mountainous tracts of theChotanagpur Region, Particularly in the inaccessible areas of Hazaribagh, Ranchi, and Gumla. Some isolated patches of their undefined habitats occur in Madhya Pradesh, Orissa and West Bengal but with little significance. Till recently, the Birhors were a wandering or nomadic tribe, rooming across the forest and mountains. Nevertheless, a section of Birhor, comprising, perhaps, the majority have been brought to be settled down in the neighbourhood of their undefined habitat, under various government welfare schemes in the past three decades. The wandering Birhors are called 'Uthḷu' whilst those who become 'sedentary' are known as 'Jaghis or Pariya'. With the passage of time, Uthlu Birhors and Jaghis Birhors are becoming mostly exclusive, while the Uthlu or Wandering Birhors are yet to develop their specific habitat, the sedentary Jaghis Birhors have developed their habitat, as they have been settled. The Birhor constitutes an interesting tribe, hitherto, unknown to the geographers, and a geographical study will certainly unfasten some of the mysteries concerning their genre de vie.

Aims and Objectives of the Study

Every work proceeds with certain specific aims and objectives for meaningful interpretations, and finding. Since the present work is concerned with the Birhors- a tribe with an 'Undefined habitation' across the forest, hill and mountain of Hazaribagh, Ranchi and Gumla, it requires an indepth study with specific aims and objectives.

One of the foremost objectives of the present work is to identify sedentary Birhor villages - vis-a-vis the limit of the habitable tracts of the wandering Birhors. Even the Uthlu (Wandering) Birhors have certain areas of their mobility in search of livelihood confined to those areas. These areas of spatial mobility require to be identified in the work . It is also proposed to study the impact of large scale depletion of the forest cover on the life of the wandering Birhor as the depletion greatly reduces the forest based resource availability. To what extent has the depletion of forest base resources affected the genre de vie of the wandering Birhors.?

The study would like to determine to what extent has non-spontaneous settlement of the Birhor under various welfare schemes changed the genre de vie of the 'sedentary' Birhor. It is proposed to study whether or not the Birhors have developed territorial feeling and to what extent has their genre de vie territorialised and regionalised ? or is it still marginalised ? The study would like to concentrate on the Birhor culture ecology in the humanistic and welfare perspectives so as to enumerate the tribe's quality of life. The Birhors are a neglected tribe in all accounts, and a geographical interpretation will be of vital importance to the social scientists.

One of the important objectives of the study is to make an in-depth geographical interpretation of the Birhor economy in the ecological perspective - characters, distributions, classification, regularity, system, primitiveness and change ones. It also proposes to study the institutional aspects, with their spatial attributes of the Birhor economy.

The work further proposes to study the spatial of the Birhor population, with a view to demonstrate how variation in composition and growth is related to the areal variations in the nature of places.

Finally, the work would try to identify and determine the morphology of the Birhor landscape particularly in the sedentary villages. It also proposes to determine the wild landscape of the wandering Birhors.

However some works on the Birhors have been done by the sociologist and anthropologists in the recent past which require to be reviewed before any formal hypothesis - statements of problems is to be developed.

Review of Literature - Large number of research works and projects have been done by the anthropologists, sociologists and to an extent by geographers on various Indian tribes in the light of their environment and genre de vie, and quite a good number of these also concentrate on demographic aspects of various tribes. Major tribes of Bihar have also been studied but very few research works seem to have been done on the Birhor tribe which is evident from the following review of the existing works and literature including those concerning with other tribes. The review is being done chronologically.

Roy (1917[6], 1925[7]) Studies the Birhor habitation in the light of the tribes, wandering nature. Mitra (1932[8]) studies the nature and incidence of cruelty among the Birhors of the Chotanagpur and makes a reference of spatial nature of Birhors' cannibalism. Bhattachariya (1953[9]) makes a graphic account of the Birhors, of the Palamu in which he seeks to identify the tribes' habitable part in the area/district. Sen, et al (1955[10]) provide an explanatory note on the Birhor. Francis (1957[11]) studies the institutional aspects of the nomadic Birhor. Sharma (1958[12]) studies the way of living of the wandering Birhor, particularly in the light of the tribes, non-specific habitable areas across the plateau region.

Sinha (1958[13], 1959[14], 1959[15]) Provides a graphic but explanatory accounts of the Birhors' changing adaptation to the natural and social milieu. The first work makes a study of relationship between the Birhor' cultural group, i.e., the Birhor showing a common mode of life, both material and mental, and its natural environment, drawing upon the biological analogy of the animal and plant life style adjusting to and exploiting its natural habitat in specific ways. The last work, however, concerns itself with description of portrait of Birhor Chief.

Vidyarthi (1954[16], 1960[17]) makes a sensual perception analysis of the Birhor in his studies. The first work intrinsically deals with the territorial specification vis-a-vis the area of the tribes, mobility in ecological perspective whilst second one studies the cultural ecology vis-a-vis the reciprocity and the adaptability that the tribe expresses through its response.

Singh (1963[18]) makes a descriptive study of the fecundity and fertility aspects of the Birhor women. The work is not substantiated by authentic data. It is a simple description and does not intend to specify the amount of change it involves in the Birhor population. Malhotra l (1963[19]) studies the leadership and ethno-political aspects of the Birhor.

Rana (1964[20]) studies the vital statistics of the Birhor of West Bengal but his work is short of analytical data therefore the work is more descriptive rather than analytical. Choudhary (1965[21]) makes an analytical study of the life and culture of the Birhor tanda. However the work does not give any specific idea of the Birhor habitation. Sachchidanand (1965[22]) out lines the contemporary variations in the Birhor way of life in the spatial temporal perspective. However , the work is short of empirical analysis. William (1968[23]) makes an explanatory study of various traits of Birhors' institution, organization and culture and seeks to comment on the tribes' lack of territorial feeling. Verma (1977[24]) studies in detail on tribal demography and compares the qualitative and quantitative aspect of the population of the Nomadic Birhor and settled santhals of Hazaribagh district.

Adhikary, (1978[25], 1984[26], 1993[27]) in his three works, makes holistic studies of the institutional aspects of the Birhor genre de vie. His first work deals status and role of women in the tribes social organisation while his second work is concerned with the social milieu of the Birhor of Sundargarh district of Orissa. His latest work deals with the perceived environment, particularly, the psycho-cultural environment of the Birhors' traditional way of living.

Oraon (1994[28]) seeks to edit a book on the Birhor. The book deals with various social and cultural organization of the sedentary and migratory Birhor of Bihar. Mukherjee and khatua (1996[29]) attempt to study the social, cultural and political aspects and organization of the Birhor of Madhya Pradesh. The work emphasises the institutional aspects of the Birhor of the State.

Sherwill (1854[30]) provides an account of the Socio-cultural structure of various tribal communities of the Danmin-i-koh area of Rajmahal areas. Hunter (1868[31], 1895[32]) makes an analysis of the ethnic division and the agricultural condition of Indian people, including those of major Indian tribes in historical perspective, Hunter presents a rich account of the tribal people of Santhal Pargana and Bhagalpur of undivided Bengal. The book specifically deals with cultural heritage of the Oraon. Hunter provides a comprehensive account of the aboriginal tribes of the sub-continent. Dalton (1872[33]) Studies the cultural heritage of the tribal societies of the north-eastern frontier, and in one of the section of the book he writes about social and cultural aspects of the tribes of the Damin-i-ko h area of the Rajmahal region.

Ball (1880[34]) studies lifestyle of the tribal people of the Damin area of Santhal Paraganas. He analyses the reciprocity between the physical nature of the area and the tribal people. Grierson (1903[35]) analyses the dialects and the languages of the tribes belonging to the Munda and the dravidian family of Eastern India and Chotangapur plateau. He also seeks to identify the regional, linguistic and dialectical pattern of the original inhabitants and natives. Crooke (1907[36]) studies the cultural ecology of the people of India. However, he denotes a section in the book on the life style of the various tribes of the subcontinent. O' Malley (1910[37]) provides the first hand information of various tribes of Bihar and Bengal in the areal, genological and genetic perspective. The account, to a greater extent, however, in a historical perspective, reflects the empirical nature of the analysis.

Reslley (1915[38]) makes an anthropometric analysis of the origin and classifications of the Indian races. Russell and Lal (1916[39]) study the cultural heritage of the tribal communities of each of the principal provinces of central, particularly of East Indian tribal people, including that of the Chotanagpur region. Hodson (1922[40]) seeks to trace out the complex historical evaluation of various Indian tribes. He also studies the way of living of these tribes in environmental perspective. Buchanan (1929[41]) carries out a statistical survey of undivided Bengal , Particularly of Bhagalpur and Santhal Paraganas and studies the cultural heritage of the Santals and Malers.

Specifically based on the work of Francies Buchanan Gantzer (1938[42]) analyses the tribal Law of the Rajmahal areas. Majumdar (1944[43]) , makes a holistic study of various races of India with their cultural contours. He also studies the region - based innovation diffusion of tribal cultures in various parts of Indian races. The work also deals with the spatial - patterns of cultural ecology of the major races and tribes.

Roy (1954[44], 1958[45],) studies various aspects of the Paharia tribes. However, he has not taken into consideration Malpaharias and Sauri Paharia tribes. His final work deals with the regional pattern of fertility among the Paharia women while the second is an analysis of Paharia culture and society of Manbhum area of Bengal. He tries to enumerate the cultural ecology of the Manbhum Paharia.

Prasad (1961[46]) basically studies the pattern of tribal cultural ecology of the Chotanagpur region, particularly in the light of the regional flora and fauna. Fortes (1962[47], 1969[48]) has edited a collection of papers which intrinsically concerns with regional pattern of marriage customs of various Indian tribes and also has made a comparative studies of marriage customs of diverse origin. Ghurye (1963[49]) traces the historical development of Indian tribes in the light of the 'sequent occupance' of the British system. Goody (1966[50]) has written about various facts of domestic life of some tribal groups which include IBAN of Borneo, Fulani and Dagaba.

Barnes (1971[51]) has presented a book which is based on the study of kinship. Fox (1971[52]) has examined the behavioural and ideological interaction between the local community and national society in pre industrial northern India. Haviland (1975[53]) has given a thorough introduction to the principles and processes of cultural anthropology. Singh and Mishra (1976[54]) analyse the regional distribution and social cultural and economic organization of the various tribes in Orissa and in their geographical perspectives and have analysed how they have responded to their physical environment.

Prasad (1977[55], 1977-78[56], 1978[57], 1979[58]) makes a few tribal studies and analyses in geographical perspective. The first work studies the internal spatial pattern of tribal society particularly in the light of the cultural alignment as being observed in the village. The second identifies the meaning and scope of tribal geography and its relationship with other branches of human geography. Tribal geography is a systematic geography and requires to be made a law-seeking subdiscipline. The third work provides information about nature and types of works which have been done in Tribal geography until 1974-75. The last work although makes an explanatory analysis of the spatial patterns of tribes it is a core study and attempts to study the impact of urbanization on the genre de vie of tribes living in the town.

Berreman (1981[59]) has prepared a collection of essays and public statements as social, political and academic controversy dealing with the perceptual truth of the tribal communities. The study analyses such works which were done between 1965-79. Chakravorty, (1981[60]) had attempted to study the political relations between tribes of Assam and the British Government and shows the development of British policy towards these tribal communities of Assam. Roy (1981[61]) studies the impact of modernity in the tribal neighbourhood which seems to have brought the tribal culture at the cross-roads of modernity and tradition and transitions.

Archer (1984[62]) has focused the principles of tribal law which Santals of the Santal Parganas now accept as defining their civil rights and duties. Karotemprel (1984[63]) has edited a collection of papers concerning socio - cultural facts of various tribal communities cf northern India .

Singh (1985[64]) studies the Tribal society of India in an Anthropo-historical perspective.

Kumar (1986[65]) has attempted to analyze and interpret the socio-cultural organization and economic structure of the Mal Paharia in the light of regional geographical complex. Saha (1986[66]) Presents a graphic account of distribution of various tribes in Tripura. He also studies their regional pattern of cultural and social perspective.

Das (1987[67]) studies the genre de vie of the Indian Tribes in institutional perspective.

Narayan (1988[68]) simply studies the changing nature of tribal genre de vie of some Indian tribes. The changing genre de vie as he observes, is result of the emerging modernity in the neighbourhood. Oraon (1988[69]) presents a holistic analysis of the Oraon genre de vie in the regional perspective. It deals with all aspects of the Oraon culture, society and politics.

Prasad (1988[70]) Simply studies the cultural ecology vis-a-vis- the reciprocity of various tribes and also analyses various indices of tribo-cultural dynamism. Rizvi (1988[71]) discusses the frequency of colour blindness among the tribal population of Gujarat. The rate of blindness varies from 0.70 among the Bill to 8.96 among Koli.

Roy (1989[72]) has edited a book which consists of analysis of various tribes of Orena, their society and culture. But none of the works could claim to be empirical in nature. Sinha (1989[73]), discusses the various spatial aspects of Religious life at the Dudh Kharia, an important tribe of the Gumla district.

Behera and Parida (1990[74]) in their paper make a humble attempt to examine the problems and treatments of the aged among the plain-Bhuiyans of Orissa. The paper is a study of koira block of Sundargarh, a tribal predominated northern district of Orissa and Bhuiyans constitute the largest tribe of this block. Haldor (1990[75]) has provided general account of economic and health conditions of the Bedia of Ramgarh hill range.

Dasgupta (1992[76]) has highlighted in his paper how the forest plays role in Birjia's life and also their closeness or affinity or dependence on forest.

Babu and Naidu (1994[77]) in their paper have focused on the marriage pattern and distance among two endogamous sub tribes of Mali namely, Manzai Mali and Bod Mali of Andhra Pradesh. Choubey (1994[78]) has discussed about the health care services to Tribal population in Baster region of Madhya Pradesh. Mukhopadhyay (1994[79]) studies regional Pattern of ethnicity of the khasi of north east India. The study also emphasises socia-cultural organization of the tribe in the areal perspective.

Mathew (1994[80]), discusses the tribal social and cultural phenomenon-vis- a- vis- the situation in Singhbhum of Bihar. The study reveals the various facts of cultural disposition of the area and seeks to make analysis of the intra-tribal cultural synthesis. However the work is short of empirical analysis.

Roy, (et al), (1994[81]) have shown how the rate of fertility among the kissan women of Orissa is declining with the increase in the marriage age. It shows a positive correlation between declining fertility and increasing marriage age.

Chib (1995[82]) has identified those regions which were once isolated because of physical inaccessibility or ethnic composition and have now been brought to the main stream but has shown how reacted differently in this regard. The work is specified on the Kinnaur in Himachal Pradesh, one of such regions.

Dutta (1995[83]) studies the territorial bases of different categories of the khasi in Meghalya, Particularly in the light of their anthrocity and makes anthrometric measurements which appear to bear high discriminatory power.

Munshi (1995[84]) seeks to identify the natural habitat of the tribal communities of the Konkan coast of Maharashtra. Mathur (1995[85]) analyses the cultural ecology of the Angami Nagas, particularly the reciprocity between the tribe and the nature. The analysis is, to a greater extent, explantary in nature.

Malik (1995[86]) seeks to highlight the changing economic pattern of the Kamars mostly as a result of the changing environment condition in the neighbouhood. Naskar's (1995[87]) paper deals with the identification of the Gotual organization and its utility among the Muria of Baster in the contemporary situation.

Devan (1997[88]) discusses the general economy and the quality of life of the tribe of Wynad of Kerala. Guru and Koshy (1997[89]) make an analytical study of health care and nutritional attitudes and infants mortality pattern among the Paraja tribe of Orissa. George (1997[90]) examines the descent organization and its corporate nature among the Mudugas of Kerala.

Jana, (et al.) (1997[91]) have given a brief account of the pattern of the land alienation among the Kora tribe of the Kharagpur region in Midnapore district of West Bengal. Mishra (1997[92]) discusses about the regional food-in-take pattern of various tribal communities of the Jharkhand region. He also studies the nutrition level of the tribal population of the region.

The above review of literature; reveals that very few works have been done on the Birhors as compared to other tribes of Eastern India, particularly of the Chotanagpur region and whatever little work has been done on the Birhors that intrinsically concerns with the institutional aspects of the Birhors' rudimentary social organization and does not concern with the spatial attributes of the organization. The proposed work, therefore, makes a spatial and systematic study of the Birhors so as to make itself distinct from the existing works.

Sources of Data

The present work is based on sources of data (i) Secondary sources and (ii) Primary sources. Secondary data has been collected from the Patna based census office, the statistical dept. of the Bihar Govt. and from some other Govt. sources which include the block offices of the concerned villages. Some data has been collected from various libraries visited for the purpose. However, it is necessary to mention here that the census officials of the Patna based unit did not cooperate with the author as they showed their inability to make available the 1991 data of the Birhor tribe, saying that the data were classified and required approval from the higher authority for their general uses in research purposes. The statistical dept., Govt. of Bihar, Patna also expressed its inability to provide relevant information about the study area and of the Birhors. The work is therefore based on 1981 census data, however attempts have been made to generate up-to-date data. It is required to be mentioned here that not much data regarding the special attribute of Birhor genre de vie and landscape morphology are available because of the lack of geographical studies on the tribe. The author has to proceed with a very limited published geographical data and literature to arrive at a meaningful conclusion.

The collection of Primary data has been based on the field survey of the sample villages. Two types of questionnaires were prepared : one for the household and the other for the village - household and village schedules (Appendix no. I and II) and the survey was undertaken in the sample villages in order to generate /collect primary data. Household and village schedules were however too extensive because they contained too many questions being framed and put with a view to collect comprehensive information of the Birhor, so a large number of questions in both schedules remained unanswered because of the types of information required were not available in the sample villages.

PROBLEMS UNDER STUDY

The above review reveals that not much work has been done on the Birhors and whatever little work has been done on them, they are mainly done by the sociologist and anthropologist. They have emphasized in their works the institutional aspects of the Birhor culture and social organizations. Thus it is proposed in the present study to make a spatial analysis of the Birhor people in the light of their geographical, social, cultural and economic characteristics since a section of the tribe is believed to be wanderers. It is also proposed to examine certain problems associated with the wandering Birhor. The problems to be studied and analysed are as follows :

(1) Where the major concentration of the sedentary Birhor occurs ? What is the habitable limit of the wandering Birhor in the study area ? Why does a section of Birhor still practices nomadism ? Are the Birhors a little known jungle tribe still ?

(2) To what extent does the Birhor settlement manifest the control of the physical features ? What is the nature of the settlement types of the Uthlu Birhor ? Is there any difference between the settlements of the sedentary and wandering Birhors ?

(3) What are the salient features of the Birhor culture and Social organization ? Do the wandering or Uthlu Birhors have social organization? What are the distinguishable aspects ?

(4) How is genre de vie of the Pariya or sedentary Birhor distinguishable

from the genre de vie of the Uthlu Birhor (wandering) ?

(5) What is the nature of the Birhor economy ? Has there been any change in their economy ?

(6) What are the salient demographic features of the Birhor population ? Are the Birhor "a vanishing tribe" ?

(7) Is there any Birhor cultural landscape worth mentionig ?

Methodological Approach

Methodology, in simple words, refers to the research technique of a discipline. It largely depends on the conceptualization of the discipline itself. It implies that as the philosophy of a discipline changes with time, its research techniques undergo a change so as to meet the requirement of widening subject matter. Every work in social and natural sciences ascribe towards an explanation and every methodological approach is required to be intrinsically based on a sound philosophical foundation. Since present geography is positivist in nature, it requires scientific explanation, hypothetic-deductive method based on an a priori model to develop the methodology which involves : a priori model; hypothesis; experimental design (definition, classification, measurement); data collection; verification procedures (statistical tests) and if the verification procedure becomes successful, it may lead to these laws and theory construction and then to explanation. In fact, the present work is a positivist - led empirical work on the Birhor tribe.

The present work comprises of the following phases of methodological approach on account of being empirical in nature:

(1) Intensive library works which involve the interpretation and enquiring of various literature and works done by the sociologists and anthropologists on the Birhor;

(2) Collection of data from the secondary sources. However not much datas were made available on Birhor.

(3) Preparation of questionnaire, based on the pattern having been emerged from tabulation, arrangement and analysis of the secondary information and data;

(4) Panel survey of certain Birhor Villages, selected on the basis of random sampling i.e. with the Questionnaires the author personally visited the village to collect primary data and for information about the Birhor.

The first two phases: Library work and collection of secondary data tend to develop the perceptual experience, image of the Birhor and an a priori model about the genre de vie of the Birhors. Preparation of Questionnaire and the sampling level towards hypothesis formulation, experimental design and, data collection. However the verification procedures would be decided at final chapter of the work : whether the entire methodological procedure until the phase of data collection is successful . If it is successful it would a positive feed back of the hypothesis - deductive explanation of the work.

Sources of Map

Village cadestral map (16 inches to 1 mile) , census map (1 inches to 8 miles) and various maps collected from various government sources , including the topographical maps of the sheet no. 72H, 73E , have been taken into consideration in the preparation of maps. However various trends of cartogram have been prepared on the basis of the data, both secondary and primary.

To substantiate the sense - perception vis-a-vis the observation of empiricism of the sample villages, photographs have been taken to authenticate the sample survey of the villages concerned so as to identify the nature of the Birhors emerging landscape.

Study Area

The study area is confined to Gumla , Ranchi and Hazaribagh districts of Chotanagpur region (Fig. : 1.1). However the Birhor population is also scattered across the districts of Lohardaga , West and East Singhbhum, Palamu, Garhwa, Giridih and Dhanbad (Appendix No. III). Following villages of the three districts Gumla , Ranchi and Hazaribagh have been selected randomly and personally surveyed :

Village	Block	District
Beti	Bishunpur	Gumla
Jehangutua	Bishunpur	Gumla
Katiya	Bishunpur	Gumla
Kaibera	Simdega	Gumla
Pahar Singh	Angara	Ranchi
Bigha	Chauparan	Hazaribagh
Dembu	Hazaribagh Sadar	Hazaribagh

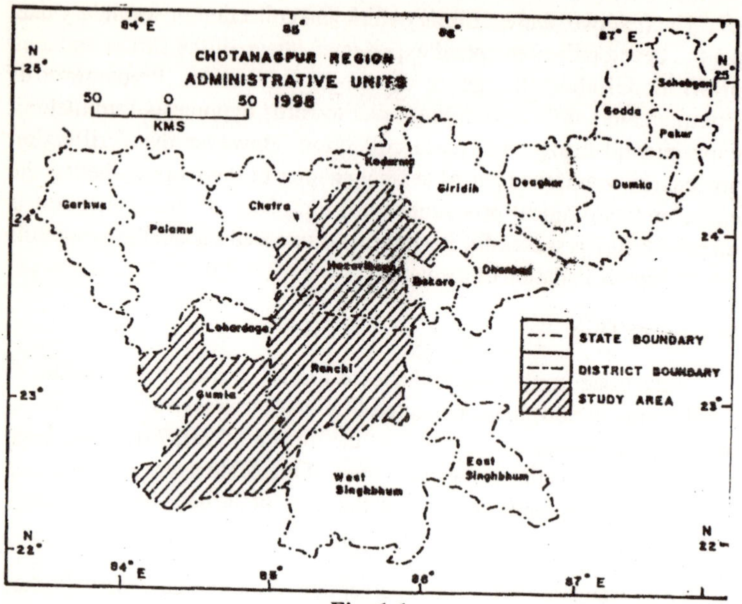

Fig. 1.1

The total number of Birhor residing in the above villages is 755 according to a latest estimate and out of which 602 have been identified and surveyed.

References :

1. Harvey, David, 1969/Ind.Ed.1984 : Explanation in Geography, Arnold-Heinemahn, London, p. 3.

2. Smith, D.M., 1975 : Patterns in Human Geography, Penguin Book Ltd, London, p.15.

3. Haggett, Peter, 1986/2nd Ed. : 'Human Geography' in R.J. Johnshon et al. (ed.), The Dictionary of Human Geography, Black Well Reference Oxford, p.206.

4. Prasad, M., 1977/1978 : 'Tribal Geography: An Enquiry into its Progress and Scope', Geographical Outlook, Vol. VIII, p. 42.

5. Kumar, A., 1986 : Tribal Culture and Economy, Inter India Pulication, New Delhi, p.2.

6. Roy, S.C., 1917 : 'A General Account of the Birhors', Journal of

Bihar and Orissa Research Society, Vol.2 (2).

7. Roy, S.C., 1925 : The Birhor: A Little - known Jungle Tribe of Chotanagpur, Man in India Office, Ranchi.

8. Mitra, S.C., 1932 : 'Notes on the Prevalence of Cannibalism among the Birhors of Chotanagpur', In J.A.S.B.,Vol. 47, pp. 478-83.

9. Bhattachariya, A., 1953 : 'An Account of the Birhor of Palamu', Bulletin of the Department of Anthropology, Vol. II, no. 2. July, pp. 1-10.

10. Sen, B.K. and Sen, J., 1955: 'Notes on the Birhors,' Man in India, Vol. 35, No.3, pp. 169-75.

11. Francis, J.V., 1957 : 'Wandering of Uthlu Birhor,' Bulletin of Dept. of Anthropology, Bihar University, pp. 58-65.

12. Sharma, K.N., 1958 : 'How the Uthlu Birhor make their living,' Vanyajati, Vol. 6 (4).

13. Sinha, D.P., 1958 : 'Cultural Ecology of the Birhor : A Methodological Illustration,' Journal of Social Research, Vol-1, pp. 86-96.

14. Sinha, D.P., 1959 : 'The Birhor and their world view', Adibasi, Vol. III, No.3 and 4, pp. 17-25.

15. Sinha, D.P., 1959 : 'Portrait of Birhor Chief ', Journal of Social Research, Vol.2, No.1 and 2.

16. Vidyarthi, L.P., 1954 : 'Nature and extent of Migration of the Birhor,' In Man and Cultural ed. Wallace, University of Pennsylvania Press.

17. Vidyarthi, L.P., 1960: 'The Birhor: A Study in Ecology, Economy and wandering', in Selected papers of the Fifth International Congress of Anthropological and Ethnological Science, Philadelphia.

18. Singh, R. ,1963: 'Reproductive life of Birhor Women,' Bulletin of Bihar Tribal Research Institute, Vol. 4, No. 1, pp.125-42.

19. Malhotra, S.B., 1963: 'Kinship Organisation among the Birhor' Bulletin of the Bihar Tribal Research Institute, Vol.5 (2).

20. Rana ,M.K., 1964: 'Demography of the Birhor of West Bengal,' Vanajati, Vol.12 (2).

21. Choudhary, G., 1965 : 'Life and Cultural of BirhorTanda', M.A. thesis,

Ranchi Univeristy, Ranchi.

22. Sachchidananda, 1965 : 'Directed Change among the Birhor', The Eastern Anthropology, Vol .9 (1).

23. William , B.J., 1968 : 'The Birhor of India and some comments on Bend organization', In Richard B.Lee and Irven Devore(ed.), Man the Hunter, Aldine, Atherton/Chicago, pp.126-31.

24. Verma, K.K., 1977 : Culture, Ecology and Population, National Publishing House, New Delhi.

25. Adhikary, A.K., 1978 : 'Status and Role of Women among the Birhor : A namadic hunting and gathering community of Eastern India,' In tribal women in India, Indian Anthropological Society, Calcutta, Publication, No. 4, pp. 39-44.

26. Adhikary , A.K., 1984 : Society and world view of the Birhor : A Nomadic, Hunting and gathering community of Orissa, Anthropological Survey of India, Calcutta.

27. Adhikary, A.K., 1993: 'The Birhor and their Universe A study on Perception and Classification of objects and Phenomena in a Oral tradition', Man and life, Vol. 19, Nos. 1 and 2.

28. Oraon, P.C., (ed.), 1994: Bihar Ke Birhor, Bihar Government Welfare Dept., Bihar Tribal Welfare Research Institute, Ranchi.

29. Mukherjee, B. M. and Khatua, N., 1996: The Birhor of Madhya Pradesh , Man and Life , Vol.. 22, No, 1-2, pp. 13-24.

30. Sherwill, W.S., 1854: Geographical and statistical report of the District of Bhagalpur, Calcutta Gazettee Office, Calcutta.

31. Hunter, W.W., 1868: The Annals of Rural Bengal, London.

32. Hunter, W.W., 1895 : A Brief History of Indian People, The Clavendon Press and Company Ltd., London.

33. Dalton ,E.T., 1872: Descriptive Ethnology of Bengal, Govt. of Bengal, Calcutta.

34. Ball, V., 1880 : Jungle Life in India, Thos. Dela Rua and Co., London.

35. Grierson, G.A., 1903: Linguistic Survey of India, Vol. II, London.

36. Crooke, W., 1907: Nature of North India , Archibald Constable and

Company Ltd., London.

37. O' Malley, L.S.S, 1910 : Bengal District Gazetteers: Santhal Paragana, The Bengal Secretariat Book Depot., Calcutta.

38. Risley, H.H., 1915: The People of India, Oriental Books, London.

39. Russell, R.V., and Lal , H., 1916: Tribes and Castes of the Central Provinces of India, Vol. 1, Rajdhani Book Centre, Delhi.

40. Hodson, T.C.,1922 : The primitive culture of India , The Royal Asiatic, Society, London.

41. Buchanan, H., 1929: 'Journal of Francis Buchanan of Bhagalpur 1810-1811', Journal of Bihar and Orissa Research Society, Vol. 15, No. 3-4, pp. 311-571.

42. Gantzer, J.F., 1938: Final report of the Survey and Settlement operations in Santal Paraganas, Patna.

43. Majumdar, D.N., 1944: Races and Cultures of India, Asia Publishing House, Bombay.

44. Roy, A.K., 1954 : 'Reproductive life of Paharia Women,' Man in India, Ranchi ,Vol. 34, No. 2, pp. 151-60.

45. Roy, A.K., 1958 : 'An Anthropometric Study of the Paharias of Manbhum,' Man in India, Ranchi, Vol. 38, No.2, p. 129.

46. Prasad, N., 1961 : Land and People of Tribal Bihar , Bihar Tribal Research Institute, Ranchi.

47. Fortes, M., (ed.), 1962: Marriage in Tribal Societies, Cambridge, University Press, Great Britain.

48. Fortes, M., 1969 : Kinship and the Social Order, Routledge and Kegan paul, London.

49. Ghurye, G.S., 1963: The Scheduled Tribes, Popular Prakashan, Bombay.

50. Goody, J., (ed.), 1966 : The Developmental Cycle in Domestic Groups, Cambridge University Press, Great Britain.

51. Barnes, J.A., 1971 : Three Style in the study of Kinship, Tavistock Publication, London.

52. Fox, G.R., 1971: Kin ,Clan, Raja and Rule, Oxford University Press, Bombay.

53. Haviland, W.A., 1975 : Cultural Anthoropology, Holt. Rinehant and Winston. Inc., New York.

54. Sinha, B.N. and Mishra, B.K., 1976 : Tribes of Orissa : A Geographical Analysis, Geographical Review of India, Vol. XXXVIII, No. 2., pp. 167-87.

55. Prasad, M., 1977 : 'Internal Structure of a Tribal Village of Chotanagpur, India', Geoscop, University of Ottawa, Canada, Vol. VIII, No. 1. pp. 58-74.

56. Prasad , M., 1977-78 : Tribal Geography: An Enquiry into its progress and Scope', Geographical outlook, Vol. XIII, pp. 41-51.

57. Prasad. M., 1978: 'Spatial Pattern of Tribes in Chotanagpur : A Case study of Jharia Town', Journal of Social Research, Ranchi, Vol. XXI, No..2, pp. 35-43.

58. Prasad, M., 1979 : Tribal Geography : An Introductory Bibliography, Classical Publications, New Delhi.

59. Berreman, G.D., 1981: The Politics of Truth, South Asian Publishers Pvt. Ltd., New Delhi.

60. Chakravorty, B.C., 1981: British Relations with the Hill Tribes of Assam Since 1858, Firma K.L.M. Private Ltd., Calcutta.

61. Roy, D.H.L., 1981: A Tribe in Transition, The Jaintia of Meghalaya, Cosmo Publications, New Delhi.

62. Archer, G.W., 1984: 'Tribal Law and Justice', Vol. I, Concept Publishing Company, New Delhi.

63. Karotemprel ; S. (ed.), 1984 : The tribes of North East India, Vemdrame Missiological Insititute, Shillong.

64. Singh, K.S., 1985: Tribal Society in India, Manohar Publications, New Delhi.

65. Kumar, A., 1986: Tribal Culture and Economy, Inter-India Publications, New Delhi.

66. Saha, S.B., 1986: Tribes of Tripura, Rupali Book Store, Agartala, Tripura.

67. Das, T.S., 1987: Life Style Indian Tribes, Vol. I, Gian Publishing House, Delhi.

68. Narayan, S., 1988 : Tribes in transition, Inter-India Publication, New Delhi.

69. Oraon, K., 1988: The Spectrum of Tribal Religion in Bihar, Kishor Vidya Niketan, Varanasi.

70. Prasad, R., 1988: Tribes : A study in Cultural Ecology and Tribal Dynamics, Amar Prakashan, Delhi.

71. Rizvi, S.H.M., 1988: 'Frequency of Colour Blindness Among Kotwalias, A Small Primitive Tribal group of South Gujarat', Tribe, Vol. XX, Nos. 1-4, pp. 37-41.

72. Roy, B.C., (ed.), 1989 : Tribals of Orissa , Gian Publishing House, New Delhi.

73. Sinha, P.A., 1989 : Religious Life in Tribal India, Classical Publishing Company, New Delhi.

74. Behera, D.K. and Parida, M., 1990 : 'Problems and Treatment of the Aged Among the Plain- Bhuiyans of Orissa', Journal of Social Research, Vol. 32-33, Nos. 1-2, pp. 166-79.

75. Haldor, A.K., 1990 : 'Aging Among the Bedia of Ramgarh hill Range', J.S.R., Vol. 32-33, Nos. 1-2, pp. 105-109.

76. Dasgupta, S., 1992 : 'Role of forest on the Socio-cultural Life of the Birjia- Some observations', Journal of Indian Anthropological Society, Vol. 27, No. 1, pp. 1-6.

77. Babu, B.V. and Naidu, J.M., 1994: 'Marriage Pattern and Distance among the two subtribes of Mali of Andhra Pradesh', South Asian Anthropologist, Vol. 5, Nos. 1-2, pp. 51-53.

78. Choubey, K., 1994: 'Allopathic and Traditional Healthcare services to Tribal population of Baster (M.P)' , Geographical review of India, Vol. 5-6, No. 2, pp. 69-76.

79. Mukhopadhyay, K., 1994 : 'Dynamics of Ethnic Identity maintenance among the Khasi of North - East India', Journal of the Indian Anthropological Society, Vol. 29, No. 3, pp. 209-19.

80. Mathew, A. ,1994: 'Tribal Situation in Singhbhum: A Critique', Social

change, Vol. 24, No. 1-2 , pp. 56-59.

81. Roy, S., (et al.), 1994 : 'Age of Marriage and Fertility among Kissan Women of Orissa', South Asian Anthropologists, Vol. 5, Nos. 1-2, pp. 55-59.

82. Chib, S.C.,1995: 'Demographic Dynamics in the Trans-Himalyan Tribal Region of Kinnaur H.P., Perspective on Socio- economic implication', Geographical Review of India, Vol. 57, No. 1, pp. 20-28.

83. Dutta, P.C., (et al.), 1995 : 'Numerical Taxonomy and group Divergence of the Khasi Population Groups', Journal of the Indian Anthropological Society, Vol. 29, No.3, pp. 222-26.

84. Munshi, I., 1995: 'Tribal Communities in their Natural environment : The Changing context in Western India', Social Action, Vol. 45, No. 2, pp.217-23.

85. Mathur, M., 1995 : 'Angami Nagas: Rituals and Environment', Man and life , Vol. 22, Nos. 1-2 , pp. 33-42.

86. Malik, N., 1995: 'Loping with Disturbed Physical Environment : A study on Primitive Tribal group the Kamars'(M.P.), Man and Life, pp. 43-47.

87. Naskar, S.K., 1995 : 'The Gotul and its Utility among the Muria', Man and Life, Vol. 21, Nos. 1-2, p.19.

88. Devan, P.K., 1997: 'Tribal wynad- Past and Present', Man and Life, Vol. 23, No. 1.2, pp. 37-44.

89. Guru, S.S. and Koshy, A.K., 1997: 'Maternal Nutrition, Antenatal care and infant Mortality. A Study on the Paraja Tribe of Orissa', Man and Life, Vol. 23, Nos. 1-2, pp. 57-68.

90. Geroge, T .C., 1997: 'Descent Organisation and Corporate action among the Mudugas at Kerala', Man and Life, Vol. 23, No. 1-2, pp. 1-12.

91. Jana, L. (et al.), 1997 : 'Dispossession of the Tribal people from their agricultural land : A case study of Koras in Midnapore', Man and Life, Vol. 23, No. 1-2, pp. 85-89.

92. Mishra, J., 1997 : 'Nature of Food with reference to Jharkhand Region' Man and Life, Vol. 23, Nos. 1-2, pp. 77-84.

2

Geographical Background

An almost quadrilateral-shaped State of Bihar can be divided into four major regions -

(a) The mountainous north west region, theTerai in the extreme north.

(b) The Great North Bihar Plain.

(c) The South Bihar Plain, South of the Ganga and

(d) The Chotanagpur Region and the Rajmahal tracts in the South i.e., South of the Bihar Scarp.

Chotanagpur region extends from 21^0 58' N to 25^0 18' N Latitude and 83^0 22' E to 87^{0}57' E longitude and covers an area of about 79714.00[1] sq. kms. with a population of 218, 43, 911.[2] Its boundaries have been marked by Bihar plain in the north, Orissa in the south, Madhya Pradesh in the west and West Bengal in the east. This plateau region is a part of ancient land block , therefore its Geological structure is not only complex but its topography is also uneven . The Chotanagpur Plateau is separated fromBihar plain by 150 metre (500') contour line, in the north. Its maximum extention is 457 kilometers as east-west and about 310 kilometres as north-South. There are four Commissionaries, 18 districts and 194 blocks in the Chotanagpur region.

Relief

Chotanagpur virtually consists of a series of plateau standing at different level of elevation, the highest general elevation at about 1,100 m. being in mid -western portion known as pat lands. From here, the land descends in all directions in a series of steps particularly towards the east until it merges gradually with the lower Ganga Plain. The Sharp breaks in the slope are marked by steep -scarps where the river courses are interrupted by waterfalls. The most characteristic features of relief are revealed in the Hazaribagh and Ranchi Plateaus standing at the same general elevation (600m) but separated by the Damodar trough. To the west of the central Ranchi Plateau rises the pat or high level mesas capped with laterites facing the former with bold steep scarps, while the east the land drops abruptly with similar scarps on the Manbhum plain. The Baghmundi highland tract attaining a height of above 600 m at places is separated from the Ranchi Plateau by the Subarnarekha river.

To the South-east, there is similar abrupt drop on the Chaibasa Plain but towards the South, it gradually turns into a lower dissected upland characterised by diverse complex topography of the Kolhan and Porhart regions. The Varying successive levels from pat land to Chaibasa plain mark the succesive uplifts of an old peneplain during Tertiary era. There has been some difference of opinion regarding the number of uplifts as well as the character and connections of different peneplains.[3] While S.P. Chatterjee.[4] has suggested the occurance of four peneplains on the central Ranchi Plateau, others do not agree to this view. Following Dunn, most of the writers regard the plateaus as the products of three succesive uplifts of the same peneplain.

The highest plateau, i.e. the pat region was uplifted above the preexistings peneplain in early Tertiary times, while the Cental Ranchi plateau together with the higher parts was block-lifted towards the late Tertiary period leaving the original peneplain marked by the Chaibasa and panch-paragana plains at the original level. The third uplift was in the nature of a tilt so that there is no steep scarp on the outer edge of Chotanagpur. All the three plateaus, upper, middle and lower, resemble each other in many respects, that is, they appear to be flat, extremely gullied, studded with low rounded hills and bordered by steep escarpments.[5] The Hazaribagh plateau on the northern side of the Damodar trough has essentially the same features and elevation . It also has two distinct surfaces; the upper Hazaribagh Plateau at 600 m (Figure 2.1) stantds engirdled by the lower Kodarma Plateau (300 m) which is bordered by steep scarps in the north but slopes gradually to the east. Westwards, in the Palamu, this Plateau exhibits highly broken relief similar to the Southern dissected portion of the Ranchi Plateau.

On the North-eastern side, the plateau continues into the Rajmahal highlands comprising a chain of lava plateaus, sculptured divided surface.[6] The volcanic Rajmahal hills extend north-south rising 300 - 450 m above the general plateau surface overlooking the Ganga in the north with steep scarps to the west . The Damodar valley lying in between the two main plateau blocks occupies the permo-triassic trough fault and exhibits a variety of topography characterized by sandstone hills e.g. Panchet and Mahudi, rising above undulating plateau Platforms at various elevations,

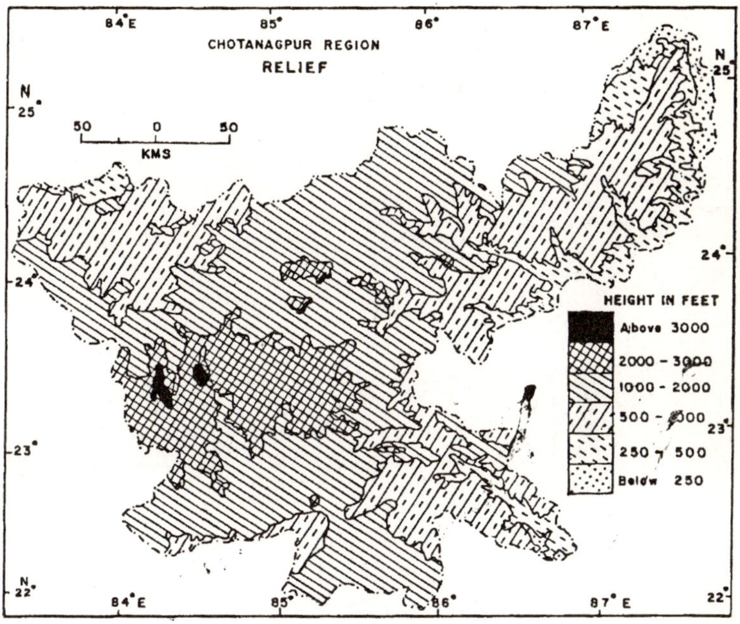

Fig. 2.1

such as the Ramgarh Peneplain and the steep sided scarps on both sides of the Damodar and scarp edge interfluves between pairs of rivers.

Drainage

Chotanagpur region is drained by various rivers and streams (Fig. 2.2.), in different directions. Among the rivers and streams are the South Koel, the North Koel, the Subarnarekha, the Damodar and the Barakar, which have developed extensive drainge basins, while the Ajay, the Mor , the Brahmani, the Gumani etc, drain the Rajmahal highlands in parallel channels towards the West Bengal Plain. The northern fringe of the plateau is drained by numerous small tributaries of the Punpun, the Phalgu, the Sakri and the Kiul rives towards the south Bihar plain. The rivers are characterized by wide shallow channels over the flat Plateau but exhibit youthful characteristics marked by steep - sided, narrow valleys or gorges, the courses being interrupted by rapids and waterfalls.

The Damodar originates from the district of Palamu, flows eastward in a structural trough between the plateaus of Ranchi and Hazaribagh. The Damodar valley corporation has executed a number of projects in the Damodar basin to control the water of this mighty river for irrigation and

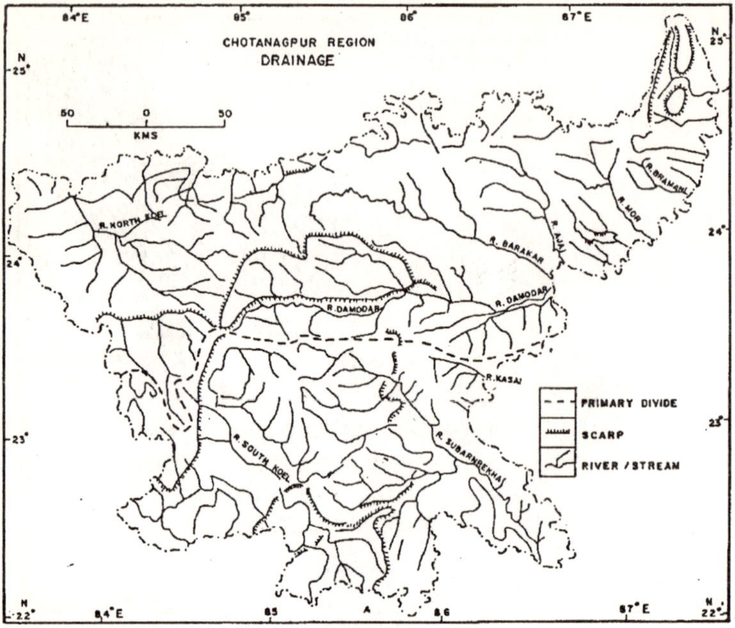

Fig. 2.2

power generating purposes and to prevent the floods. The corporation's main dams are Tilaya, Konar, Maithan and Panchet.

The Subarnarekha originates from near the junction of the Ranchi and Hazaribagh district in the Ranchi plateau. It flows through the district of Singhbhum in the state. It flows in a south - easterly direction. Hundrufall is situated on the Subarnarekha on the scarpedge of the Ranchi plateau.

The Barakar rises from the district of Hazaribagh and flowing through the district of Dhanbad falls into Damodar. The North Koel eminates from the western part of the Ranchi district and falls into Sone after flowing through middle of the district of Palamu, on the other hand, South Koel flows through the Singhbhum district and joins the Sankh. A dam has been constructed at 'Kutku' in Palamu district across the North Koel river under the Koel Karo multipurpose project for hydal power generation and irrigation purposes . Subarnarekha project is also a multipurpose project for irrigation, water supply and flood contol. Dam has been constructed at Chandil across the Subarnarekha river.

The Ghaghri fall about 7 kilometres from Netarhat has a drop of 43 metres. Rajrappa waterfall about 25 kilometers east of Ramgarh is another waterfall, remakable for its scenic beauty. The Burhaghah fall (142 metres) on the Burha river is said to be the highest waterfall located west of Mahuadanr. Motijhara is in Santhal Paragana, Gutamghagh in Palamu, Hirnifalls in Singhbhum etc. are other important water falls of the Chotanagpur plateau.

There is a nucleus of the drainage axis on an elevated tract of the plateau South of Piska near Ranchi. The three drainage axis radiate from this elevated tract of the country which divides the main river basins of the region-

(a) The eastward drainage axis forms watershed between the Damodar and the Subarnarekha basins.

(b) The westward drainage axis forms a semi-circular water-parting till it takes a south eastern loop to turn west and reaches eastern limit of the state.

(c) The southward drainage axis radiating from the elevated tract near Piska-lodma road forms the divide between the Subarnarekha and the South Koel basins.

A few minor drainage axis like the vindhyan scarp, pat, Rajmahal, Dhanjori etc. also occur.

The Subarnarekha, South Koel, the Mor rivers provide distinct example of superimpositon.

The Chotanagpur's rivers regime is highly fluctuating with continuous flow only during the monsoon season and either competely dry bed or disconnected pools of water during the rest of the year. The rivers rise suddenly after the monsoon downpour but after a few hours they quickly subside.

Owing to their traverse course mostly on the peneplain surfaces, the over all drainage pattern is dendritic signifying limited structural control, even though they flow over rocks of varying character and hardness. However, there are several local variations depicting different types of drainage patterns. Some of the fault-guided river e.g. the Damodar have remarkable straight courses. A variety of the trellis pattern is seen in the Damodar Valley where a series of parallel faults have resulted in alternating bands of strong and weak rocks which give the drainage a 'fault trellis' pattern. The Trellis pattern is also visible in the folded structures of

Chotanagpur where alternating weak and strong rocks have been truncated by stream erosion. The Sankh reveals a barbed drainage pattern where its tributaries join it in boathook bends pointing upstream. In north Palamu ' angulate' pattern has developed under the influence of joints in the granite-gneiss areas. Radial pattern can be marked over the plateau tops in pats, the central Ranchi plateau and the Hazaribagh plateau.

Geology

The Chotanagpur region is composed mainly of Archaean granite and gneiss (Fig. 2.3) with patches of Dharwar rocks (Phyllite, Mica, Schists etc.) on the northern and sourthen margins.. The southern margin is very conspicuous in the iron ore and kolhan series constituting greater part of the Singhbhum district. The Singhbhum Supergroup marks the onset of proterozoic and is made up of rift - related deposits. It is the main litho-assemblage of this province covering vast area encircling the SGP. The rock assemblage has been classified into Dhanjori, Chaibasa, younger iron-ore and Dalma groups.[7] Dalma group is composed of mafic- ultramafic pyroclasts with thin bands of Quartzite, Phyllite and auriferous tuffs in the lower part and basaltic lava flow, pillow lava and agglomerate in the up-

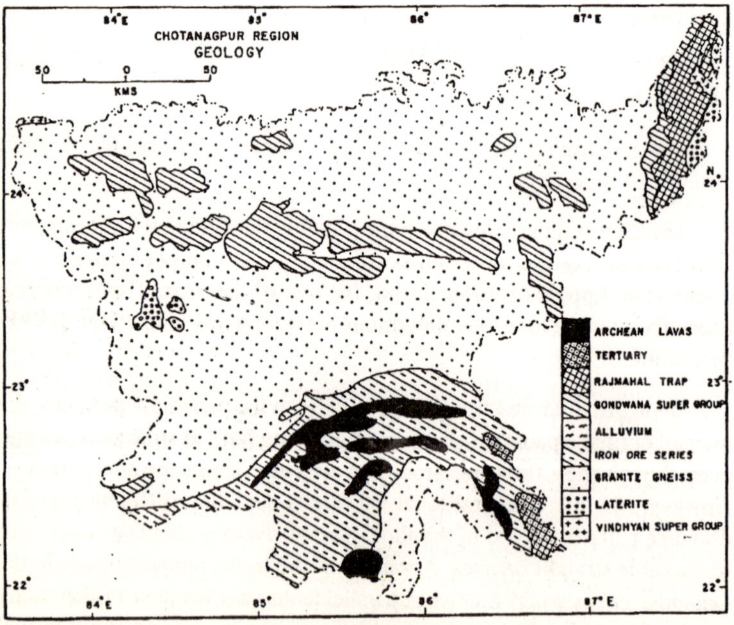

Fig. 2.3

per part. Kolhan group is made up of underformed and unmetamorphosed platforms deposits of conglomerate, sandstone, shale and limestone. Dalma range marks the belt of Archaean lava flows. "The Structural base of the region is provided by a series of batholithic intrusions of granite into Dharwar strata, which were intensively metamorphosed by orogenetic movements. The earliest floor, on which the Dharwars were deposited has not been recognized since it was subsequently metamorphosed".[8] This part of Chotanagpur is characterised by complex geological structure.

The great shear or thrust zone runs approximately ENE- WSW and E-W for nearly100 miles turning to the SE near the eastern end . There are two almost parallel thrust zones to the north of the great shear zone, one marking the northern limit of a broad belt of lavas (Dalma Traps) and the other further north. They are almost parallel to the Satpura trend and converge near Goilkera, east of Chakradharpur.

In the structural trough of the Damodar valley occur Gondwana rocks consisting of sand stone of great thickness with some slates and clay. The pat land on the western margin is covered with Deccan trap which is converted into laterite and bauxite due to weathering.

The Rajmahal hills in the south-eastern fringe of the plateau are also covered with lava flows which were probably linked with the initiation of the Himalayan orogeny.

Eruption of the Rajmahal Traps in the Early cretaceous (C 116 Ma. Dalrymple and Lanphere 1974; Baksi 1986; Baksi et al 1987) was roughly synchronous with the final fragmentation of Gondwana and formation of the eastern Indian ocean basin. The Rajmahal[9] Volcanic rocks constitute part of the Gondwana Supergroup and cover an area of about 4100 sq.km. in the eastern part of the Indian shield. They overlie the Dubrajpur Formation (Upper Triassic - Lower Jurasic), and in places overstep into the Barakar formation (Permian) and Precambrian basements. Gravity studies of the Rajmahal Hills show that the Gondwana supergroup sediments were deposited over a rifted and highly - faulted shield margin. The faults may subsequently have acted as channels through which the lava erupted. The Rajmahal basalt and the Gondwana supergroup sedements are known to continue towards the east and south under the Bengal Basin,and beneath the Gangetic alluvium to the north (Mukhopadhyay et al. 1986) . The general elevation of the Rajmahal Hills varies from 150mt. to 250 mt. with individual peaks attaining heights ranging from 457 to 505 mt. The lava flows show a gentle dip towards the east and north following the basement topography at the time of eruption. Fifteen basalt flows were observed and up to 28 flows have been identified in boreholes by the Geological Survey of India (Mukhopadhyay et al. 1986). Individual flows range in thickness from < 1 mt to about 17 mt. Although eruption of the Rajmahal basalts appears to have been relatively quiescent, there is evidence in the lava pile of minor explosive activity characterised by the presence of pyroclastic deposits (tuff, agglomerate, scoria, pumice, volcanic breccia and ash flows). The inter trappean beds are largely tuffaceous, but include argillaceous and arenaceous units. Vindhya Supergroup occupies the western most part of Bihar where are exposed the lower two subdivisions of this group - Semri group and Kaimur group. Semri group representing lower Vindhyans is found in the north western part of Palamu district.[10]

Climate

The Climate of Chotanagpur is a part of the climatic pattern of the Indian Sub-continent . The Chotanagpur plateau enjoys monsoon type of climate with marked seasonal rythms of weathers.[11]

The hot weather begins in March . It is marked by a continuously rising temperature between March and May. The mean temperature ranges around 29 degree C. and above which causes atmospheric low over the north eastern part of the plateau. The hot wind popularly known as 'loo' increases the temperature by a few degrees in the northern fringe of Chotanagpur. The plateau is almost immune from the influence of loo[12] The winds blow from the west , but gradually a calm prevails during late summer. Light rains occur during April, which come with the Norwesters of West Bengal.

Rainy season starts after the hot seasons and continues upto October The rain is the gift of the south west monsoon which originates in the Bay of Bengal. The normal date of the onset of monsoon in Bihar is from 7th June in the north east and east to about 15th June in the western end of the state. The temperature gradually decreases with the onset of the South-West monsoon. The winds during these months commonly blow from east and south -east . However, their velocity decreases with the advance of the season. 80% of the annual rainfall comes during this season. The average annual rain ranges between 100 and 150 cms. The pattern of rainfall shows a decreasing trend from south to North and also from east to west. Local rainfall variations are due to topographic diversities. The following table shows the districtwise total rainfall during 1991-92 and number of rainy days (Table 2.1).

Table 2.1

Name of District	Total Average Rainfall in M.M.(1991-92)	Rainy Days
Dumka	1233.7	66.5
Deoghar	1051.9	61.8
Godda	1088.4	60.0
Sahibganj	1487.3	62.6
Dhanbad	1251.1	70.1
Giridih	1133.2	61.4
Hazaribagh	1419.0	58.6
Ranchi	1168.3	60.8
Gumla	1391.7	67.3
Lohardaga	1303.1	67.3
Palamu	1105.8	46.2
East Singhbhum	874.2	46.2
West Singhbhum	1126.0	60.4

Source : Bihar Ankaro May, 1993. p. 177

Above table 2.1 shows that Sahibganj and Hazaribagh district have recorded highest total average rainfall duing 1991-92 with figures of 1487.3 and 1419.0 mm respectively, on the other hand East Singhbhum has recorded the lowest total average rainfall during 1991-92 with figure of only 874.2 mm. The maximum rainy days recorded in Dhanbad are 70.1 . While Palamu and East Singhbhum have recorded the lowest rainy days i.e. 46.2 days each during the same period.

The rainy days generally concentrate in the rainy season because the remaining period of the year is practically rainless. The highest rainfall occurs at the high Netarhat pat,where the rainfall is over 200 cm. The Chaibasa plain gets the lowest amount of rainfall.

The varying elevations of the highlands of Chotanagpur determine the nature of precipitation. The pats with an elevation of over 900 metres and Ranchi - Hazaribagh plateaux with an elevation of over 600 metres record higher rainfall than other parts. The Damodar and the Subernarekha basins form natural corridors for the march of the saturated south west monsoon to cause heavy precipitation in their topographically favoured areas.

The South-Western part of the Chotanagpur highland seems to be the land of unity between the westerly and easterly branches of the summer monsoon favouring convective ascent to account for heavy precipitation in that segment of the Highland.[13]

The winter season begins from November and stays upto February. During this period, the region experiences anticyclonic conditions. The wind blows from the north -west, but the actual direction of the wind is controlled by the local relief features. The temperature remains between 16degree C. and 18 degree C. and this period is characterised by clear blue sky and fine weather. The days are slightly warm and sunny but the nights are cold.[14]

Soil

The soil of Chotanagpur varies according to the nature of parent rock. The plateau is covered with the charactrristic red soil[15] of the gneiss and granite surface with the exceptions of (a) loose sandy soil developed over Gondwana sand stones in the Damodar Valley, (b) the high level lateritic soil over the pats and (c) regur and lateritic soil over the lava surface of theRajmahal highlands.

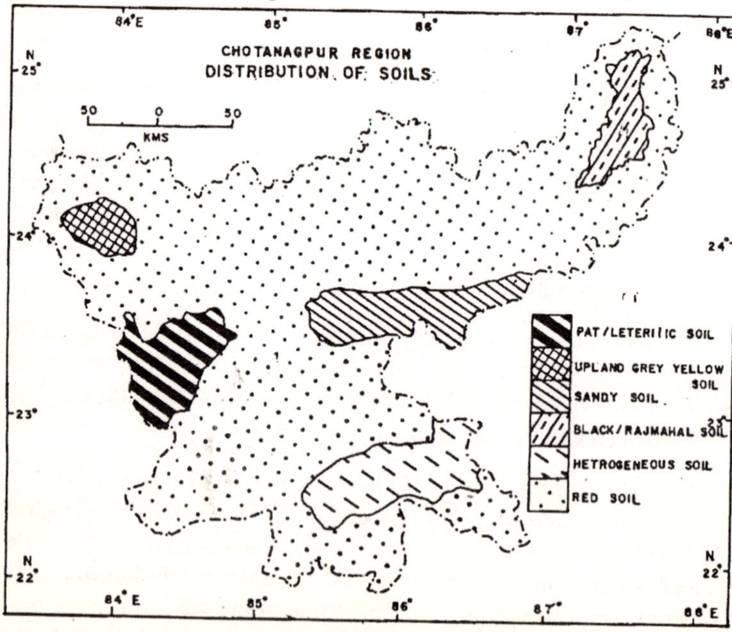

Fig. 2.4

Red soil (Fig. 2.4.) is found in Ranchi, Deoghar, Dumka, Giridih, Hazaribagh, Palamu and Garhwa while soil of Singhbhum and some parts of Dhanbad district is a mixture of Red and Black.

The soil over the gneissic and granitic surface is deep red or even black in colour because of the presence of highly ferroginous biotite and hornblends. This soil is generally thin, sandy or gravelly on the uplands but thick and loamy in valleys and depressions.

The lateritic soil of the pat (now some parts of Gumla and lohardaga) and certain localities in Singhbhum is infertile. Pat region, the western higher plateau of Chotangpur is capped by laterities which have developed under hot and humid conditions over the basalts.[16] The typical red colour is due to high content of iron oxides. The pat soils are devoid of the plant constituents and hence are infertile . The removal of the acidic reaction of the laterite soil can render fertility to it.

The Regur[17] of the Rajmahal highlands is basaltic containing siliceous matter, kaoline and potash as well as magnesia and iron oxides. The black clay developed over it is sticky when wet and retains moisture for a long time but becomes hard though friable when dry. It is very fertile.

Sandy soil is found in Dhanbad and eastern Hazaribagh . Soils vary from redish yellow to greyish yellow in colour . They are moderately deep soil and their fertility level and cropping pattern is the same as the major catenary soils .

The depth and fertility of the differnt soils are highly variable according to the details of topography and rock consitituents.

Upland grey yellow soil is found in newly constructed districts of Garhwa and some parts of Palamu district. They have developed on Shales, silts and low grade metamorphic rocks. Their texture is medium to heavy and their colour varies from grey to yellowish grey.

Hetrogeneous soils are found in central and eastern parts of singhbhum district . The soils are a happy mixture of different types of rocks . The red and yellow soils are found on the uplands where as black and dark grey soils are found in lowland.

Natural Vegetation

Although much of the original vegetation cover has been depleted by reckless cutting and grazing. Some pockets of valuable forests lie intact in the inaccessible parts of Chotanagpur region. There are two types of forest found in Chotanagpur region -

(1) Dry Deciduous Vegetation : This type of vegetation ia found where rainfall is below 1200mm.[18] The dry deciduous forest is found along the fringes of Hazaribagh and north -western fringes of Chotanagpur in palamu.The forest is a mixture of Sal, Bamboo, Amaltas, Semal, Harra, Khair, Palas and Mahua. The growth of the trees is generally stunted . The canopy rarely rises above 50feet. The leafless period is more pronounced than in the moist types of forests . In Palamu the most important tree is sal.

(2) Moist Deciduous Vegetation : This type of vegetation is found in the areas where rainfall is above 1200mm. The vegetation ranges from stunted open growth on southern slopes of Chotangpur region .Western higher plateau and their descending slopes are clad with thick forest. High rain and summer temperature favour wild and luxuriant forest in this part of the country in the districts of Ranchi, Palamu and Hazaribagh.

The chief charcteristic of deciduous trees is that the tree shed their leaves in autumn. The leafless period starts during late March to early April. At this time the ground is littered with dry brown leaves and the scarlet blossoms of palas, butea frondosa and butea superlea give a fascinating red look to the forest. Gradually new leaves start sprouting from the trees. Also in the midst of deciduous trees the presence of evergreen trees is not uncommon.The evergreen vegetation is mostly found as undergrowth,but tall trees are also present along with Sal.The grassland of moist deciduous vegetation of Chotanagpur includes zoo species of grass,the most common of which are sabai and spear grass.

Sal[19] is the most important tree in the forest of Chotanagpur region. Sal has many species. Gamar(Gualina arborea) ,kend (Diospyros melamoxylon), Anjan (Harduriker), Karri (Ponamia glabura), Pipal, Gular, Bargad etc. (tree of fig family), Palas and Khajur, Mahua, and Bamboo(Dendrocalamas strictus) are also found . Palas grows mostly in the wasteland.

The best quality forests with respect to thickness and height are found in extreme south in Singhbhum, whereas, the north and north-west fringes and outliers of Chotanagpur are covered with scrubs.[20]

Landuse

Land-use analysis is an important aspect of geographical studies in agricultural geography. Land-use[21] in an area is the cumulative outcome of historical events, the interaction of economic forces with the natural environment and values of society. In order to know the extent to which land is being used and to understand the variation in its use and productivity, it is necessary to pay more attention to land capability analysis in a field study.

In general , land use classification[22] has two components-

(1) The assessment of physical quality and agricultural potential of land.

(2) The assessment of land quality under the prevailing set of socio-economic circumstances.

Table 2.2
Land use figures of Chotanagpur

Land use categories	Area in hectares	Percentage of area
1. Forest	2313,692	29.03
2. Barren and unculturable land	573,552	7.20
3. Non-agricultural land	608,369	7.63
4. Culturable waste land	330,724	4.15
5. Permanent pasture land and other grazing	106,966	1.34
6. Miscellaneous trees and groves	73,516	0.92
7. Other fallow land	885,025	11.11
8. Current fallow	1069,901	13.42
9. Net sown area	2008,236	25.20
10. Total Chotanagpur	7969,881	100.00

Sources : Bihar State Land use Report 1988-89.

Table 2.2 shows that more than 29% of the land of Chotanagpur plateau is under forest. The highest percentage of land under forest cover lies in Hazaribagh District (48.36 %), followed by Palamu (43.68%), Giridih (34.03%), Lohardaga (29.06%), Singhbhum (28.02%) and Gumla (25.53%).

Dhanbad district has the highest percentage of its land given to barren and unculturable land and non-agricultural land , being 14.34 and 25.62 respectively. Dumka has the highest percentage of its land under culturable waste and permanent pasture and grazing being 7.28 and 5.37 respectively. Ranchi has the highest percentage (17.43%) of current fallow land.

The cultivated land are confined either to flat plateaus at varying heights or to valley bottoms where terracing is possible. Godda and Dumka have the highest percentage of net sown area with 39.24% each. The per capita cultivated land is 0.56 acre.

Agriculture in the Chotanagpur plateau is essentially traditional. Of the total land area of the Chotanagpur , 20.082[23] sq. km. of land are cropped annually. The method of cultivation is backward and the productivity of land is low. Rice, the chief crop is grown in the river valleys and in terraces on the slopes. Best rice land is in the lowlands. The net lowlands are known as the 'Don' land and dry uplands as 'Tanr' Lands.

The land situated near the home stead is known as 'Bari' lands and are the most fertile parts of the upland . While rice is the staple cereal, it is supplemented to a great extent by 'Marua' and 'Gondli' the two most commonly grown millets and by maize. The importance of rice appreciably declines from the wetter east and south to the drier west.

Dr. E. Ahmad has identified different crop-associations for Bihar, out of which following crop-associations have been found in the Chotanagpur region.

1. Rice-Maize-Gram-Palamu.

2. Rice-Ragi-Fruits-Vegetable- Ranchi.

3. Rice-Maize-Ragi- Hazaribagh.

4. Rice- Maize-Fruits and Vegetable- Dhanbad.

5. Rice-Maize-Gram-Singhbhum.

Most of the crops grown in the region fall in three categories -

(1) ***Bhadai Crops (Autumn) :*** Bhadai crops are sown in June and July and harvested in August and September. They are grown on uplands with autumn rice, maize, millets and other coarse grains. Paddy is the dominant crop with nearly 40% of the total area under this harvest. It is important in Ranchi and Hazaribagh districts where the land is generally high. Marua another important crop on the flat Ranchi.Plateau accounts for 20% of the Bhadai acreage. Vegetables are grown near Urban centres and Industrial areas.

(2) ***Aghani Crop(Winter) :-*** They are sown in June and July and harvested in December. Aghani crops are important over the entire plateau. Paddy is the dominant Aghani crop and covers between 70% and 80% land in all districts. Other crops of this harvest including sugarcane. Til, Surguja and Jowar gain importance in the lower plateau areas of Singhbhum and Panch Paragana plains. Its importance decreases in the Upland area of Ranchi and Hazaribagh. Other crops namely pulses and oil seeds etc. account for nearly 10% land but they are grown on Uplands.

(3) ***Rabi Crops (Spring) :-*** These are sown in October - November and harvested in March-April. They are restricted only to the upland areas with irrigation facilities because of insignificant winter rains and dearth of moisture in the soils. The Chief rabi crops are pulses , wheat, barley and oil seeds. Pulses are grown everywhere but wheat and barley are localized in 'bari' lands adjacent to settlement. Oil seeds such as castor, til, lineseed and mustard together account for l0% of the total land under Rabi.

The fourth agricultural season is Garma (summer) but the acreage under this harvest is very small and is mainly confined to the production of vegetables on irrigated ' bari' lands. They are sown in March and harvested in May.

Industry

Chotanagpur has emerged as an important industrial region in the post independence period mainly after the completion of second five year plan. The location of Industries in Chotanagpur has been governed chiefly by the availability of minerals, suitable structural base and an adequate labour force. The Industrial development has largely taken around Jamshedpur, Ranchi, Dhanbad and Bokaro.

There are many important industries in Chotanagpur region.:-

(1) ***Iron and Steel Industry :-*** Iron and steel industry is the most important industry of Chotanagpur region. Chotanagpur has two major iron and steel plants. They are situated at Jamshedpur and Bokaro Steel City respectively. Jamshedpur plant was established in 1907 and Steel output began in 1911. Bokaro steel plant was established in 1964 with soviet collaboration and production began in 1974 . Jamshedpur plant is situated in the region of metallic ores. Most of the raw materials are brought from a radius of 175 kms. The factory gets coking coal from Damodar valley coal region, Limestone and dolomite from Panposh and Sundergarh, manganese from

Gua and Manoharpur mines and Sundergarh and Chromite from Chaibasa mines. While Bokaro steel plants gets limestone from Birmitrapur, iron ore from Jamda and Sasanda, coal from Kargali, Raniganj, Jharia, transport facility of Chandrpur - Muri- Ranchi - Rourkela line.

(2) ***Aluminium Industry*** **: -** Aluminium is derived from bauxite mines in Lohardaga. The Indian Aluminium Company Limited is located at Muri on the Subarnarekha valley.

(3) ***Cement Industry*** **:-** Bihar is the 8th largest producer of Cement among the States in the country. Cement is a limestone based industry. Other raw materials needed are coal and Gypsum. The present working units are situated at Chaibasa (Jhinkpani) and Sindri.

There are many other industries located in different parts of the Chotanagpur region. A Heavy Engineering plant was established at Ranchi (Hatia), in 1958. Chemical fertilizer industry is situated at Sindri (1951). Ranchi and Jamshedpur have emerged as Centre of T.V. assembling, electronic goods and drugs. Kodarma is a Centre of micanite produced from mica waste, mica bricks and mica papers plant. Bidi industry has flourished in Sahibganj, Singhbhum, Giridih, Dhanbad, Gumla and several other districts of the plateau due to the availability of Tendu leaves.

Bihar has evolved not less than 14 industrial zones[24], out of which following are situated in the Chotanagpur region.

(1) Mica Industrial Belt
(2) Damodar Basin industrial Belt
(3) Upper Subarnarekha Basin industrial Zone
(4) Lohardaga Bauxite mining Area.
(5) Jamshedpur Industrial Zone .
(6) South- Eastern Singhbhum Industrial Zone
(7) South Singhbhum Mining Industrial Zone

Population

The total population of Chotanagpur Plateau Region has been recorded as 2,18,43,911 in 1991 census, which is 25.26% of the total population of the Bihar State. The density of the Chotanagpur region has been recorded as 274 persons/sq.kms. while the density of Bihar is recorded as 497 person /sq.kms. The percentage of tribal population in the Chotanagpur region is 24.45 to the total population of the Chotanagpur region while the figure is 7.66% for the whole state.

Following table shows the growth of population of Chotanagpur region:-

Table 2.3
Growth of population of Chotanagpur region

Year	Population	% of Decennial Growth
1951	94,66,153	16.06
1961	1,07,36,428	13.42
1971	1,42,28,238	32.52
1981	1,75,85,661	23.59
1991	2,18,43,911	24.21

Source : Various census reports.

The table 2.3 shows that between 1961 to 1971 there is a remarkable growth of population. The rate of growth of population between these periods has been registered as 32.52% while the rate of growth of population between 1981-91 shows a declining trend i.e. 23.59%.

The region has registered a remarkable growth since 1951 especially in the minerally rich district of Dhanbad and Singhbhum districts. The growth of heavy industries, increase in mining activities and development of agriculture in the Chotanagpur region accelerated the pace of population growth.

Regional pattern of population growth:-

Table 2.4
District wise growth of population

Name of District	Growth Rate in Percentage (1981-91)
Godda	20.71
Sahibganj	20.50
Dhanbad	26.46
Giridih	28.52
Hazaribagh	29.35
Gumla	13.44
Lohardaga	25.72
Palamu	27.83
East Singhbhum	16.98
West Singhbhum	20.58
Dumka	23.05
Deoghar	31.64

Ranchi	21.42

Sources:- Bihar Ankaro may, 1993, p. - 23

The table 2.4 shows that the highest growth rate is recorded in Deoghar district being 31.64 percent between 1981 - 91. This is not only the highest in Chotanagpur plateau region but also in the whole of Bihar. The region has been fast developing as a pilgrimage cum tourist centre. A large number of people prefer to settle in Deoghar because of its salubrious climate.

On the other hand, the lowest growth rate has been recorded in Gumla being only 13.44 percent during 1981-91. This is not only the lowest in Chotanagpur region but also among the other districts of Bihar .

Hazaribagh, Giridih and Dhanbad have recorded 29.35, 28.52 and 26.46% respectively during 1981-91.

On the other hand, East -West Singhbhum and Sahibganj have recorded 16.98, 20.58. and 20.50 percent respectively during 1981- 91.

Regional Variation in Density

The density of population in a region depends on the supporting capacity of land and the existing level of resource utilization . According to 1991 Census, Dhanbad is the most densely populated district (Table-2.5) with 892 persons per sq.kms. Here, mining and manufacturing industries offer better employment opportunities. East Singhbhum with a density of 456 persons per sq. kms. Ranchi,Hazaribagh and Dumka districts have comparatively lower densities of 287,255 and 240 persons per sq. kms. respectively . Palamu and West Singhbhum have low densities of 192 and 180 persons per sq.kms. respectively, while the lowest density has been recorded in Gumla district . This may be attributed to their forested and inaccessible terrain with dissected uplands and steep scarps.

Table 2.5

Nature of Population in Chotanagpur region, 1991

Name of District	Total Geographical Area in Sq. Kms.	Total Population	Density of Population Persons per sq. kms
Ranchi	7698.00	2214048	287
Gumla	9077.00	1153976	127
Lohardaga	1491.00	288886	193

East Singhbhum	3533.00	1613088	456
West Singhbhum	9907.00	1787955	180
Palamu	12749.00	2451191	192
Hazaribagh	11165.00	2843544	255
Giridih	6892.00	2225480	322
Dhanbad	2996.00	2674651	892
Dumka	6212.00	1495709	240
Deoghar	2479.00	933113	376
Sahibganj	3405.00	1301088	382
Godda	2110.00	861182	408
Chotanagpur Region	79714.00	21843911	274
Bihar	173877.00	86374465	497

Sources:- N.I.C. Bihar State Unit 1991.

Tribal Population

Chotanagpur plateau has 91.34 percent of the total tribal population of Bihar in 1991. The highest percentage of tribal population to total

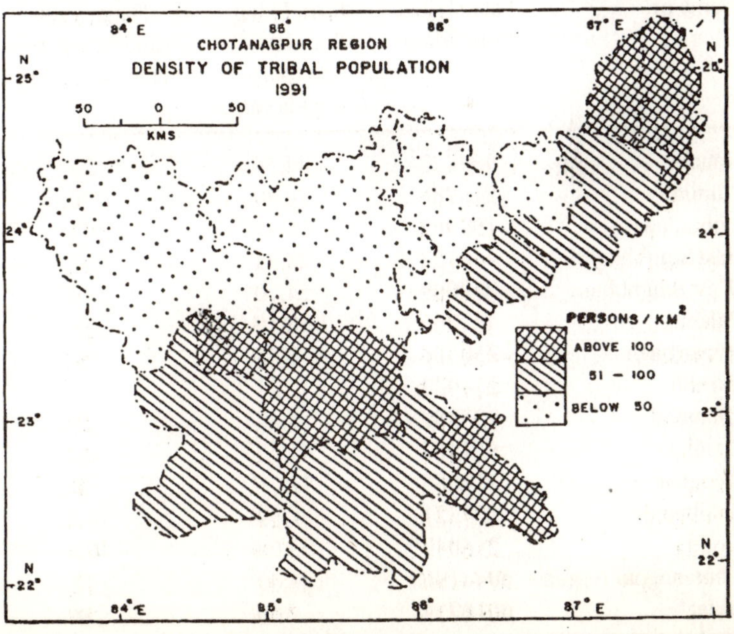

Fig. 2.5

population is in the Gumla district i.e. 70.80. Lohardaga, West Singhbhum and Ranchi comes second, third and fourth respectively in this term , where as this percentage has been recorded as 56.41, 54.70 and 44.56 percent respectively (Table 2.6).

Density of Tribal population in Chotanagpur region is presented by Table 2.6 and Fig. 2.5. Chotanagpur region can be studied in three categories on the basis of density of tribal population :

(a) Areas above 100 persons per sq. km. : This includes all those districts which have 100 persons per sq.kms. It includes the district of Ranchi, Lohardaga, East Singhbhum, Sahibganj and Godda.

(b) Areas of 51-100 persons per sq. kms : It includes the districts of Dumka, Dhanbad, Gumla and West Singhbhum.

(c) Areas below 50 persons per sq. kms. : It includes the district of Palamu, Hazaribagh, Giridih and Deoghar.

Table 2.6

Tribal population in Chotanagpur region, 1991

Name of District	Total Tribal Population	% of Tribal Population to total population	Density of Tribal Population Persons / sq. km.
Ranchi	964422	44.56	125
Gumla	816988	70.80	90
Lohardaga	162964	56.41	109
East Singhbhum	466752	28.94	132
West Singhbhum	978069	54.70	98
Palamu	443266	18.18	35
Hazaribagh	250586	8.81	22
Giridih	271924	12.21	39
Dhanbad	225282	8.42	75
Dumka	621484	41.55	100
Deoghar	119085	12.76	48
Sahibganj	507321	38.99	148
Godda	216047	25.08	102
Chotanagpur region	6044190	24.45	75
Bihar	6616914	7.66	38

Source :- N.I.C. Bihar State Unit, 1991

Chotanagpur plateau comprising South Chotanagpur, North Chotanagpur, Santhal Pargana and Palamu divisions in the State of Bihar is the abode of the tribals.

There are thirty different Scheduled tribes in Bihar, some of them are small while others number more than a lakh. They are Proto-Australoid racial stock. Most of them speak languages of the Austric linguistic group (Mundari, Santhali, Ho, Kharia etc.). The Oraon and the Sauria Paharia speak languages that are in Dravidian linguistic group. Most of the Tribal communities understand Nagpuria (Sadari or Sadani, a variant of the Magahi dialect.). They are generally bilingual. 91.34 percent of the total tribal Population of the State reside in the region. The rest of the total tribal population of the State are scattered in the neighbouring districts of Bhagalpur, Munger and hilly tracts of Rohtas and West Champaran district. Some of the Oraons, locally known as Dhangers are found in the West Champaran and Santhals in the district of Purnia and Katihar.

In 1991, the tribal population of Bihar comprises 7.66% of the total population of the State. The most among them are the Santhal followed by the Oraon, the Munda, the Ho, the Kherwar, the Kharia and the Bhumij. These seven tribes taken together consititute about 86% of the total tribal population of the State. Majority of the tribes in the state are primarily dependent on low land paddy cultivation.

Out of the 30 tribal communities, nine (one Hill Kharia is the sub-group of the other) are identified as primitive groups in the state. Among these are the Birhor, the Asur, the Korwar, the Sauriapaharia and the Hill Kharia (sub group of the kharia) are considered to be the most primitive groups.

There are some social groups of population in Bihar who are anthropoligcally tribe, like Tharu of Champaran, Kheturi at Deoghar, Pergha of Basukinath etc. but since they have not been enlisted in the scheduled list therefore they are not the schedluled tribes.

The most significant point about Bihar with reference to tribal population is that Bihar has the pride of having demographically number one tribe of India i.e. Santhal and also for having economically number one tribe of India i.e. Munda.

Transport

There are various kinds of Transport systems (Fig. 2.6.) available in

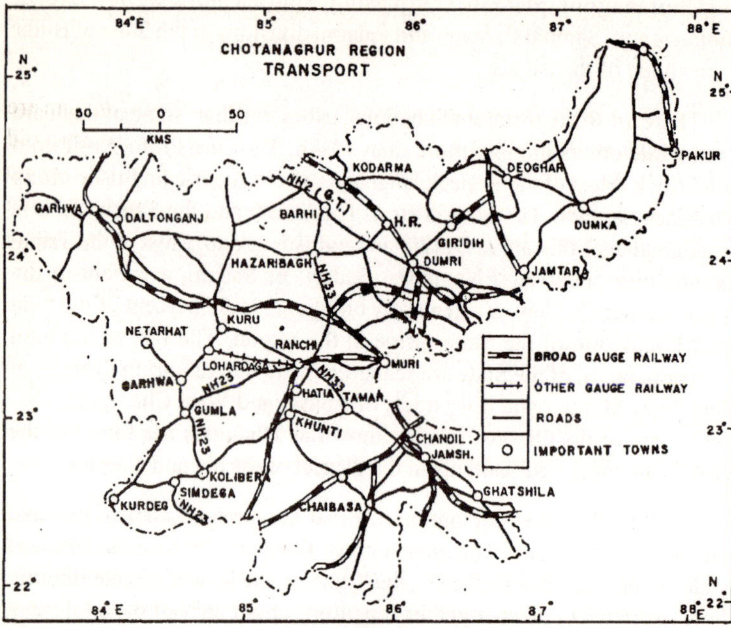

Fig. 2.6

the Chotanagpur region . Railway is the chief means of transport in mining and industrial areas. The main line of the eastern railway was built in 1871, While the south-eastern main line and Raniganj, Jharia extension were opened between 1876-1900. The grand chord line connecting Dhanbad with Gaya traversing through the Hazaribagh Plateau was completed in 1906. The Barkakana loop passing through the coalfields of the Damodar valley could be completed by 1929 because of its slow and gradual extension. The significant addition to the rail network has been the Chandrapura - Muri- Ranchi- Rourkela line which runs diagonally over the Ranchi plateau and was opened to traffic during 1960's.

The highest density of railways is found in the lower Damodar valley where coal mining and mineral industries are concentrated. The Subarnarekha basin has also a dense network of railways where heavy metallic industries and several mining centres are located. But sparsely populated, dissected and forested region of western Palamu, south -western and western Ranchi, north-eastern Hazariabgh have poor network of railways. Northern Chotanagpur is served by Eastern Railway where as the Southern parts are served by South-Eastern Railway. Both zones converge on Howarh. The dissected forested terrain of Chotanagpur presents a major problem for the expansion of rail network. Important links with other regions, are provided by the Bombay - Hawarh line passing through Jamshedpur and the Hawarh - Mughalsarai Grand Chord passing through Dhanbad and Kodarma. Another line to Delhi is by Muri-Daltonganj- Chunar loop. Smaller branches connect Jamshedpur and Ranchi with the mining areas of Badam Pahar and lohardaga respectively. The railway lines of Chotanagpur carry heavy traffic consisting of mineral and manufactured products and their importance in this respect is well reflected in their trackage.

Roads are more important for passenger traffic in the dissected terrain of the Chotanagpur plateau. Ranchi, Jamshedpur, Dhanbad, Chaibasa, Chakradharpur, Barhi and Daltonganj etc. are important nodal centres from where metalled roads radiate in different directions. The important highways are :-

(1) The Grand Trunk Road (N.H.2) which joins Calcutta with Delhi via Dhanbad and Dehri.

(ii) National Highway No. 33 conncets Patna with Jamshedpur via Kodarma, Hazaribagh and Ranchi and, at Bahragora, Joins National Highway No. 6 (Calcutta -Bombay).

(iii) State Highway connecting Muri, Ranchi and Daltonganj and

(iv) Ranchi-Chaibasa- Jamshedpur State Highway.

There are many other all weather matalled roads which provide link between all major cities and towns.

The average road density/sq.km. is 0.2 k.m. or 854 persons /.km. About 30% region is 8 km. away from the roads.

The rivers are not fit for navigation due to their seasonal character and rock beds.

Ranchi is connected with Patna and Calcutta by Indian Airlines. There are small landing stations at Jamshedpur, Chaibasa, Chakulia, Hazaribagh, Bokaro, Dumaka and Daltonganj etc.

References :

1. Census, 1991, N.I.C. Bihar State Unit.
2. Ibid.

3. Ram, L.N., 1968 : "Determination of Uplifts through Profile studies in South-East Chotanagpur", Transactions, Indian Council of Geographers, I.G.U., Vol. 1968. pp. 117-20.

4. Chatterjee, S.P., 1940 : "Gneissic Topography of the Ranchi Plateau", Geographical Review, No. 1, pp. 45-48.

5. Chatterjee, S.P. (Director), 1968 : Selected maps from the Planning Atlas of the Damodar Valley Region, Explanatory notes, Map 7.

6. Singh, R.P., 1960 : 'Geomorphological Evolution of the Highlands of Rajmahal', NGJI, VI (I),

7. Singh, S.P., (et al.), 1997 : 'Geology of Bihar - An Overview' Souvenir, Department of Geology, Patna University, p. 22.

8. Singh, R.P., 1970 : Geomorphological Evolution of Chotanagpur Highland, NGSI (Varanasi), p. 14. often Quoted text.

9. Ghose, N.C., (et al.), 1996 : 'Flow stratigraphy of selected sections of the Rajmahal basalts, eastern India', Journals of South East Asian Earth Science, Vol. l3, No.2, pp. 83-93.

10. Malltiar, K.K., 1991 : 'Geology' in Ram, L.N. (ed.), 'A Systematic Geography of Bihar', Geographical Society, Department of Geography, Patna University, p. 6.

11. Shankar, U., 1991 : 'The Chotanagpur Plateau', in L.N. Ram (ed.) : A systematic Geography of Bihar, Geographical Society, Dept. of Geography, Patna University, p. 190.

12. Singh, R.P. & Kumar, A., 1970 : Monograph of Bihar, Bharati Bhawan, Patna, p. 17.

13. Singh, R.P. : op. cit, p. 19.

14. Shankar, U. : op. cit., p. 191.

15. Singh, R.L., (ed.), 1989 (reprint) : India : A Regional Geography, National Geographical Society, Varanasi, p. 655.

16. Singh, R.P. and Kumar, A., op. cit. p. 29.

17. Singh, R.L. (ed.), op. cit., p. 556.

18. Singh, R.P. and Kumar, A., op. cit. p. 25.

19. Sharma, R.K., 1991 : 'Vegetation' in Ram, L.N. (ed.), 'A Systematic

Geography of Bihar', Geographical Society, Department of Geography, P.U., p. 45.

20. Ibid, p. 46.

21. Singh, J. and Dhillon, 1991: Agricultural Geography, Tata Mcgraw Hill, Pub. Co., New Delhi, p. 344.

22. Husain, M., 1996 : Systematic Agricultural Geography, Rawat Publication, New Delhi, p. 256.

23. Shanker, U. : op. cit., p. 194.

24. Singh, R.P. and Kumar, A. : op. cit., p. 151.fc

3

Primitive Subsistence Economy

The organization of activity to produce goods and services for given consumers may be referred to economic system. The central problems are: what to produce, how to produce it and whom to produce it for: to allocate human resources to supply wants when there is a scarcity of the factors of production, most of which have alternative uses. Any economic system should be able to determine the need of society for goods and services, ensure the correct allocation of the factors of production to industry, provide and maintain investment, distribute goods and services by matching supply to demand and utilize resources efficiently. The mode of production is the way in which society organizes production which shows spatial variation in temporal perspective. Marxists claim that the system of ownership of means of production is the foundation of all social systems and the superstructure politics and ideology of a society - takes its character from the mode of production. Marxism claim the mode of production , especially the capitalist mode, reinforces and reproduces the status Quo. In the primitive, communal mode of production , land and raw materials are commonly owned and labour requirements are shared In the slave mode of production, the labour is a chattel who may be bought and sold. under a feudal system. The proprietor owns the land and most of the produce, but the peasant who is tied to the land may win some of the factors of production. Under capitalism, the worker may sell his labour for a wage but does not own the factors of production. It is the foremost task of the geographers to recognize the fact hat each mode of production creates its own geography vis-a-vis the landscape.

Economy is indicative of a functional whole of the unit of the land to which it is manifested and regardless of the size of the unit, it reflects interdependence of various cultural phenomena, leading to areal association. Economy is an indication of culture vis-a-vis the social organization of the community with identifiable territorial features. Economy, therefore, manifests the genre de vie of the community. The tribal economy which is indicative of what is called 'rudimentary' social organization intrinsically manifests a primitive subsistence culture.

Tribal Economy in General

The tribal culture is Cognated to tribal economics and the economic system of the tribal can be understood in the purview of the cultural factors [1]. In the conventional wisdom of economic science, non-economic features , like social and cultural relations are considered non-essential though they are the tribal realities for the very organization of their economic process. Economy is an important constituent of the community life and plays a deciding role in the formation of the cultural and social structure of society . The economic life of the tribal people helps us to understand an important feature of their culture.

For an assessment of the tribal economy, specially analytical concepts are necessary because social organization and cultural - kinship, political organization , religion - affect economic organization and performance. So, directly and sensitively in tribal communities, only a socio-economic approach which considers explicitly the relationships between economy and society is capable of yielding insights and generalization of any importance.

The scientific study of the tribal economy, in its direct form, was first done by two economists, D. S. Nag and R. P. Saxena. Nag[2] makes an extensive field tour of the contiguous areas of Madhya Pradesh like Mandla, Bilaspur, Durg and Balaghat and studies the Baiga economy in the context of the general economic theories, laying emphasis on the sources of economy of the Baigas. Saxena[3] follows the model of Nag and studies the tribal economy of the western hills in Madhya Pradesh and presented the tribal economy of five tribes who inhabited the area. Prior to these studies, a number of accounts were given about the tribal economy in different ethnographic monographs of the tribals. Vidyarthi gave a good account of the male economy which revolves round hill cultivation. Rai[4] studies the tribals in the context of their home forest and hills and tried to show that economy is based on forest irrespective of their economic types. The problem of getting the basic facts of economic life in a small non-monetary economy of the tribal people, is of specific nature.

It is very difficult to find a simple and precise definition of the tribal economy. The socio- economic structure of the tribal communities intrinsically differs from that of the non- tribals or advanced groups of communities. They have a simple technology which fits well with their ecological surroundings and conservative outlook. Moreover their economy can be said to be subsistence type. They practice different types of occupations to sustain themselves and live on 'marginal economy'.

A tribe is usually considered as an economically independent group of people having their own specific economy and thus having a living , pattern of labour, division of labour and specialization ,gift and ceremonial exchange, trade and barter, credit and value, wealth, consumption norms , capital formation, a land tenure and good - tangible and intangible- economic status. All these have their own speciality which identify the tribal economy in the broader set-up of Indian economy[5].

The characteristics of the tribal economy may broadly be viewed in three ways[6], (a) the structure of the tribal economy, (b) The tribal economy as a socio-economic and cultural system and (c) economic characteristics of the tribal economy.

The structure of the tribal economy is generally based on the forest and the sea . The simple technology and absence of technological aids is the other structural feature of the tribal economy. At the socio- economic and cultural level of the family, is a unit of both production and consumption. The community itself acts like a cooperative unit, and the tribal communities living in a village or locality are economically interdependent . The distribution is generally based on gift and ceremonial exchange.

Following are the fundamental characteristics of the tribal economy-

(1) Forest based economy- Birhors of Bihar ,the Chenchus of Andhra Pradesh.

(2) Unit of production, consumption and pattern of labour being the family - Birhors set out for materials like fibre, chop etc. with their families.

(3) Simple technology - Birhors use very ordinary Jungle knife to procure forest raw materials and rope-making is manually done.

(4) Absence of profit in economic dealings - the barter system fulfills one's requirements but does not give any profit.

(5) The community : a cooperative unit — Birhors trap the hares or monkeys collectively.

(6) Gift and ceremonial exchange - Gift giving and hospitality to social intimates is an important part of their economy.

(7) Periodical markets - Weekly market is the mirror of the tribal culture in India in general, .

(8) Interdependence - under this system each caste group is expected to give certain standardized services to the people of other castes .

(9) The economic Institution of Dhangar - The agriculturist tribes get a helping hand in their agricultural activity .

There are several sources of livelihood for the tribes. But on broad definitions many scholars have blocked out some widely distributed types. Generally speaking, tribals in almost every case have a mixed economy. The economic system of any Indian tribe can not be exclusively placed in a particular typology in its strict sense. The fact that a tribe uses all available means to eke out its subsistence and combines minor forest produce collection with cultivation or shifting cultivation. simple cultivation with food collection indicates the complex economy of these people . At the same time, the tribes men have their primary means of economy and this characterizes their typology. The typology reflects the various grading from hunting and food gathering to the industrial phase.

Majumdar and Madan[7] have provided the following six fold classification of the tribal economy-

(1) Food Gathering :- The Birhors , the Kharias, the Chenchu, the Malapantaram, the Khadar, the Paliyan , the Paniyan , the Yanadi and the kurumba are the food-gathering tribes.

Kadar practices food gathering and even shifting cultivation . They collect fruits, edible roots and honey from the forest and combine the same with the fruits , hunting and chase. All food gatherers are hunters and fisherman, hunting and fishing being, strictly speaking , form of food gathering.

(2) Agriculture :- Agriculture gets the central place in the economic activity of the tribal people in India. However, economic life is nowhere static and rapid changes are taking place. Prominent examples of agricultural tribes are the Oraon, the Munda, the Bhil, the Santhal , the Kharwar, the Baiga, the Korwa, the Gond , the Ho and the Assam tribes.

The most primitive of tribal agriculturists are not much different from the food gatherers. The Kamar, the Reddi, the Baiga and similar primitive agriculturists have never been able to reach beyond the level of neolithic economy . The Kamars live on the inefficient and wasteful shifting axe cultivation, known locally as dahi, hunting , fishing, honey collecting basket making and petty trade . Their economic life is very underdeveloped and depressed like that of most other Indian tribes.

(3) Shifting Axe Cultivation :- It is usually practiced in tropical and sub- tropical realm of the world. In tribal India , Shifting cultivation is widely prevalent, though it is known by different names in different region . The Nagas call it Jhum, the Bhuiya distinguishes two forms of it, dahi and koman, the Marias of Baster call it Penda, the Khonds refer to it as podu, and the Baigas call it bewar.

Shifting axe cultivation consists of felling down trees on a hill -side, a little before the sowing season and setting them on fire. (If all the trees are cut down then the Bhuiya call it dahi; if only bushes and shrubs are placed round the trees and then burnt, they call it koman). By the time of the sowing season the unit is covered with a layer of ashes. Then seeds are scattered and rarely sown in these ashes. After some time the seeds take root and grow, nourished by an occasional shower of rain . The crops are scarce and of inferior quality. In few years, the soil becomes impoverished in the absence of ploughing and manuring and a new stretch of the forest is brought.

Some section of the Naga people like the Rengma Naga are experts in terrace cultivation which is easily possible on a hill slope. Elsewhere in India, among the Bhil , the Gond, the Munda, the Santhal , the Khasi and other tribes plough cultivations similar to that practised in the non-tribal villages in India.

(4) Handicrafts :- Many subsidiary occupations like handicrafts are undertaken in the various tribal zones. These include basket making, Spinning and weaving . The Maria Gonds distill spirit from the forest produce. Functional classes among the Saora , the Kond and the Gond devote themselves to cow herding , metal working, weaving , cane working, pottery and so on. The Korwa and the Agaria are well known iron-smelters , producing tools for local use only, their techniques being very crude. The Ghasi makes gut from the fibrous tissues of animals . The Tharu depends upon farming, manufacture of furniture, household utensils , baskets, musical instruments, weapons, rope and mats.

(5) Pastoralism :- Toda presents a classic example of pastoral economy, their social and economic organization being built around their buffaloes. The Bhotiya of north U.P. are midway between pastoral and agricultural economies. The Todas obtain their living by drawing directly upon milk and milk products and by exchanging the same with neighbouring people to acquire other necessities of life . The buffaloes are ubiquitous figuring in all aspects of life. They or their milk play the prominent part in the socio-religious and ritual of the tribe . The daily life of Toda men is mainly devoted to the maintenance and care of their buffaloes and dairies.

(6) Industrial Labour:- Industrialization and urbanization in the tribal neighbourhoods have intrinsically affected primitive genre de vie of the various tribal communities across the country in general and Bihar , Madhya Pradesh and Bengal in particular .

The Birhor Economy :- The Birhor economy is intrinsically reflective of a primitive subsistence culture which is partly sedentary and partly migratory in nature. Sedentary in the sense that some group of the community have been settled down by the government in some villages of Ranchi, Gumla and Hazaribagh. Nevertheless, the perceptible change has occurred in the economy of the Birhors. Their economy essentially concentrates on (i) hunting and fishing (ii) collection of forest spices. Even the Birhors who have been settled in the past three decades are yet to come out of the primitive economic system.

Culturally speaking, the Birhors have a food gathering and hunting type of economy.[8] Birhor economy centres around the forest . The forest provides them food, drink, shelter and material for their livelihood. Primarily, Birhors depend on forest for three things-

(a) Wild roots and fruits which they eat .

(b) Chop fibres (Bauhina Creeper) from which they make rope and

(c) Small animals e.g. monkey, hare etc. which they hunt or trap for flesh and skin.

Besides these, they also collect wood from the forest and they prepare 'crude vessels' from this wood for sale . The plants , fibres and animals on which the Birhor depend for their livelihood do not provide a continuous supply as these regions are characterised by a tropical climate. As such, the forest resources at one place are limited for exploitation and thus they often face the threat of starvation, hence they have to move with their camps at short intervals from forest to forest in search of food and other materials.

There is a division of labour in Birhors, based on age-sex differentiation . Adult Birhors have to do the hunting and collect chop fibres which draw them away from their tandas .On the other hand, women have to collect edible fruits, tubers, roots, and look after the household affairs and remain mostly near the settlement site.

The Birhor economy, to a grater extent, is family -specific rather than community- specific because each family consisting of couple and the children enters the forest, procures ,fibres, processes them and prepares variety of rope. The family spends one or two days in the forest and then returns back to its huts with raw materials and fruits so that for some time the member can work in the huts for a period. It is the females who usually stay back and do the work while the males move out . The Birhors use forest materials for their subsistence in a more primitive way [9]. The Birhors exploit the forest for their raw material requirement in groups, collect the fibres on the family level but trap the hares or monkeys collectively.[10]

There is cooperation at family level as well as tanda level in some economic activities. Rope-making is done with the help of family members, while hunting is done with the help of family members of a tanda. This type of cooperation is based on a principle of reciprocity.

The collection of forest Resources:- The collection of forest resources is one of the most important economic activities of the Birhors. They collect their food items from the forest.

Food Gathering :- Birhors engage themselves throughout the year to collect roots, tubers, fruit, flower and leaves, according to availability of these items. The following table 3.1 shows the availability of various edible roots, tubers, fruits, flowers and leaves in different seasons. Mahua flower holds an important place in their food habits. Alcoholic drink is also prepared from mahua. The roots like piska , kharia, kesar, barnai are also preserved and have important place in their diet. The forest also provides them herbs.

Table 3.1
Month wise food gathering by Birhor

Month	Nature of Food	Name of Article
Chait	Flower	Mahua (Besisa Latifloa) Gulgul (Cochlos pevem grossyiam.)
(March - April)	Fruits	Pair (Buchanania Latifolia), Kend (Dyosphrous melanoxylon),
	Leaves	Bathua (Chenopodium album). Koniar.
	Roots	Khania, Kesor, Piska.
Baisakh	Flowers	Mahua, Kachnar Korea.

	Fruits	Bel, Baher, Pithona, Piar.
(April - May)	Leaves	Chakwar, Koniar, tender Leaves.
	Roots	Kesor, Kharia, Barnai, Piska.
Jeth	Fruits	Gambar, Kend, Piar, Pipal.
(May - June)	Leaves	Chakwar, Koinar, Pipal, Pankar.
	Roots	Khania, Piska, Haser, Kulo.
Asharh	Fruits	Kussam , Dori, Bar, Bel, dates.
(June - July)	Leaves	Kena, Chakwar, Chirchoni.
	Roots	Peckchi, Khania, Dura.
Sawan	Flower	Mosiphul.
(July-August)	Fruits	Jamun, Mosiphul, Pinora.
	Leaves	Chakwar, Kena, Kerma.
	Roots	Barnai, Piska.
Bhado	Leaves	Khnia, Gurman, Kena, Kodo.
(August-		
September)	Stem	Kareil.
	Roots	Piska, Barnai, Pathal, Kohnra,
Aswin	Fruit	Kainta, Bhet.
(Sept.-Oct.)	Root	Khania, Pitaru.
Kartik	Fruits	Baher, Ber.
(Oct.-Nov.)	Leaves	Purn, Kena.
	Roots	Khania, Piska.
Aghan	Fruits	Baher, Ber, Sarifa.
(Nov.-Dec)	Leaves	Kudrum, Bathua.
	Roots	Bernai, Khania,, Piska.
Magh	Flowers	Gulgul, Jirhul, Kachanar.
	Fruits	Ber, Pipal, Doomar.
(Jan. - Feb)	Leaves	Gurman.
	Roots	Kesor, Bernai, Piska.
Phagun	Flowers	Jirhul, Mahua.
(Feb. -March)	Fruits	Ber, Pipal.
	Leaves	Gurman.
	Roots	Haser, Bhirwa, Dura.

Source : Verma, K.K., 1977 : Culture, Ecology and Population, National Publication, New Delhi, pp. 38-39.

Generally, women and children collect the fruits, nuts and roots. The collections of tubers is carried on by sharpened stick. Some devices such as a net; bags or wooden bowls are used for carrying things like seeds, fruits, nuts, leaves etc. The above table 3.1 shows the availability of edible roots, fruits, leaves and flowers in different months of the year.

Hunting and Trapping :- This is one of the main occupations of the Birhors which runs through out the year. Except during monsoon, Birhor has to go everyday for hunting and trapping. Birhor traps monkey, wild rats, squirrels, rabbit, wild fowls etc. Males take part in daily hunting which is done in a collective way. The nets are placed in line in the vertical position and the whole group splits into two or three units and one unit remains near the nets to catch the arrivals when entrapped. The people beat the bushes with their sticks in order to drive the animals towards the nets. As soon as the animal goes near the nets, it is entrapped and caught. Trapping the birds requires much more patience. Small children below 10 yeas of age are not taken for hunting. The nets are usually of three types;-

(1) Turn Jhali - It is made of threads available in the market and used for trapping fowls, squirrels etc.

(ii) Bara Jhali- This is made of chop-fibre, bigger in size and is used to trap rabbits and monkey etc.

(iii) Gira Jhali- This net is used for fishing. It is round like a basket of two feet diameter.

Inter-tanda hunting expedition- Inter tanda association is found in Hunting. Once in a year people from other tandas are called for a collective hunt. This annual hunting expedition is known as Disum Sendra (or regional hunt). During this ceremony, sexual taboo is very strictly observed. Males usually participate in the hunt.

The Birhors eat monkey flesh and the skin is sold in the market. The price of the animals skins varies according to their size. Occasionally they use animals skin for drum making . Rabbits are sold in the market.

Chop Fibre collection and Rope making:-

The Chop fibre collection and rope making are one of the main sources of livelihood of the Birhors. Both man and women participate in the economic activity. The chop fibre is extracted with the help of tangi (axe) from the following trees.[11]

(i) Mahulan Lati,
(ii) Kumbhi,
(iii) Parambhi,
(iv) Kachnar Kuthul,

After removing the fibres they soak them in water for a day or so to make the fibre soft. The fibre is separated into threads by the use of finger nails and then the rope is made. The rope is sold in the near by weekly market or neighbouring villages.

Honey collection and Fishing :-

During the months of march to May and October to November , the Birhors do the work of honey collection. Generally young Birhors do this job. Among the Birhors, there is a custom that the first who sees the honey comb becomes its owner. In case two case or more persons see it simultaneously they all share it equally. Birhors catch fish from rivers and fields from the months of August to October. Fishing is usually done with the help of Gira Jhali or by drying up shallow water. Following Table -3.2 shows the month wise occupational pattern of Birhors.

Table 3.2
Month wise occupational pattern of Birhors

English month	Vernacular month	Source of Livelihood
May - June	Jeth	Rope manufacturing, Honey collection, Hunting.
June - July	Asharh	Wooden raw materials sale, Honey collection, Rope Manufacturing
July - August	Sawan	Wooden raw material sale, Rope manufacturing.
August - Sept.	Bhado	Wooden raw material sale, Fishing, Rope manufacturing.
Sept. - Oct.	Aswin	Chop fibre collection and Rope manufacturing, Fishing.
Oct. - Nov.	Kartik	Rope manufacturing, Hunting, Honey Collection.
Nov. - Dec.	Aghan	Rope manufacturing, Paddy collection, Hunting.
Dec. - Jan.	Push	Rope manufacturing, Hunting.

Jan. - Feb.	Magh	Rope manufacturing , Hunting.
Feb. - March	Phagun	Rope manufacturing , Hunting.
March - April	Chait	Rope manufacturing , Honey collection, Hunting.
April - May	Baisakh	Rope manufacturing , Honey collection, Hunting.

Source : Verma, K.K., op. cit. p.42

Above table - 3.2 shows that Rope-making is the main source of livelihood. This is main sources of income as this has its own sale value.'The adoption of rope-making craft by the Birhor, their exclusive forest economy undergoes modification and with their food habit, social behaviour and nature of wandering have undergone change'.[12]

From the foregoing discussion, it is evident that the Birhors are gatherers of wild roots and fruits, chop-fibres and trappers of lower form of animals. The natural environment and the forest resources, the flora and fauna are largely important in determining the nature of their food products, the size of the tanda, their social organisation and their nomadic life.[13]

Hunting and fishing as well as collection of forest materials constitute the main economy of the Birhors on account of being wandering nature of genre de vie. They also practice primitive subsistence farming wherever they go in course of their mobility. In fact, the wandering Birhors practice shifting cultivation to a limited extent , and grow different categories of coarse crops. However, a section of the Birhors who were settled to become sedentary in the past few decades, under different Government schemes now practice agricultural activities with the help of traditional implements, nevertheless, the government schemes seek to provide them with certain basic cultivation- specific requirements such as providing seeds, fertilizer and water. These Birhors, however are yet to identify themselves with the agricultural system of any specific nature.

What is important about the Birhors is that the tribe has not carved out its habitat. A very few of them may have been settled but the great majorty still servives on hunting and gathering and which involves movement form one place to another. Because of their wandering nature which is intrinsically confined to Ranchi, Gumla and Hazariabgh districts, they have not come out with their cultural and / or economic landscape, resulting into non agricultural pursuits. Rudimentary social organization with non-sedentary migratory nature appears to be the main reason. The Birhors have not developed the 'territorial feeling vis-a-vis the territoriality' for them, like other tribes of the Chotanagpur region. This is, perhaps, the main reason that they heavily rely on the forest and water bodies for their sustenance and intrinsically lack 'sustainable economic system'.

However, it is reported at the Tribal Research Institute Ranchi, in course of consultation that massive government aids to a greater extent sustain their livelihood, in spite of the fact that they were brought to settled down to become sedentary tribe with lands provided to them under the welfare scheme.

Economic Transformation of the Birhors :-

There has been some short of changes in the structure of the Birhor economy. But number of Birhor's economy to a greater extent thrives on the primitive system of hunting and collection of forest species and, also to an extent on the shifting cultivation. This is largely because of the fact that the tribe, on account of its wandering/nomadic nature, has not developed its own specified habitat vis-a-vis the economic landscape which would have brought subsistence primitive nature to a modern- urban specific agriculture system.

It is equally interesting to note that the Birhors prefer to wander across the forests and mountains of the region. The Chotanagpur Region particularly the districts; Ranchi, Hizaribagh and Gumla are quite rich in minerals and a large number of quarries have been set up but this has not attracted the Birhors in large number to work in the mines. This may be attributed to the primitive perception of the Birhors and their close link - up with the flora and fauna of the area they roam across.

The Birhor economy, to a large extent, is yet to be influenced by the economic transformation taking place in their 'neighbourhood' mostly as a result of the spread of education, industrialisation and urbanisation. The social phenomena in the tribal Chotanagpur are fastly changing as the structure of economic systems of various tribes are experiencing a change over from the primitive subsistence economy through industrialization to an industrial or even to 'post industrial society'.

Changes in the Occupational pattern of Tribe in General

Most of the tribes of the Chotanagpur Region, e.g. the Santhals, the

Oraon, the Munda & the Pahariya have experienced structural changes in their occupational patterns i.e. from primary occupation through secondary, to the tertiary and quarternary occupation in the past fifty years, since independence. Industrialisation and urbanisation that the Chotanagpur region experienced since the Launching of the first- five year plan and the beginning of the regionalisation vis-a-vis- the micro and macro- level planning for the whole region that newer opportunities for the locals and natives began to come up and the tribes with territorial specification vis-a-vis- habitat were the main beneficiaries.

Rapid spread of literacy across the region has essentially benefited the enlightened tribe and education has spread among them which to a greater extent, has changed their perception towards economic occupation and more and more tribal youth irrespective of age and sex are drawn towards the tertiary and quarternary occupation. The rapid spread of education has to a large extent, reduced the out-flow of the tribal people to neighbouring states : West Bengal, Orissa , Madhya Pradesh and to the North -East.

With the spread of infrastructure, particularly with the construction and repair of road- ways, most tribal village markets have been linked up with big markets and the central places which now facilitate to and fro movement of goods, products and even ideas. This has facilitated 'reciprocity' between the rural tribal markets and urban markets which has an obvious impact on the structure of tribal economy.

The spread of infrastructure has sought to integrate various parts of the Chotanagpur region and the phenomena, both cultural and economical tend to be associated as a whole so as to create a new geographic pattern in which newer economic opportunities have been created which now lead to cooperative movements. A large number of co-operatives of various occupation have come into being which seek to train the tribes to change their traditional genre de vie.

Large number of commercial and rural banks have come into being as result of rapid industrialisation and urbanisation. These banks provide financial loan to the tribal people to start their own occupation at a very reduced rate of interest. They also provide loans to tribal students for studies.

Tribals have developed new potato and vegetable varieties to cope with the rising demand of industrial and urban centres in their neighbourhood viz, Ranchi, Bokaro, Rourkela, etc. The tribal of Bero near Ranchi developed a rainy season potato to earn money from eastern India.

Most of the tribes of the region other than the Birhors and whose occupation structure has changed , have come to attract the importance of labour union in their occupational pattern. Tribal labour union have come up both in the industrial areas and mining centre . The union apprises the tribes of their rights and duties and usually fight for the protection of the development rights and save these from exploitation. The labour unions, to a greater extent, have enlightened the perception of the tribes. They have created a sustained concept of saving among the tribes which has brought about or a shift in their consumption patterns from need-based to impersonal need.

The emergence of commercial aptitude among the tribes in the past few years has intrinsically made their 'genre de vie' competitive but not mutually exclusive. They are becoming more and more commercial in their out look even in agricultural produce, they prefer to grow cash crops rather than the cereals. The collection of forest species which used to be subsistence type, has now become commercial in nature.

The government protection to tribal land and the introduction of the land- mortgage act and their subsequent rescheduling have greatly helped tribal genre de vie, making the tribes conscious of their immovable property. The tribal lands which were earlier forcefully occupied by non-tribals, have been recovered and handed over to them. However comprehensive land reforms act is a vital necessity.

More and more tribal youth, regardless of their age and sex, are moving into the tertiary and quarternary occupation because of employment reservation being provided to them under the law, both, in public and private sector. This has greatly changed their traditional and primitive economic system.

The study reveals that the Birhor economic genre de vie has experienced some short of changes. In spite of Government efforts significant number of the Birhor economy still sticks to subsistence primitive forest and hunting type. This is largely attributed to the fact that they are yet carve out their economic landscape across the territories they roam about. However, other tribes of the Chotanagpur region have experienced changes in their occupational pattern because of a number of socio-economic factors, besides the specification of their economic landscape across their habitats.

References :

1. Vidyarthi, L.P. and Roy, B.K. ,1976 : The Tribal Cultural of India, Concept Publishing Company, New Delhi, p. 93.

2. Nag, D.S., 1958 : Tribal Economy : An economic study of Baiga, Bhartiya Admijati Sevak Sangh, New Delhi.

3. Saxena, R.P., 1964 : Tribal economy in Central India, Firma, K.L.Mukhopadhya, Calcutta.

4. Rai, B.K.,1967: Nature and Man : A study of interaction between man forest in Chotanagpur, Ph.D. Thesis, Ranchi University, Unpublished.

5. Vidyarthi and Rai , op. cit., p. 97

6. Ibid., p. 98

7. Majumdar , D.N. and Madan, T.N., 1986 : An Introduction to Social Anthropology, National Publishing House , New Delhi, pp. 196-200.

8. Vidyarthi, L.P., 1958: cultural types of Tribal Birhor, Journal of Social Research, Vol. - 1 (1), p. 77.

9. Vidyarthi and Rai, op. cit., p. 101.

10. Ibid., p. 104

11. Verma, K. K., op. cit., p.41.

12. Vidyarthi, L.P. , 1964 : Culture Contours of Tribal Bihar, Punthi Pustak, Calcutta, p. 232.

13. Sinha, D. P., 1958 : 'Cultural Ecology of the Birhor - A Methodological Illustration', Journal of Social Research, Vol. 1 (1), p. 28.

4

Settlement Pattern

The word 'settlement' in human geography is referred to any form of human habitation from a single house to the largest city, whilst 'culture' reflects man's moral and material refinement and/or development over time. Hence 'culture' seem to be 'cause' and the 'settlement' is its effect. Settlement and culture, therefore, seems to be inseparable and settlement is a geographical manifestation of cultural expression. A settlement reflects not only man's response to his environment but also the religious and social customs of the society. It is through the human occupance that what the German called 'Urlandschaft' changes into 'Kulturlandschaft'. The postulate is that the settlement plays the most significant role in the evolution of 'cultural landscape'. Otto Schluter[1]and the Carl sauer[2] emphasized the importance of settlement in landscape morphology. It is through the process of occupancy that settlement comes into being and which shows a wide variance from region to region because of the peculiarities of the physio-cultural alignments[3]. A setlement is an occupance unit representing an organized colony of human beings, showing the reciprocal relationship of human occupance features and environment[4]. In geography, the study of settlement is done in the light of the spatial attributes of the social organization and occupational structure, and accordingly, the settlement be divided into (i) Urban settlement; and (ii) Rural settlement. An urban settlement is defined as a residential area of a city containing a cluster of individuals of similar culture and/or interest, in which the occupants are involved either in secondary or tertiary or quarternary occupation. A rural settlement is a complex entitled as a result of the varying arrangement of dwellings and Parcels of land. It is the expression of arrangement of rural dwellings or geographical entities to express the grouping of dwellings and their interrelationships[5]. A rural settlement is , therefore, an organised colony of sedentary human beings together with their residences and other buildings and the paths and streets over which they travel. One of the distinguishing aspects of the rural settlement is that the occupants are intrinsically involved in primary occupation and the social organization is primitive subsistence type. It is mainly an agricultural workshop and its shape and arrangement are often in strict accord with the kind of work, the agricultural technique and the way the soil is used[6].

Settlement of The Study Area

The study area of the present work spreads over Hazaribagh, Ranchi and Gumla districts of Chotanagpur region. The study area consists of mountains, plateaus, spurs and valleys, or in other words, the study area is a heterogeneous in terms of relief and intrinsically manifests areal differences and variations. The rural settlements are, therefore, characterized by hilly terrain, poor accessibility, forested landscape and tribal organization[7]. Settlements normally occurs on spurs, ridges, tops, divides and slopes above the valley bottoms with cultivation below in the valley. As the region has dissected terrain, settlements do not seem to consist of larger clusters. It is interesting to note that settlements in the study area usually occur slightly away from the river basins and as a result small settlement clusters have grown up which are commonly hamleted. Settlements are also found away from the main thorough fares[8].Rural settlements in the study area are of various types:

1. Compact settlement,
2 Semi-compact settlement,
3. Hamleted settlement,
4. Semi-sprinkled settlement,
5. Sprinkled settlement,

A compact settlement consists of a number of buildings with streets which are irregular in width and layout. The dwelling are closely spaced or the dwellings develop into clusters[9]. A semi-compact settlement is an intermediate type between the zones of compact and sprinkled settlements. The basic characterstic of the settlements is the presence of one nucleated site with one or two hamlets around the main site[10].

The hamleted settlement consists of a number of physically separate house clusters in close proximity to each other and closely interrelated in day to day social and cultural life, although usually separated by tracks of cultivable land.

The cluster spreads over a wide area[11]. The semi-sprinkled settlement is distinguished by the presence of several smaller hamlets and separate individual habitations spread over the entire mauza or around the main site[12]. A sprinkled settlement is characterized by the presence of complete dispersal of houses over the entire village area and relatively

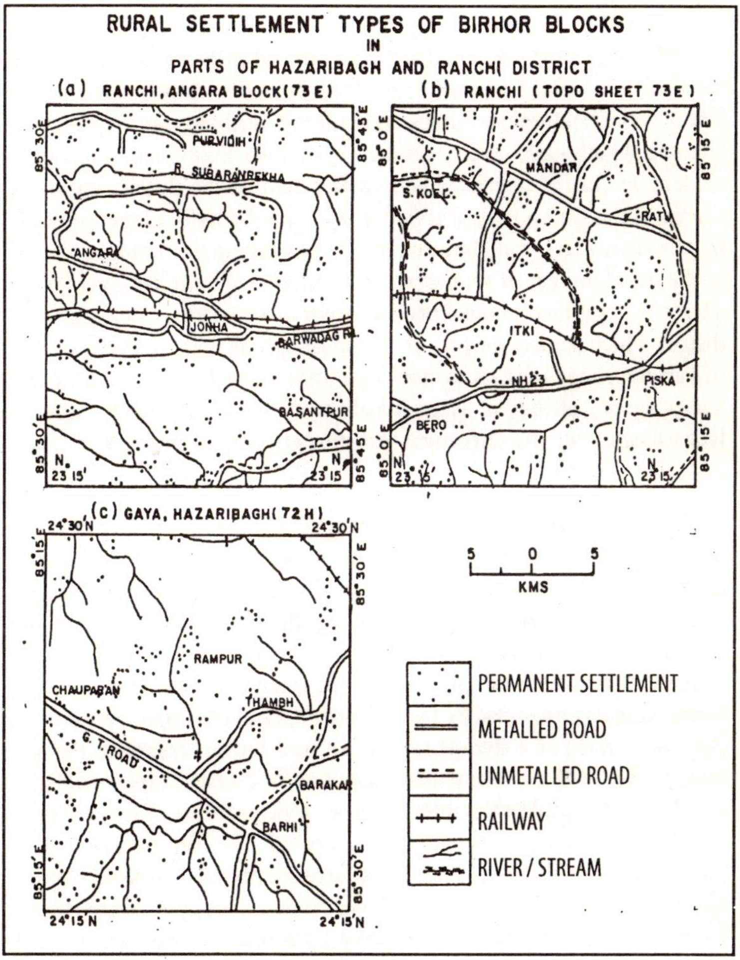

Fig. 4.1

long distances between the dwellings[13].

The rugged areas of the study area: Hazaribagh, Ranchi and Gumla districts possess more uneven or irregular distribution of settlements while the relatively flat area of the districts reveal more or less even distribution of settlements. In the rugged physical area of the study area, settlements tend to grow on uplands (tanr) away from the river basins and utilize the lowlands or river basins for cultivation. The following discussion reveals the types of rural settlement in the district of the study area.

Hazaribagh District

Physiographically, the district consists of hilly terrain, plateau surface and flat upland as well as forested upland with poor accessibility. The physical/natural resources and cultural attributes are unevenly distributed which have direct bearing on the distribution and size of rural settlements in the district. The southern part of the district consists of scarps of the Damodar and is dotted with tiny hamlets. Upper portion of the district suffers from the scarcity of water during the summer, resulting in the development of semi-sprinkled settlements near the river valleys. The semi-sprinkled settlements also occur in the south western part of the district which neglect the role of rolling landscape with a number of peaks of varying shapes and sizes in the evolution of such a type of settlement. The size of settlement is relatively very small. However, near the Hazaribagh town the settlements are mostly compact perhaps, due to the influence of urbanization.

Semi-compact and semi-sprinkled settlements usually occur in the areas of more even terrain of the district which have agricultural land and mica and coal mines. The occurance of natural resources is the main reason for such types of settlements, eg. the lower Barakar basin has a semi-compact settlement. Sprinkled settlements occur in the western part of the district where the plateau surface merges imperceptibly with the North Koel basin divided by the Chatara plateau. The upper portion of the Barakar basin has the semi-sprinkled whilst the lower basins has the semi-compact settlements. The upper reaches of the Damodar basin in the district show hamleted settlements because of the presence of varying nature of erosional features, steep and gentle scarps. The distribution of settlements is relatively sparse. The steep scarps are dotted with widely sparsed tiny hamlets. However, in the relatively flat surface of the district where the presence of the water sources is not a problem, a semi-compact settlement seems to have grown up. Nevertheless, the topographic control is reflected in the settlement type of the district.

Ranchi and Gumla Districts

Ranchi and Gumla districts are characterized by rough terrain particularly in their western parts but relatively flat upland in the eastern part of Ranchi district intrinsically presents contrast in the distribution of settlements. Uneven distribution of settlements occur on the rough terrain whilst comparatively flat topography and balanced distribution of agricultural lands in the eastern part of Ranchi district lead the growth of compact and semi-compact settlements. Sprinkled and/or dispersed settlement are found in the southern parts of both the districts because the areas are undulating in nature and intersected by numerous streams and are also studded with rocky hills and isolated peaks. The South Koel basins and the southern scarps of the Ranchi plateau have mostly semi-sprinkled settlements. Hamleted settlements are rare and occur at wide intervals.

The higher southern scarps of Ranchi plateau, on account of its rough terrain and steep slopes, exceeding over 500 m, is densely forested and hence is dotted with tiny hamlets while semi-sprinkled settlements occur on the lower scarps of the plateau of Ranchi district.

The western Gumla district is highly dissected and rugged and therefore has distinct settlement types. The pat areas are dissected by the tributaries of the river North Koel and the Burha river into many isolated meoas and steep scarpements. They are marked by isolated tiny hamlets . Settlements are isolated here. As the district consists of several rocky spurs of varying heights alternating with deep gorges and valleys, it has many spur settlements along the spurs of the hills and scarp settlements along the scarps. In area where the forests have been cleared for agriculture, semi-sprinkled settlements have grown up. The Simdega plateau of the district with the steep scarp and intervening gorges and valleys have led to the growth of tiny hamleted settlements. The area of rugged relief have widely sparsed isolated hamlets. However, the basins of the rivers Sankh and Deo all mainly dotted with semi-sprinkled settlements. The above discussion intrinsically reveals that the settlements in the study area are controlled by the physical features[14].

Size of Rural Settlements in the Study Area

The size of rural settlements depends very much on the distributional pattern of settlements. The physical nature of the topography and demographic structure as well as inter-village distances usually influence the size. " Where settlement sites are located at relatively long distances, settlements are larger while the villages having several sites within the uneven boundary possess smaller settlement units. The larger settlements generally cover 5-10 hectares of land and are compact in form whilst the disperse settlements generally possess several settlements sites."

The compact villages occuring in the homogeneous resource areas are relatively of larger size than the other settlements like hamlets and individual habitation.The large compact settlements occur at a distance of one to 2.5 kms. While the smaller hamlets in the same homogeneous resource area occur at a distance of less than half a kilometre. Sprinkled settlements genrally have very small hamlets distributed in the entire village lands at a very short distances interspersed by cultivated fields, gardens, pasture lands, patches of forests and small tributaries of streams. In the study area where there is good net of drainage, the river divides which are generally unsuitable for cultivation form a good site for habitation. As a result these settlement units are not nucleated at a site. Almost every river divide is utilised for habitation and the adjoining valleys are used for cultivation. Thus the size of the settlement in these areas is generally small and the inter village distance is short.

The average size of settlement in the study area ranges from 200 to 500 persons. However, there are regional variation in the distribution of size classes of villages. Hazaribagh district has roughly 45 percent of villages having less than 200 persons while 32 per cent villages having population ranging from 200 to 500 persons. Over 45 percent villages in Ranchi district have population ranging from 200 to 500 persons and 20 percent villages have population less than 200 persons. Gumla district has roughly 40 percent villages with population of less than 200 whilst 38 percent villages have population ranging from 200 to 500 persons.

Because of economic constraints, physical hardship, poor accesibility and rudimentary tribal organization, the size of villages in the study area is generally small. Medium and large seized villages are not common.

Settlement Pattern of the Study-Area

Agglomeration of dwellings and their placing at crossroads with a distinct external layout is known as settlement pattern. The arrangement of dwelling is guided by roads, cart-tracks, water facilities and other social amenities. The village cart-tracks and lanes form the skeleton of internal layout of the village. The buildings located in the space within the skeleton determine the shape and form of the village[15]. The geometrical pattern of individual houses determine the internal structure of the village. The settlement is very much dependent on the configuration of the site surface water, in nature of soil, water bodies, ancient architecture, the shape of cultivated fields, and the village street pattern.[16]

Various kinds of settlement and/or village pattern occur in the study area which are as follows :-

Rectangular Pattern :

The most common village pattern where nucleated settlements occur is roughly rectangular. One of the main reasons for this pattern is the shape of the cultivated fields. Most of the houses remain rectangular with their main axis from north to south and east to west. In compact settlements the rectangular and square blocks of land give rise to greater concentration of dwellings which produce the rectangular pattern. Compactness requires houses to be as close to each other as possible[17].

Hollow Rectangular Pattern :

This pattern develops around an unbuilt open space in the middle of the village. It is most frequent in zones of strife where the central vacuum space was once occupied by the old fort of the local chieftan around which the villages congregated. The presence of a church or a tribal worshipping and/or water body also cause the rise of such pattern of village.[18]

Square Pattern :

The square pattern appears to be the beginning of the rectangular pattern. Such a pattern usually comes into being when the rural dwellings tend to develop at the cross-road of cart-tracks or roads. It is also related to some features restricting the extension of village outside a square space. The square field pattern also gives rise to a square pattern[19].

Chess-Board Pattern :

The chess-board or grid iron pattern denotes a right angled mesh of streets with or without a central rectangular market place[20]. The intersection of lanes and cart-tracks creates rectangular sub-blocks giving the form of chess-board.

Linear or Elongated Pattern :

The linear pattern develops when the rural dwellings come up along a navigable water way or road or along a railway track. The settlement growth is prolonged in one direction.

Radial Pattern :

The growth of this pattern is controlled by the radiating character of cart tracks and lanes. The convergence of lanes in a circular village with five straight lines result in a radial pattern. In the centre of the habitation there may be a well or a primary school or a shop. The dwellings tend to develop along the radiating road.

Irregular Pattern :

It is one of the most common village pattern in the study area. It generally consists of larger villages than the average of compact settlements. In this pattern houses are hirdled in an irregular fashion without any definite plan. The larger villages generally consist of several tolas having different forms and when compiled , do not provide any pattern. Some of the villages in Gumla do have such pattern.

Double Nucleation Pattern :

In double nucleation, two settlement units which have grown up simultaneously or one after another on a single site are found in close proximity. A double village is also called "double dorfer"[21]. Their revenue and administration are dealt separately in spite of their similar geographical conditions. A nala or road, a mound, a tank, river or a channel may separate these double nulceated settlements.

Amorphous Pattern :

An amorphous pattern settlement courts of human hamlets scattered over the mauza. Though, each hamlet by itself is more or less rectangular but their relative arrangement is so irregular that no pattern emerges and such settlements can best be termed as amorphous.[22]

L-shaped Pattern :

It is the common village pattern found at several sites where two linear forces meet at right angles to each other. This village pattern is a subsidiary pattern of the rectangular or square form. When two roads and cart tracks attract the dwellers to settle in that direction the L-Pattern comes into being.[23]

The above discussion on the village pattern reveals that the pattern is essentially controlled by site characteristics approach by cart-tracks, geometrical disposition of internal lanes, field pattern and also by the occurrence of cultural features, water bodies and by any other conspicuous man made phenomenon such as the tribal organization. The most common and evenly distributed village patterns in the study area is the rectangular pattern. It is more particularly found in the villages having compact and semicompact rural settlements. There are also several nucleated villages in the areas of semi-sprinkled and sprinkled type of settlements which are mostly rectangular or square in Ranchi, Gumla and Hazaribagh districts. However, the hollow rectangular pattern occurs in eastern Hazaribagh district.

The linear or elongated villages have developed in the Damodar basin in Hazaribagh and in the Koel basin in Ranchi district, mostly along the river courses, particularly the water problem becomes acute during summer. The linear pattern has developed in the districts where long cart-tracks and village lanes occur. In the hilly Gumla and Ranchi areas this pattern is common. Radial village pattern has developed also in the hilly Ranchi and Hazaribagh plateau. A few examples of circular pattern have been identified on the Ranchi plateau, however, this is not a common pattern.A few villages with fan pattern occur in the hilly areas of Ranchi and Hazaribagh district but the irregular villages pattern is again found to be common in hilly and plateau surface of the study area. A few L-Shaped villages occur in the hilly Gumla district. The radial village pattern mostly occurs in south western Ranchi plateau whilst hollow rectangular pattern in lower Hazaribagh plateau. The square pattern is common in the neighbourhood of Ranchi and Hazaribagh urban centres whilst the chess-board pattern occurs in the upper reaches of Ranchi and Gumla districts. The amorphous patterns of settlements are mostly found on the outer fringe of the study area but major concentration of such village pattern occurs in Gumla district.

Types and Pattern of Birhor Settlement

Hardly any consistent literature is available on the types and patterns of the Birhor settlement and whatever little is available, does not seem to be enough for a meanigful and/or rational interpretation. Nevertheless, in the following discussion an attempt is made to enumerate the types and patterns of the Birhor settlement, so as to give a synthetic treatment to the Birhor settlement study.

The sedentary Birhor settlements tend to occur on the hilly areas near the forest and the wandering Birhor settlements usually occur in the inaccessible, rugged and forested areas but their settlements are of the most temporary in nature. The word 'settlement' however does not seem to be relevant in the case of the Uthlu or wandering Birhor. Uthlu Birhors build their houses with reeds, bamboos , leaves etc[24]. Since they wander in small groups particularly in the forests, they build their small temporary sheds in 'parallel rows'. They leave on abandoning their sheds. Sheds are about 1.5 meters in height, Uthlu Birhor settlement which is most temporary act, occurs in the forested rugged terrain and is hamleted because individual shed or jhopri comes up within the shortest possible time when the 'tanda' decides to stay on a particular place for some time. The individual sheds are constructed in parallel rows with an intervening space, hence the pattern is parallel.[25]

Most of the Birhor villages in the Ranchi plateau do have semi-sprinkled and sprinkled settlement because of the rugged physical terrain in close proximity to forests. However, the Birhor villages in the Khunti area are of hamleted type. The Birhors prefer to build their houses close to the forests so that they can secure their sustenance without much hindrance since their economy is forest-based primitive types.At the foot of the ridges and hills where forests exist, the Birhor villages have developed in a haphazard manner, resulting in the growth of semi-sprinkled settlements.

In the forested Simaria and Barkagaon anchals of Hazaribagh district, the Birhor villages have isolated home-steads, e.g. Muresatoli, Semrateri, Jori, Hanri and other villages. However, the Birhor villages, on the whole, in Hazaribagh district are of semi sprinkled nature because of the presence of rolling landscape with a number of peaks with varying shapes and sizes. The Birhor villages in the Bishnupur anchal of Hazaribagh consists of both semi-sprinkled and hamleted types, reflecting the influence of the physical terrain and the adjoining forests. Besides, the occurrence of spring and small river in the vicinity also seems to have led to the growth of such village types.

Highly dissected and relatively highland areas of Ranchi and Gumla districts, with many meson and steep escarpments have isolated tiny Birhor hamlets. However, the Birhor settlements, on the patches of relatively flat surface which have been recently cleared of forests and a few small streams traverse across the surface, and the 'Birhors have switched over to agriculture from their forest gathering occupation, to a greater extent, semi-compact types. Tiny hamleted to semi-sprinkled Birhor settlements occur on the rugged but dissected Simdega plateau.[26]

However, a few examples of semi-compact Birhor settlements can be found on the flat pleateau surface of the study area in close proximity of the urban centres where, apart from the topographic influence, the social situation in the neighbourhood also seemed to have played a decisive role. It is important to note that Birhor tribal organization hardly plays a role in dividing the type of settlement, rather the role of physical belief and forest is significant[27]. Lack of compactness may be attributed to (i) lack of territorial feeling, (ii) since the Birhors are a forest tribe their, genre de vie intrinsically reflects hunting of various herbivorous and carnivorous animals to sustain their lives, they become fearless rather to an extent, ferocious but not cruel. As a result, they do not feel the necessity of living together in congregation (iii) the Birhors like to remain isolated from other tribes of the locality and prefer to have their settlements on the hill tops and mountains, as they are suspicious about other tribes (iv) rudimentary but primitive social and economic organizations. The Birhor settlements in the study area are of recent origin. Till recently the Birhors were a wandering tribe moving from forest to forest across the rugged mountainous terrains. With the depletion of forests, felling down of forests and forest clearing, the Birhors were forced to abandon their wandering genre de vie and settled down on the outskirts and on fringe areas in an haphazard way. A section of the Birhor tribe is still roaming and wandering across the forest but a great majority of them have settled down spontaneously. However, some Birhors have been settled in the past three decades as a part of the government sponsored plan.

The geographic conditions that determine the size of Birhor settlements are more or less the same that influence the distribution and types of rural settlements. Sprinkled and semi-sprinkled Birhor settlements in the study area have very small hamlets distributed in the villages at a very short distance intersperersed by cultivated fields, gardens, pasture lands, patches of forests, and small tributaries of streams. The siz of the Birhor settlement in the study area is comparatively small and the average distance between the settlement is short.

The size of Birhor villages ranges from less than 75 to 300 persons, as compared to 200 to 500 persons of other tribal villages in the study area.[28] The size of the Birhor villages can be classified into the following three categories :(i) Villages with less than 75 persons, (ii) villages with 75 to 149 persons, and (iii) villages with 150 to 300 persons. The first category of villages with less than 75 persons requires to be called the 'very small size village' whilst the second category villages is known as the 'small size villages' and the third category village with a population, ranging between 150 and 300 population would be identified as the 'medium range size villages' in the tribal perspective.

In the study area, the small, size Birhor villages predominate which roughly proximate around 67. 60% percent notwithstanding the regional variation within among the Birhor villages in the study area, 70 percent Birhor villages in Hazaribagh district belong to the category of the very small size whilst the corresponding percentage for the same category and/or size for Ranchi and Gumla district stands to 65 percent and 68 percent respectively. Similarly 25 percent Birhor villages in the study area belong to the second category with 35 percent in Hazaribagh; 27 percent in Ranchi and 13 percent Birhor villages in Gumla belong to the category of the small size village. 3.40 percent Birhor villages in Hazaribagh, 2 percent each in Ranchi and in Gumla belong to the third category of the medium size range of villages[29]. In fact 7.40 percent village in the study area belongs to the, third category of the village size.

These three categories of size of Birhor settlements in the study area reveal that (i) the growth of the Birhor population in comparision to other tribes does not seem to be too smooth, rather the growth is slow, (ii) the process of territorialization of the Birhor settlement is rather slow and intermittent, (iii) the process of economic transformation from the forest inclined primitive subsistence system to the sedentary agricultural system is a recent phenomenon and the change-over appears to be intrinsically belated and (iv) the Birhors are yet to completely abandon their nomadic character-vis-a-vis in the rudimentary social tribal organization.

Most of the semi-sprinkled and sprinkled types of Birhor settlements on the hill tops and also on the higher surface of the pats in Ranchi and in Gumla neighbourhood, are mostly rectangular and square pattern, though some examples of hollow rectangular do occur in some villages which are situated on the flat plateau surface.

The linear or elongated village pattern is a common Birhor village pattern in the study area. Linear Birhor villages are found mostly on the northern and southern fringe of the study area along the cart track small tributaries of them, nalas, roads and also along the ridge tops (fig.4.1.)

The irregular development of hamlets on the higher rugged surface of western Ranchi and Gumla district has led to the growth of amorphous Birhor villages. However, irregular development of cart tracks and lanes in a haphazard manner also seem to have been the prime reason for the amorphous Birhor villages in western Hazaribagh district.

Some Birhor villages, particularly those which have been settled a bit long ago where the tribe has increasingly become sedentary in the recent past and where it has built up, its places of worship, the dwellings tend to develop in circular ways around the places of worship. These circular Birhor villages occur on the flat plateau of Ranchi and Hazaribagh. Still on the higher pat area, a few example of terraced Birhor villages can be found where the Birhors have started cultivation on the patches of cultivated lands on different altitudes in some villages. A few examples of double nucleated Birhor villages can be found in study area particularly in Gumla and Hazaribagh districts where the relief consists of isolated hilly tops with intervening spurs and basins. The dwellings have come upon the hilly flat tops in an isolated manner. The forest also plays a significant role in the pattern of the Birhor villages.

However, the common patterns of the Birhor villages are rectangular, hollow rectangular, circular and linear pattern which instrinsically manifest the impact of physical nature of the areas and the emerging Birhor cultural ecology, particularly the adoptive nature of the Birhor genre de vie to the new environment. As more and more Birhors are becoming sedentary, their traditional life style is changing in their village pattern.

Birhor House Types

Houses are the fundamental requirements of human beings as they provide shelter and protection from the rigorous climate. They are universal elements of the cultural landscape of permanently occupied region. The agglomeration of houses marks the origin of human settlements. Their character is related to the environment and to the cultural heritage of the people[30]. The geographical location of a region greatly influences the character of rural house types which are the results of adaptation to the physical conditions. They show the influence of relief, geology, climate, vegetation and of social and economic condition in the internal structure as well as external form of the houses[31]. These factors play an important role in the function, size and shape of houses[32]. In the study area, laterite soil, bamboo, grass, reed and vegetative matter are the leading materials used for the construction of dwellings.

The amount of rainfall, and its infirmity, however determine the various forms of walls and roof. The nature of the roof is an index of the climate determinant[33].

Economic activities, cultural heritage, tribal organization determine the dwelling types and their layouts. The study area shows a greater regional variation in the tribal character and organization. Most of the major tribes of the Chotanagpur region carved out their habitation across the study area. Therefore, there are differences in house type of various tribes. The Birhors are perhaps the poorest tribe in the area with their primitive subsistence economy and culture, a section of the tribe is still practicing nomadism. The Birhors have become sedentary in the past two to three decades.

Majority of the Birhor houses belong to the category of the 'Rudimentary House Type' which roughly approximate 82 percent of all Birhor houses. These houses have only one room and the same room is used for cooking food and taking rest. In such rudimentary houses the family deity is kept in right corner while the Kitchen is specified in the left where the family utensils are kept. Grains are kept hanging from the ceiling. The Birhors keep their domestic animals and other forest produce in the same room. Since the Birhors are a poverty stricken tribe, they build such rudimentary houses. These houses do not have ventilation and so they remain completely dark even during the day time. Houses have small doors and are made of bamboos, grasses and leaves. There is no privacy being maintained in such houses. Though the rudimentary Birhor houses occur every where in the study area the greatest concentration occurs in Ranchi and Hazaribagh districts.

The semi-sedentary Birhors who are undergoing social transformation in the recent past usually build their dwellings which are called as 'straggling house Type' which occur mostly in the forest, summits and hill tops of the study area. These houses are characterised by walls built with mud ,reeds, grass, bamboo and sticks covered with thatched roofs. The doors are small and such houses do not have ventilations. The straggling houses of the Birhor reflect the primitive character of the tribe. The Birhors live together with their domestic animals. These houses are one-roomed and small.

The Uthlu Birhors put up temporary sheds or jhopri in the midst of the forests. Such sheds are made of leaves and bamboos. The Uthlu Birhors build such shed every year mostly before the onset of the rainy season. They start abandoning the sheds or Jhopri with the coming of spring. The height of the temporary sheds or Jhopri of the uthlu Birhor is less than 1.75 metre from the ground.

One - roomed houses premodinate in the Birhor villages with 82 percent of the total households. These Birhor houses are 2.75metre long and 1.75 metre wide. These one-roomed houses, mostly have bamboo wetly or reed walls and thatched roofs. In most cases the roof are covered with leaves. The average height of ceiling is 2.75 metre from the ground.

Two- roomed Birhor houses are not much common in the study area because of the relatively poor economic condition of the tribe. However, two- roomed Birhor houses do exist in some anchals of Hazaribagh and Ranchi districts, particularly where the rehabilitation scheme has been launched by the Government. Two- roomed Bihor houses have mudwalls with thatched roofs, but some of these have tiled roofs. Many such houses have separate verandahas and cattled sheds and open spaces in front of the room. The average length of the room is 3.5 metre x 2.75 metre.

Most of the Birhor houses in the study area are built with reeds, bamboos, thatch and leaves etc, which intrinscally manifest (i) the primitive subsistence economy of the tribe and (ii) the influence of the rugged terrain and the control of forest. These Birhor houses are quite small in size. The roof of such houses consists of bamboos covered with leaves. The dwellings are one- roomed with no window. The building materials are locally available and the Birhors themselves collect them and build the structure. Such Birhor houses account for nearly 74 percent of all Birhor houses in the study area though there is district wise variation, 78 percent in Ranchi district, 81 percent in Gumla and 73 percent in Hazaribagh.

However, some Birhor houses in the study areas, particularly on the rolling landscape of the plateau surface are built with mudwalls and thatched roof. Such houses are more common in Hazaribagh district, though few examples are found in Ranchi and Gumla district. Under the Government rehabilitation programme, recently settled Birhor houses in the study area, have been built with brick walls and tiled roof and also with brick walls and cemented roof.

Though the rectangular house type is the most common feature of the sedentary Birhor in the study area, the wandering or the Uthlu Birhors in the study region do construct Beehive type houses with bough and twigs. These houses do not have solid wall and only shallow gulten surround them. These are the most temporary houses.[34]

The mudwall, in fact accounts for little over 70 percent of the total Birhor house holds in the study area. However, the district- wise percentage of mudwalls of the Birhor house holds shows not much variation, e.g. 70

percent in Hazaribagh, 73 percent in Ranchi and 71 percent in Gumla district. The remaining percentage is shared by the walls made of vegetative materials, grass, leaves, reeds, bamboos and bricks. In the rugged higher surface and forested areas, walls constructed of bamboos, , grass, leaves and reeds etc. account for 23.13 percent of the total Birhor households and the remaining percentage of walls are made of bricks and stones. Walls constructed with bamboos, grass, reeds and other vegetative materials are significant among the poorest of the poor Birhor. More than fifty percent of Birhor houses made of mudwalls are occupied by individual family group and small families consisting of 2 to 4 persons.

Roofs thatched with grasses, leaves and vegetative matters predominate in the region and 78 percent of the roofs are of this type while the remaining 22 percent are accounted for by the tiled roofs. Thatched roof with bamboos splinting grass, leave and vegetative matters are frequently used because of their easy availability in the neighbourhood. Thatched roofs are very common among the Birhors of the study area which also reveal the poor economic conditions of the tribe. These materials however, are easily available in the Birhor habitat of the study area.

It has been empirically stated that the Birhor house holders in the study area intrinsically suffer from the lack of general amenities to meet the basic requirement of the tribe[35]. Except in the case of Anchal/Block head quarters and the Thana head quarter, the distance of centres of other amenities lies between 2 and 8 kilometres. However, the great majority of the Birhor settlement and/or villages lie at relatively greater distance from the the centre of the territorial social services.The Birhor villages in the study area are relatively at greater distance from the metalled road. The average distance of the Birhor villages to the metalled road and bus stand is 6 kilometre. Although there are some local variation within the study area, e.g. in Gumla, it is 7 km., in Hazaribagh district the average distance between the Birhor village and the metalled road is 5 km and in Ranchi it is 6 km.The Educational facilities are non-existent in the Birhor settlements of the study area. The Birhor children have to travel an average distance of 5 km, to reach primary schools. However, the literacy among the Birhor is necessarily very poor and the school dropout is maximum. The medical facilities including dispensaries, hospitals and doctor are again very meager and inadequate. Keeping in view of the need of such facilities, Birhors have to travel an average distance of 6.5 km to meet these requirements in Birhor village in the study area.

The Birhor villages usually lack in other facilities, pucca wells, drains, and community hall. The geographic distance is an important factor for their backwardness. Their rudimentary social organization along with their primitive subsistence occupation requires to be considered as an important factor[36].

To sum up, the Birhor villages have variable settlement types from being hamlated to sprinkled ,semi-sprinkled and semicompact types. Most of the Birhor villages are rectangular and linear in shape and pattern. Birhor houses are usually made of reeds, bamboos, vegetative matters and mud. Some houses have brick - walls and cemented roofs. However, most of the houses are thatched roofed. The Birhor villages are all devoid of power, infrastructure facilities. The territorial social services, including health care, education, communications are not available in the neighbourhood of Birhor settlements which result in their backwardness and isolation from the main streams of the tribal life of the various tribes of the study region.

References :

1. Schluter, Otto, 1906: Die ziele der Geographic des Menchen. R. Olderbourg, Munich.
2. Sauer, Carl, 1925: The Morphology of the Landscape, University of California Press Berkeley.
3. Singh, R.L and Singh, K.N. (ed.), 1975: Readings in Rural Settlement Geography, National Geographical Society, p. 7.
4. Singh, R.L.,1975: ' Meaning and Objectives and Scope of Settlement Geography,' In Singh R. L. and Singh, K. N., (ed.), Readings in Rural Settlement Geography, pp. 4-5.
5. Aurosseau, M., 1920: 'The Arrangement of Rural population', Geographical Review, Vol. 10, p.223.
6. Trewartha, G.T. (et al.), 1967: Elements of Geography, Physical and Cultural, Mc Graw Hill, Co., London.
7. Sinha, V.N.P., 1969: 'Houses and House types of the Chotanagpur Plateau,' Geographical Knowledge, Vol. 2, p.91.
8. Sinha, V.N.P., 1976: Chotanagpur Plateau : A Study in Settlement Geography, K.B. Publication, New Delhi, p.76.

9. De La Blache, P.V., 1922: Principles of Human Geography, New York.

10. Mandal, R.B., 1979: Introduction to Rural Settlement, Concept Publishing Company, New Delhi, p.137.

11. Singh, R.B., 1975: 'Rural settlement types and their distribution: Examples from Varanasi district, India,' In Singh, R.L. and Singh K.N. (eds.), Readings in Rural Settlement Geography, National Geographical Society, Varanasi, p. 233.

12. Singh, R.L., 1955: 'Evolution of Settlements in Middle Ganga Valley', National Geographical Journal of India, Vol. 1, p.100.

13. Trewartha, G.T. (et al.) op. cit. p.559.

14. Sinha, V.N.P.,op. cit. pp. 69-70.

15. Ahmad, E., 1942: 'Rural Settlement Type in U.P,'Annals of the Association of the American Geograpers, Vol. XLII, pp. 223-46.

16. Dickinson, R.C., 1934: 'The Town Plans of East Anglia: A Study in Urban Morphology', Geography, Vol. 19, p. 37.

17. Mandal, R.B. 1979: Introduction to Rural Settlements, Concept Publishing Co., New Delhi, p. 137.

18. Ibid.

19. Ahmad, E., 1962: 'Indian Village Patterns', Geographical Out look, Vol. III, p. 11.

20. Dickinson, R.E., op. cit. p. 74.

21. Ahmad, E., 1962 : 'Indian Village Patterns', Geographical Out look, Vol. 3, p. 11.

22. Sinha, V.N. P., op.cit. p. 91.

23. Sinha, V.N.P., op. cit. p. 91.

24. Singh, R.P. and Kumar, A., 1976: Evolution of Man and Racial Study (Hindi), Bihar Hindi Granth Academy, Patna, p.201.

25. Mukherjee, S., 1980: 'The Birhor of Bihar and W. Bengal', Geographical Review of India, Vol. 4, No. 2, pp. 48-54.

26. Sinha ,V.N.P., op.cit., pp. 68-69.

27. Mikherjee, S., op. cit., pp. 48-54.

28. Sinha, V.N.P., op. cit.,pp. 70.

29. Mukherjee, S., op. cit.,pp. 48-54.

30. Sinha, V.N.P., op. cit., pp. 95-96.

31. Sharma, R.C., 1972 : Settlement Geography of Indian Desert, Kumar Brothers, New Delhi.

32. Singh, L.R., 1965 : The Terai Region of UP : study in Human Geography, Allahabad, p. 37.

33. Kumar, Alok, 1985 : Tribal Culture and Economy : The Mal Paharias of Santhal Paragana, Inter- India Publication, New Delhi, pp. 88-89.

34. Sinha, V.N.P., op. cit., p. 103.

35. Vidyarthi , L.P., 1960 : 'The Birhor : A Study in Ecology, Economy and Wandering ,' Paper submitted at the 54th International Congress of Anthropology and Ethnological Science, Philadelphia, U.S.A.

36. Choudhary, G., 1965 : Life and Culture of Birhor Tanda, Unpublished, M.A., Dissertation, Ranchi University, Ranchi.

5

Demographic Features

Growth of Population

The growth of population means changes in size of population, whether increase or decrease. Positive and negative growth of population is an interplay of three factors, namely birth, death and migration. The growth of population is not a separate aspect of people's existence but the outcome of these distinct factors. The growth of population passes through series of four stages. In the first stage, both the birth and death rates are high and population increases slowly. In the second stage, the death rate falls and the birth rate goes high, therefore, the population expands more or less explosively. In the third stage, the birth rate also falls sharply so that the increase of population is slow. Finally, both the birth and death rates stabilize at a low figure, therefore, the population increases slowly unless it is spurred by new development. This is called the demographic transition and the theory, although, was originally developed by W.S. Thompson[1], but in the form of a significant idea, it was developed by F.W. Notestein.[2] However, it is yet to become a law.

As regarding the growth of Birhor population, it has experienced a mixed trend during 1901-1961 and has shown an increasing trend after 1961. During 1901-1911 the population of this tribe witnessed and/or experienced probably the highest increase by 138.92%. In 1901 there were only 848 Birhors in Bihar and the number increased sharply to 2026 in 1911. Thus, the net growth was of the order of 1178 persons. However, during 1911-21 the population decreased to 1363, and the net decrease was 663 persons, that is, a decline by 32.72%. This decrease in the Birhor population may be attributed to a number of factors such as disease, epidemics, lack of minimum required amenities.

After 1921, Birhor's Population increased continuously till 1941. In 1931, the population increased to 1870 and in 1941 to 2530. Thus there was an addition of 507 heads during 1921-31 and 660 heads during 1931-41. The respective percentage growth was 37.20 and 35.29 during these decades.

Table 5.1
Growth of Birhor Population (1901-2011)

Year	Birhor population	Growth	Percentage growth
1901	848	-	-
1911	2026	1178	1138.92
1921	1363	-663	-32.72
1931	1870	507	37.20
1941	2530	660	35.29
1951	-	-	-
1961	2438	-92	-3.64
1971	3464	1026	42.08
1981	4377	913	26.36
Projected	Arithmetic	Geometric	
1991	5346	5865	
2001	6315	7857	
2011	7284	10528	

Source :Various Census Reports

During 1941-61 the population decreased slightly by 3.64 percent. There were 2530 Birhors in 1941 and their population decreased to 2438 in 1961, the net decrease during this period was 92 persons.

The population of Birhor has increased steadily since 1961. Their population was 2438 in 1961, which increased to 3464 in 1971 and 4377 in 1981.The net increase was 1026 during 1961-71 and 913 during 1971-81. The percentage increase was 42.08 during 1961-71 and 26.36 during 1971-81. This increase in population seems to be due to decrease in their death rate due to the Government sustained policy to provide them basic required minimum health care facility and also a large section of the Birhor population started becoming sedentary abandoning their migratory habit. After independence, the birth rate was high during 1961-71, but during that period the growth showed a relatively declining trend. Population during 1971-81 again showed an increase. Nevertheless, some of the sedentary Birhor families probably adopted the government sponsored family welfare measures, that is why, the percentage growth of population decreased during 1971-81 in comparison to 1961-71.

The data regarding the actual population of Birhor is not available for the year 1991, but an estimate may be made on the basis of the past trend of growth. According to the arithmetic progression, the population of

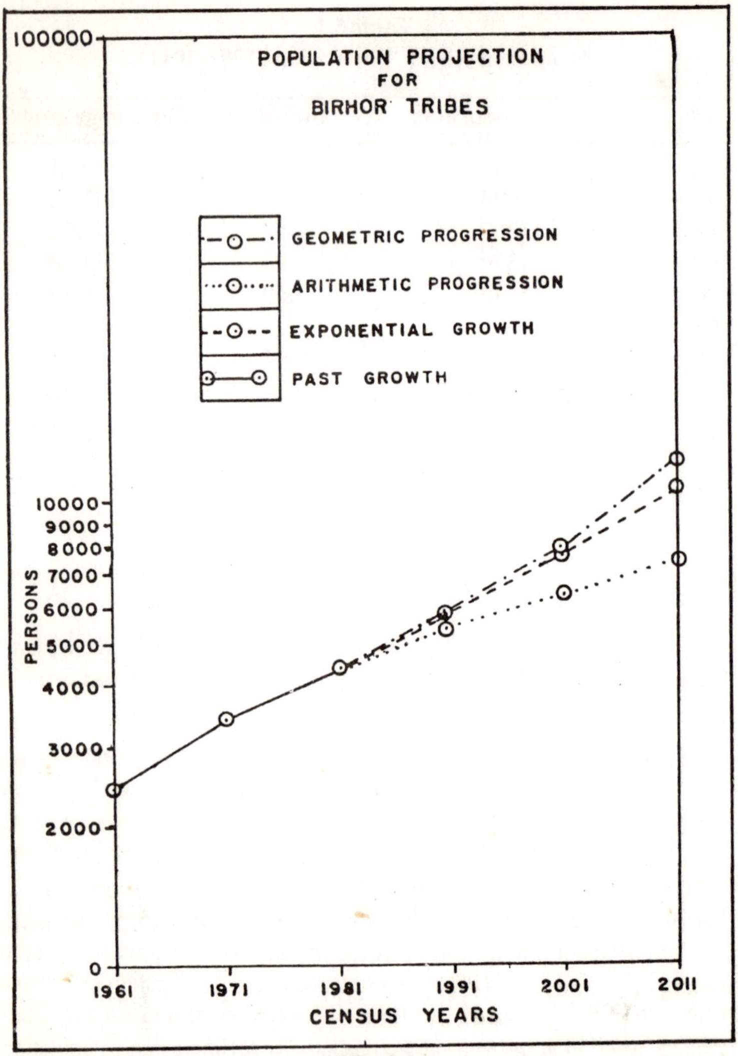

Fig. 5.1

Birhor is expected to be 5346 in 1991, 6315 in 2001 and 7284 in 2011 (Table - 5.1 and Fig. 5.1). But according to geometric progression, it is estimated to be 5864 in 1991, 7857 in 2001 and 10,528 in 2011(Table 5.1 and Fig. 5.1). The geometric progression seems to be acceptable as the population of any region or section grows geometrically. The geometric trend also fits suitably on the semi-log graph.

Marital Status

Marital status includes four types of people. The first are those who are never married, males or females. The second category includes those who are married, males and females. The third includes those women whose husband is dead or those men whose wife is dead, widow and widower. The fourth category includes male or female who are divorced or separated, basically divorcees. Regarding the marital status of Birhor in 1961, a little more than half (50.54%) of the males were never married, but the percentage of never married female was lower i.e., 44.44%. This is because the age of marriage of male Birhor is higher than that of the female Birhor. This has resulted in higher percentage of married females (47.39%) than that of married males (45.50%). The number of widows is more than double of widower. Only 3.30% of the males are widower as against 7.92% widows. This is due to difference in the age of marriage of males and females. Less than one percent of the males and females are divorcees.

Table 5.2
Birhor Marital Status-1961

	Total Population			
	MALE		FEMALE	
	No.	Percentage	No.	Percentage
Never married	612	50.54	544	44.44
Married	511	45.50	580	47.39
Widowed	40	3.30	97	7.92
Divorced or separated	8	0.66	3	0.25
Total	1211	100.00	1224	100.00

Source : Census of India, 1961 -SCT-II, Part- A.

In 1971, the martial status has changed slightly as is evident from Table 5.3. The percentage of "never married" males decreased to 49.58% and that of never married females increased to 46.75%. However, in both the cases the number of unmarried males has remained higher than that of unmarried females due to lower age of marriage of females than that of males. The figures show that the percentage of married males (46.16%) and females (46.46%) has been almost the same.

Table 5.3
Birhor Marital Status -1971

	MALE		FEMALE	
	No.	Percentage	No.	Percentage
Never married	885	49.58	785	46.75
Married	824	46.16	780	46.46
Widowed	72	4.03	110	6.55
Divorced or separated	1	0.06	4	0.24
Unspecified status	3	0.17	-	-
Total	1785	100.00	1679	100.00

Source : Census of India - 1971, ST-II.

The figures for the widowers, widows show the same pattern as being experienced in the previous census (1961). The percentage of widowers is (4.031) and that of the widows is 6.5percent which is higher over the widowers. Less than one percent of the Birhors were divorcees. This shows a strong family bond among the Birhors. However, up to 0.17 percent Birhors are in the category of unsepecified status.

Table 5.4
Birhor - Marital Status, 1981

	Total		Total population			
			MALE		FEMALE	
	No.	Percentage	No.	Percentage	No.	Percentage
Never married	2041	46.63	1105	49.02	936	44.09
Married	2073	47.36	1029	45.65	1044	49.18
Widowed	232	5.30	105	4.66	127	5.98
Divorced or separated	31	0.71	15	0.67	16	0.75
TOTAL	4377	100.00	2254	100.00	2123	100.00

Source : Census of India 1981, Series - 4. Bihar, part IX

The above table shows that the percentage of unmarried males and female both witnessed a declining trend from 1961 to 1981.The number of unmarried males slumped down to 49.02% but that of the unmarried females the number declined to record only 44.09%. Unmarried females in 1981 as against 44.46% in 1971 and 46.75% in 1961. This shows that the age of marriage of females has been lowered down. This has resulted in the continuous increase in the percentage of married females since 1961. In 1961 only 46.46% females were married and it increased to 47.39% in 1971 and 49.18% in 1981 respectively. But the percentage of married males has remained almost constant since 1971 as it was 45.50 in 1971 and 45.65 in 1981. As regards widowers and widows, the gap between their percentages has decreased sharply. In 1981 only 5.98% females became widows as against 4.66% widowers. This is due to the fact that the percentage of widowers has increased and that of widows decreased. This may be explained by a decrease in the difference of age of marriage of males and females. The percentage of divorced or separated males and females has again been less than one percent.

The combined figures of the total population shows that 46.63% of the total Birhors were never married in 1981, 47.36% were married, 5.30% were widowed and 0.71% were divorced or separated.

Table 5.5 shows the age-wise marital status of Birhor males and females in 1961. This table shows that 0 -14 age group has the highest percentage of unmarried males and females. 15-44 age group has the highest percentage of married males and females and 45 and above age group has the highest percentage of widows and widower. Age group 45 and above has the highest percentage of divorced or separated males, while all the higher percentage of female divorcees to 15-44 age group.

Age and sex structure of the population of Birhor in 1961 is also given in table 5.5 (Fig. 5.2).

As regards the age group of all persons, 46.82 % males and 43.30 % females are below 14 years of age, 39.64 % males and 43.55% females in 15 - 44 age groups and about 13 % of both sexes are above 45 years of age.

The age, sex, and marital status of Birhors in 1971 have been shown in Table 5.6 (Fig. - 5.2)

In the 0 - 14 age group the percentage of unmarried males has increased and those of unmarried females have remained almost constant. But the percentage of both males and females unmarried have decreased considerably. The percentage of both married male and female have increased in 15 - 44 age group. The percentage of both widows and widowers

Table 5.5
Birhor : Age and Sex Structure and Marital Status -1961.

	Age -Group - 0-14				Age- Group -15-44				Age -Group -45 +			
	M.	%	F.	%	M.	%	F.	%	M.	%	F.	%
Never married	505	82.52	497	91.36	102	16.66	44	8.09	5	0.82	3	0.55
Married	60	10.89	33	5.69	356	64.61	454	78.28	135	24.50	93	16.03
Widowed	1	2.50	-	-	19	47.50	32	32.99	20	50.00	65	67.01
Divorced or Separated	1	12.50	-	-	3	37.50	3	100.00	4	50.00	-	-
Total	567	46.82	530	43.30	480	39.64	553	43.55	164	13.54	161	13.15

[Source-Census of India,1961 ,Table SCT -II Part-B.]

Table-5.6

Birhor-Age And Sex Structure And Marital Status -1971.

	Age -Group - 0-14				Age -Group -15-45				Age-Group -45 +			
	M.	%	F.	%	M.	%	F.	%	M.	%	F.	%
Never married	749	84.64	717	91.34	131	14.80	66	8.41	5	0.56	2	0.25
Married	19	2.31	27	3.46	587	71.23	637	81.67	218	26.46	116	14.87
Widowed	-	-	-	-	22	30.56	24	21.82	50	69.44	86	78.18
Divorced or Separated	-	-	-	-	1	100.00	4	100.00	-	-	-	-
Unspecified	1	33.33	-	-	2	66.67	-	-	-	-	-	-
Total	769	43.08	744	44.31	743	41.62	731	43.54	273	15.30	204	12.15

[Source-census of India- 1971,Series-4, Bihar, Part-V- A,Table-S.T.-II.]

Table 5.7
Birhor- Age , Sex And Marital Status -1981.

	Age-Group 0-4		Age- Group 5-9		Age -Group 10-14		Age-Group 15-19	
	M	F	M	F	M	F	M	F
Total	265	291	326	334	303	152	194	183
%	11.76	13.71	14.41	15.73	13.44	11.87	8.61	8.62
Never %	265	291	326	334	281	212	147	74
Married	100.00	100,00	100.00	100.00	92.74	84.12	75.77	40.44
Married	-	-	-	-	21	40	43	101
%	-	-	-	-	6.93	15.87	22.16	55.19
Widowed	-	-	-	-	-	-	-	2
%	-	-	-	-	-	-	-	1.09
Divorced or	-	-	-	-	1	-	4	6
Sepaarated (%)	-	-	-	-	0.33		2.07	3.28

Cont

Age-Group 20.49		Age- Group 50-59		Age -Group 60 and above	
M	F	M	F	M	F
871	854	180	114	115	95
38.64	40.23	7.99	5.37	5.10	4.47
81	25	1	-	4	-
9.30	2.93	0.56	-	3.47	-
730	781	155	90	80	32
83.81	91.45	86.11	78.45	69.57	33.68
50	39	24	24	31	62
5.74	4.57	13.33	21.05	26.96	69.26
10	9	-	-	-	1
1.15	1.05	-	-	-	1.06

Source-Census of India, 1981-Series - 4- Bihar , part (IV)Special Table for S.T.(4 to7

have increased in the 45 + age group. All divorced males and females belong to 15 - 44 age group.

Table 5.7 gives a detailed account of age, sex and marital status of Birhors in 1981. All persons below the age of 9 are unmarried, but 6.93% male and 15.87% females in 10-14 age group are married. In 15-19 age group 22.16% male and 55.19% females are married and just one percent female is put into the category of widow. 2.07% males and 3.28% females in this age group are divorcees or separated. In the upper age group (above 20) an overwhelming proportion of both males and females are married. In 20-49 age group 83.81% males are married, 9.30% unmarried, 5.74% widower and 1.15%divorced or separated. But 91.45% of females are married, 2.93% unmarried,4.57% widow and 1.05% divorced or separated in this age-group. Almost similar is the case with 50-59 age group with the exception in the increase of widow or widower and the decrease of unmarried. The percentages of widow and widower have increased sharply above 60 years of age, recording 27% for males and 65% for females.

Age and Sex Structure

Age and sex structure of the population of Birhors in 1981 is also given in Table 5.7 (Fig. 5.2). Out of a total of 4377 persons, 2254 are males and 2123 are females. Thus, males constitute 51.5% of the total population. It is significant to note that below the age of 9, the number of females is higher than that of the males, but above that age, the number of males are everywhere higher than those of the females. This indicates higher rate of births of female child than that of male child. But, owing to the neglect of female child, their early marriage and considerable number of deaths during pregnancy and delivery, the ratio of females decreases above the age of 9. The second most important thing to note is that the difference between the numbers of males and females is found in 50.59 age group (180 males and 114 females) and the least significant difference at 5-9 age group (326 males and 334 females). The proportion of males and females in different age-groups may further be seen in the table and the map depicting age and sex structure.

Literacy and Level of Education

For an archaeologist or anthropologist the term 'literacy' may refer to a cultural fact pertaining to the development of a society's capability to make use of writing for various specific purpose. For a population

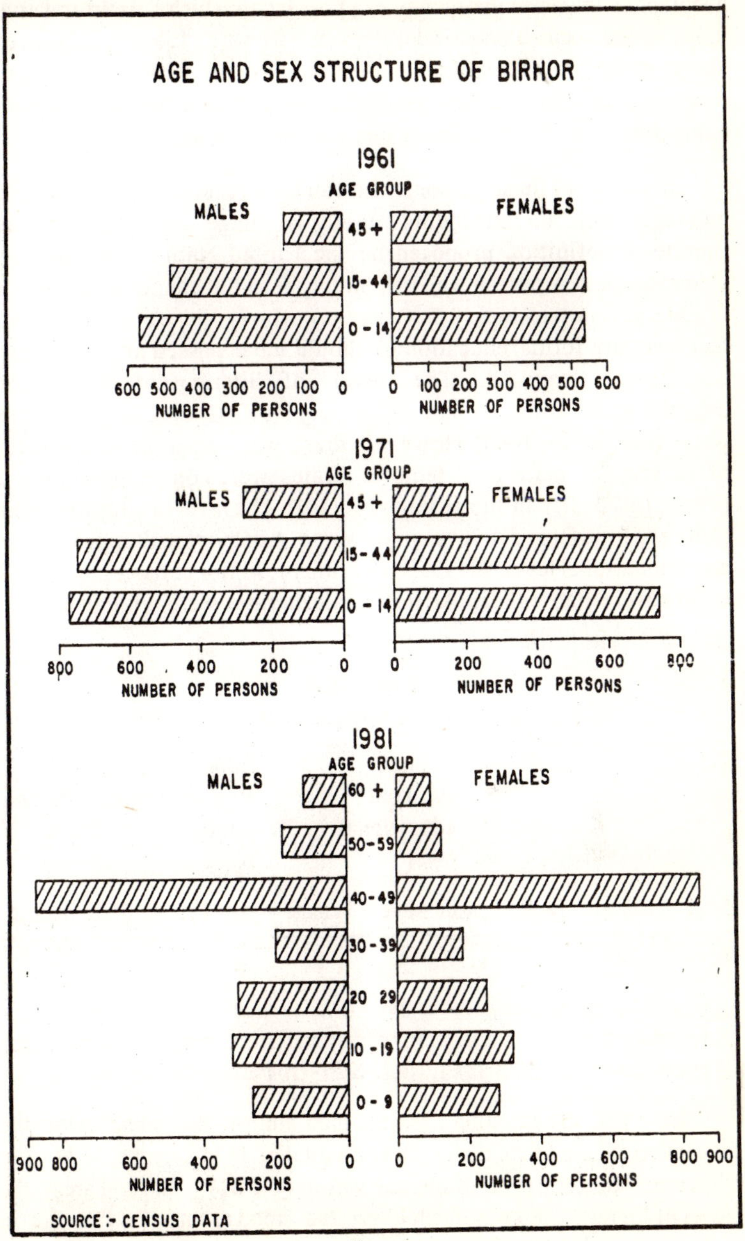
AGE AND SEX STRUCTURE OF BIRHOR
1961
AGE GROUP
MALES
FEMALES
45 +
15-44
0 - 14
600 500 400 300 200 100 0
0 100 200 300 400 500 600
NUMBER OF PERSONS
NUMBER OF PERSONS
1971
AGE GROUP
MALES
FEMALES
45 +
15-44
0 - 14
800 600 400 200 0
0 200 400 600 800
NUMBER OF PERSONS
NUMBER OF PERSONS
1981
AGE GROUP
MALES
FEMALES
60 +
50-59
40-49
30-39
20 29
10 -19
0 - 9
900 800 600 400 200 0
0 200 400 600 800 900
NUMBER OF PERSONS
NUMBER OF PERSONS
SOURCE :- CENSUS DATA

Fig. 5.2

geographer, literacy is that quality of a population which is a fairly relative index of the socio-economic development of an area. Literacy influences not only the migration of population but also the fertility, mortality, economic pattern, etc. and eradicates poverty and mental isolation, cultivating peaceful and friendly international relation.

In India, all those persons who can both read and write a simple message with understanding in any language are classified as literate, a definition proposed by the United Nations Population Commission.[3] A person who can merely read but cannot write is not literate. It is not necessary that a person, who is literate should have received any formal education or should have passed any minimum educational standard.[4] The level of literacy of the Birhor population of Bihar is extremely very low. Only 2.71% of them were literate in 1961. However, there was variation in the level of literacy of male and female. Males were comparatively more literate (4.70%) than the females (0.74%). The level of education was also very low. Out of 4.70% male literate, 4.05% were literate without any educational level, 0.49% were primary, Junior or basic passed and 0.16%, were matriculates. All the female literates were without having any formal education.

Table - 5.8

Birhor - Education Status in Rural Area, 1961

Total		lliterate		Literate With out educational level		Educational Level Primary junnior basic		Educational Level Matriculation And above	
Male	Female	Male	Female	Male	Female	Male	Female	Male	female
1214	1224	1157	1215	49	9	6	-	2	-
100.00	100.00	95.30	99.26	4.05	0.74	0.49		0.16	

Source: census of India-1961,Table-SCT-III-Part-B.

In 1971, the situation has remained almost the same with the exception of the urban males. Out of a total of 3464 persons 3377 were illiterate. Thus, the level of literacy was only 2.51%. In rural areas, the level of literacy was even much lower that stood around 2.44%. But in urban areas, 17.65% of the Birhors were literate :

Table - 5.9

Birhor : Educational Level Rural- 1971

	Total		Illiterate		Literate without educational level		Primary Junior basic		Matriculation and above But below graduate		Graduate and above	
	M.	F.	M.	F.	M.	F.	M.	F.	M.	F.	M.	F.
No	1776	1671	1697	1666	57	3	21	2	1	-	-	-
%			95.55	99.70	3.21	0.18	1.18	0.12	0.06	-	-	-

Sources : Census of India- 1971, Table. S.T. III Part A.

Table - 5.9 Shows that 95.55% of the Birhor males were illiterate in the rural areas as against 99.70% illiterate females. Out of only 4.45% literate male, 3.21% were literate without any educational level, 1.18% were educated up to primary, Junior or basic level and 0.06% were matriculates and above but below graduate. Out of 0.30% Literate female in the rural areas, 0.18% were literate without educational level and the rest 0.12% were educated up to primary level. Numerically, out of 1776 rural males only 79 were literate and out of 1671 rural females only 5 were literate. This speaks about the low level of literacy and education of the Birhors of rural areas.

Table - 5.10

Birhor : Educational Level - Urban-1971

	Total		Illiterate		Literate		Primary		Matri-culat-ion		Non-tech-cal		Technical	
	M.	F.	M.	F.	M.	F.	M.	F.	M.	F.	M.	F.	M.	F.
No.	9	8	6	8	1	-	1	-	1	-	-	-	-	-
%			66.67	100.00	11.11	-	11.11	-	11.11					

Source : census of India-1971,Table -S. T. -III, Part-A.

The level of literacy among urban people was comparatively higher only in case of male population in 1971. Out of 9 males, 6 were illiterate and 3 literate. Thus illiterates constituted 66.67% of the total urban males, and the level of their literacy was only 33.33%. Out of 3 literate, 1 was literate without any formal education, 1 was educated up to primary level and 1 was up to matriculation level or higher secondary level. As compared to males, all the 8 urban female were illiterate.

In 1981, the level of literacy of Birhor improved considerably. Out of the total of 4377 persons, only 4125 or 94.24% were illiterate. Thus, the level of literacy increased to 5.76% over the previous figure of 2.51% recorded in 1971. Both the rural and urban areas experienced improvement in the level of literacy. In rural areas 4.23% of he Bihors were recorded to be literate. In urban areas the level of literacy increased sharply to record 49.32% literate.

Table - 5.11
Birhor : Educational Level in Rural areas -1981.

	Male No.	%	Female No.	%
Total Population	2188	100	2041	100
Illiterate	2033	92.91	2017	98.82
Literate, A.Non Formal	3	0.14	-	-
(without B.Formal	84	3.84	17	0.83
educational Level)				
Primary	48	2.19	7	038
Middle	10	0.46	-	-
Matriculation	8	0.37	-	-
Higher Secondary	2	0.09	-	-
Non-Technical	-	-	-	-
Technical Diploma	-	-	-	-
Graduate and above			-	

Source : Census of India - 1981, Series 4 - Bihar, Part IX (IV) Special table S.T. (4 to 7).

Table 5.11 Shows the level of literacy and educational pattern of Birhors in the rural areas in 1981. It is evident from this table that 92.91% males and 98.82 females were illiterate. Thus, 7.09% males and only 1.18% females were literate. This is an improvement over the figure of 1971. As regard the level of education, it was higher among males than among females. Out of 7.09% male literate, 0.14% received non-formal education and 3.84% formal education without educational level. Among the rest 2.19% received education up to the primary level, 0.46% up to middle standard, 0.37% up to matriculation or secondary, intermediate or pre-university level. Both the levels of literacy and education were lower among the females than among the males. The level of female literate in rural areas was only 1.18%, the number of literate female being only 24 outs of a total of 2041 females, out of them 17 received formal education without educational level and 7 received education upto primary level. No female crossed primary level education in rural areas.

Table 5.12

Birhor : Educational Level in Urban Areas, 1981

	Male No.	Percentage	Female No.	Percentage
Total Population	66	100	82	100
Illiterate	22	39.39	49	59.75
Literate A.Non Formal	-	-	-	-
(Without educational B.Formal level)	13	19.70	9	10.97
Educational Level				
Primary	5	7.58	6	7.32
Middle	11	16.67	8	9.76
Matriculation	8	12.12	4	4.88
Higher Secondary	2	3.03	1	1.22
Non TechnicalDiploma	-	-	-	-
Technical Diploma	-	-	5	6.10
Graduate Degree	1	1.51	-	-
Technical Degree	-	-	-	-

Source: Census of India-1981 . Series - 4, Bihar, Part IX, (iv), Special table for (S.T. 4 to 7).

In urban areas, the levels of literacy among both males and females increased sharply during 1971-81. In 1981, 60.61% males were literate as against 33.33% literate urban males in 1971.Similarly the level of urban female literacy improved from zero in 1971 to 40.25% in 1981. There has been similar improvement in the level of education of urban male and female Birhors. Out of a total of 60.6% male literate, 19.7% received formal education, without educational level, 7.58% received education up to primary level, 16.67% up to middle level, 12.12% up to matriculation or secondary, intermediate or pre university level and 1.51% received graduate degree other than technical degree. Similarly, among 40.25% female literate, 10.97% received female education without educational level 7.32% up to primary level, 9.76% up to middle level, 4.88% up to matriculation or secondary level, 1.22% up to higher secondary, intermediate or pre-university level and 6.10%were having technical diploma or certificate not equal to degree.

Religious Structure

Religious structure of the Birhor tribe shows that an overwhelming majority of them believed in Hinduism vis-a-vis the genre de vie The religious structure of this tribe in 1961 is shown in Table - 5.13. This table reveals that out of a total population of 2438 persons 2355 were Hindus and 83 Sarmas.

Table 5.13
Religious Structure of Birhor, 1961

	Male	%	Female	%	Total	%
Hindu	1169	96.29	1186	96.90	2355	96.60
Christian	-	-	-	-	-	-
Sarmas	45	3.71	38	3.10	83	3.40
Total	1214	100.00	1224	100.00	2438	100.00

Source :Census of India,1961, Table SCT IV, Part- B.

Thus, Hindus formed 96.60% of the total population and Sarmas 3.40%. Almost similar position is found in male and female Birhors. 96.29% males were Hindu and 3.71% Sarmas (living In urban areas). Similarly 96.90% females were Hindu and the rest 3.10% Sarmas.

In 1971, there has been a change in the religious structure of Birhors. Out of a total of 3464 persons, 3336 were enumerated as Hindu, 35 as Christian and 93 as others. Thus, Hindu constituted 96.30% of the total population. The rest 1.01% were christian while 2.69% believed in other systems. In rural areas the composition was almost the same as 96.46% of them were Hindu, 0.84% Christians and 2.70% believed others. But in urban areas christians also formed a considerable proportion of the population, out of a total of 17 Birhors living in urban areas, 11 were Hindu and 6 were Christians, constituting 64.71% and 35.29% of the total urban population respectively.

As regards the sex-wise religious composition of Birhors in 1971, the proportion of female Hindus is everywhere larger than that of male Hindus. In rural areas 97.19% of the females were Hindu as against 95.78% males. Due to this only 0.24% female were christians as against 1.41% males. Others constituted of 2.81% of males and 2.57% of females. Similar was the case with urban area, where Christians had a sizeable proportion, 75% of the urban females were Hindu as against 55.56% urban males. Contrary to it only 25% of the urban females were Christian as against 44.44% urban males.

Table 5.14
Religious Structure of Birhor, 1971

	Total	M.	F.	Christian M.	Christian F.	Hindu M.	Hindu F.	Other M.	Other F.
Rural	1 3447	1776	1671	25	4	1701	1624	50	43
Percentage		100.00	100.00	1.41	0.24	95.78	97.19	2.81	2.57
Urban	17	9	8	4	2	5	6		
Percentage		100.00	100.00	44.44	25.00	55.56	75.00		
Total	3464	-	-	35		3336		93	
Percentage		-	-	1.01		96.36		2.69	
Rural	3447	-	-	29		3325		93	
Percentage		-	-	0.84		96.46		2.70	
Urban	17	-	-	6		11		2.70	
Percentage		-		35.29		64.71		-	

(Source: Census of India- 1971, Table S.T.-V.)

In 1981 the proportion of both Hindu and Christian Birhors has decreased and that of others increased. Out of a total of 4377 persons, 4186 were Hindu, 28 Christian, 1 Muslim and 162 believed other faiths. Thus, Hindus constituted 95.64% of the total populations, Christian, 0.64%, Muslims 0.02% and other 3.70%. In 1981 also the proportion of Christians was higher in urban areas as compared to rural areas. But both in rural and urban areas their proportion has decreased since 1971. In 1971, Christian constituted 0.84% of the population of rural areas, but in 1981 it further decreased to 0.07%. Similarly, in urban areas their proportion decreased from 35.29% in 1971 to 16.89% in 1981. Consequently the proportion of Hindu Birhors has increased to 83.11% in 1981 in urban areas as compared to 64.71% in 1971. The only Muslim and 162 others were enumerated in rural areas.

So far as the sex-wise religious composition is concerned, in rural areas 95.61% of the males were Hindus as against 96.50% females. There was one Muslim male, one Christian male and two Christian females. Among others, 94 were males and 68 females, constituting 4.29% and 3.33% of their population respectively. In urban areas 84.85% of the males were Hindus and 15.15% Christians. Similarly 81.70% of the females were Hindu and 18.30% Christians.

Table 5.15
Religious Structure of Birhors, 1981

	Rural				Urban			
	M.	%	F.	%	M.	%	F.	%
All Religion	2188		2041		66		82	
Hindu	2092	95.61	1971	96.57	56	84.85	67	81.70
Muslim	1	0.05	-	-	-	-	-	-
Christian	1	0.05	2	0.10	10	15.15	15	18.30
Sikhs	-	-	-	-	-	-	-	-
Budhists	-	-	-	-	-	-	-	-
Jains	-	-	-	-	-	-	-	-
Others	94	4.29	68	3.33	-	-	-	

Sources : Census of India - 1981, Series; 4-Bihar, Part - IX (iv) special tables for S.T. 4 to 7.

Occupational Structure

Occupational structure refers to the distinct economic activities of the people. The total population can be classified into two groups-economically active or workers and economically inactive or non-workers. In 1991 census, workers have also been divided into main workers and marginal workers. If a person has worked for 185 days or more during the reference year, he is treated as main worker. But if a persons has worked for less than 185 days or six months during the reference year he is treated on marginal worker. Non-workers include all such activities like the household duties in own house or at relative's, places, students, retired person and those living on royalties, rent, pension etc.

Table 5.16 gives an account of the occupational structure of the Birhor in 1961. It is clear from table 5.16 and Fig. 5.3 that 57.34% of the total population were workers and rest 42.66% were non-workers. Among the workers, 20.39% were cultivators, 12.16% agricultural labourers, 6.22% were engaged in mining, quarrying, fishing, hunting, etc. These workers may be called primary workers, constituting 38.77% of total workers. 55.51% of the workers were secondary workers, out of them 53.51% were engaged in household industries and 2% in manufacturing other than household industries. The rest 5.72% of workers were engaged in other services. No Birhor was engaged in trade and commerce, transport and communication and construction.

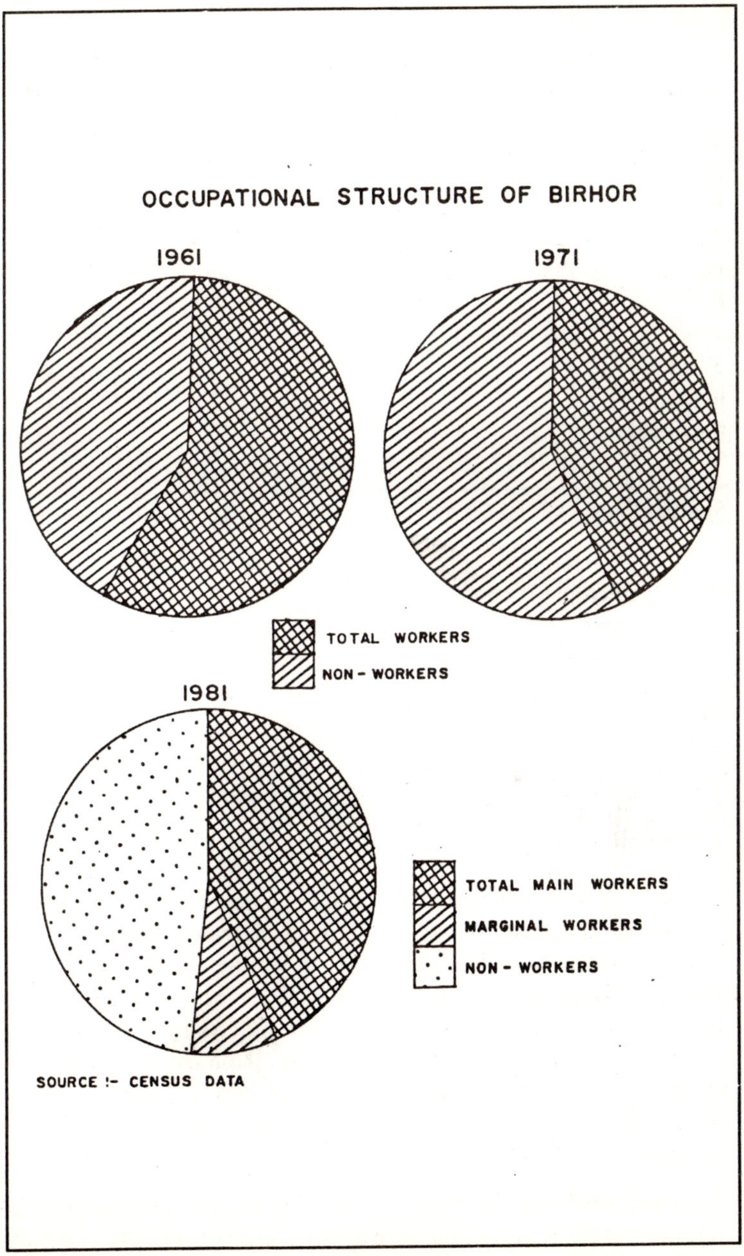
OCCUPATIONAL STRUCTURE OF BIRHOR
1961
1971
TOTAL WORKERS
NON - WORKERS
1981
TOTAL MAIN WORKERS
MARGINAL WORKERS
NON - WORKERS
SOURCE :- CENSUS DATA

Fig. 5.3

Table 5.16
Occupational Structure of Birhor -1961

Total Workers (I-IX)	I	II	III	IV	V	VI	VII	VIII	IX	X
Male 729	132	79	65	374	14	-	-	-	65	485
Female 669	153	91	22	374	14	-	-	-	5	555
1398 57.34% to total population	285	170	87	748	28	-	-	-	80	1040, 42.66% of total population
%	20.39	12.16	6.22	53.51		2.00-		-5.72		

Source- Census of India 1961.Table-SCT-I-Part-B.

I - Cultivator.
II - Agricultural Labourer.
III - Mining, Quarrying , Forestry.
IV - Household Industry.
V - Manufacturing.
VI - Construction.
VII - Trade and Commerce.
VIII- Transport and Communication.
IX - Other Services.
X - Non Workers.

In 1971, there has been some changes in the occupational structure of this tribe. It is seen from table 5.17 (Fig. 5.3) and the percentage of worker decreased to 42.73% and that of non-workers increased to 57.27%. Similarly, there has been an increase in the percentage of agricultural labourers (31.35%) those engaged in mining, Quarrying, fishing, hunting (11.22%) and manufacturing other than household industries (5.271%). In the rest of the occupation, their percentages have decreased. The decrease has been sharp in the case of household industries (35.67%), cultivators (15.41%) and other worker (1.08%).

There appears to be spatial variation in the occupational structure of Birhors in 1971. In urban areas, workers constitute 52.94% of the total workers against 42.67% in rural areas. The proportion of all occupational groups of workers in rural areas was the same as in the total population.

But in urban areas cultivators and agricultural labourers constituted 33% of total workers against 47% in rural areas. 22% of workers were engaged in mining and quarrying and 33% in manufacturing other than household industries in urban areas where other workers constituted 11% of total workers against 1% in rural areas.

In 1981, the percentage of workers has remained almost the same. Main workers form 43.41% of the total population, marginal workers 8.02% and non-workers 48.57% (Table 5.18 and Fig. 5.3). The proportion of cultivators has decreased continuously since 1961 recording only 11.89% in 1981, and that of agricultural labourers increased to 22.95%. This shows the poor economic condition of Birhors. Similarly, the figures for livestock and forestry etc. have increased to 15.63% and those for mining and quarrying decreased to 0.58%. The proportion of industrial workers has increased from 41%. In 1971 to 45% in 1981. There has been an increase in the rest categories of workers.

This general pattern of occupational structure is also seen in rural areas. But there are some differences in the pattern exhibited in urban areas. The most significant occupational group in urban areas is comprised of those who are engaged in industries (33.33%), followed by other services (27.78%), mining and quarrying (19.44%) and transport, storage and communication (11.11%).Cultivators, agricultural labourers and those engaged in live stock, forestry, fishing etc. are very insignificant in urban areas, but they are very significant in rural areas.

The above discussion reveals certain basic salient features. The growth of the Birhor population during 1961-81 shows a steady growth, though the rate is not much rapid as compared to other tribes of the Chotanagpur region. The reason for the steady growth of the Birhor population may be attributed to various factors which include among other things - accessibility to health and medical services and nutrition. The marital status does not seem to be disproportionate to the pattern found in the Birhor population. The young population constitutes the bulk of the Birhor population. The age and sex structure show a concave trend downward.The level of literacy and education among the Birhor shows slow growth, notwithstanding some intermittent increases during 1961-81. Not much variation can be seen in the religious structure of the Birhor and the nature of the adherence to the various religious belief and iconography. The occupational structure for the period does not appear to be more dynamic but it is intrinsically stationary.

Table 5.17
Occupational Structure of Birhor - 1971.

	Total Workers		I		II		III		IV	
	M	F	M	F	M	F	M	F	M	F
Urban	6	3	2	-	-	1	-	-	2	-
Total	9		2		1		-		2	
%	52.94		22.22		11.11		-		22.22	
Rural	1047	424	208	18	312	151	105	44	14	1
Total	1471		226		463		149		15	
%	42.67		15.36		31.48		10.13		1.02	
Total	1480		228		464		149		17	
Population 3464										
%	42.73		15.41		31.35		10.07		1.15	

Cont

V				VI		VII		VIII		IX		X	
A		B											
M	F	M	F	M	F	M	F	M	F	M	F	M	F
-	-	1	2	-	-	-	-	-	-	1	-	3	5
3				-	-					1	-	8	
33.33				-						11.11		47.06	
351	177	42	33	-	-	-	-	-	-	14	1	729	1247
528		75		-	-	-	-	-	-	15		1976	(57.33%)
35.67		510		-	-	-	-	-	-	1.02			
528		78		-	-	-	-	-	-	16		1984	
35.76		5.27		-	-	-	-	-	-	1.08		57.27	

Source : Census of India - 1971,Series - 4-Bihar, S. T. -I- Part-B.

M.- Male.

F.- Female.

I- Cultivator. II- Agricultural Labourers.III- Live Stock,Forestry. IV-Mining and Quarring. V- Manufacturing, Services, A-Household Industry.B-Other than Household. . VI- Construction. VII-Trade and Commerce. VIII-Transport,Storage,Communication. IX-Other Service.X- Non Workers.

Table 5.18
Occupational Structure of Birhor - 1981.

	Total Workers		I		II		III		IV				V	
												A		B
	M	F	M	F	M	F	M	F	M	F	M	F	M	F
Rural	1276	588	201	25	275	160	217	80	2	2	436	269	104	63
Total	1864		226		435		297		4		685		167	
%			12.12		23.34		15.93		0.21		36.76		8.96	
Urban	342		-	-	1	-	-	-	7	-	-	-	12	-
Total	36		-	-	2.78		-	-	7		-	-		12
%									19.44		-			33.33
Total	1900(43.41) to total Population		226		436		297		11		685			179
%	100.00		11.89		22.95		15.63		0.58		36.06		9.42	

VI		VII		VIII		IX		X		XII			XII	
M	F	M	F	M	F	M	F	M	F	M		F	M	F
3	-	2	1	-	-	37	7	72	279	840	117	36		46
3		3		-		44		351		2015		82		
0.16		0.16		-		2.36								
1		1		4	-	8	2	-	-	31	80	2		15
1		1		4		10				111		17		
2.17		2.78		11.11		27.78								
4		4		4		54		351		2126		99		
0.21		0.21		0.21		2.84		8.02		48.57				

Source : Census of India ,1981,Series-4,Part-IX ,Special Table for S.T.(1to3).

M. - Male.
F. - Female.
I - Cultivator.
II - Agricultural Labourers.
III - Livestock ,Forestry ,Hunting, Plantation.
IV - Mining and quarrying.
V - Manufacturing, Servicing- A-Household, B- Other than Household.
VI - Construction.
VII - Trade and Commerce.
VIII- Transport, Storage and Communication.
IX - Other Services. X- Marginal Workers. XI- Non Workers. XII- Seeking/Available for Work

References :

1. Thompson, W.S., 1929: 'Population,' American Journal of Sociology, Vol. 34, pp. 959-75.

2. Notestein, F.W., 1945: 'Population :the Long View,' in Sehultz, T.W., (ed.), Food for the world, Chicago University Press, Chicago.

3. Golden, H.H. : 'Literacy', International Encycelopaedia of the Social Science, Vol. 9, McMillan Co. and Free Press, p. 415

4. Census of India, Series - 4, Bihar, Paper 1 of 1982, Final Population table, p. 7.

6

Cultural Pattern

Culture is one of the most complex, yet important concepts in social science, culture is best approached historically. It is pointed out, however that in the course of the modern period, the meaning of culture has changed from reference to skilled human activity, to reference to the whole set of activities of a human group and the refined individual spirit and finally to the collection of intellectual and artistic activity deemed to indicate and produced by such spirits[1]. It calls for attention to the need to recover from this history the ways in which the changing meaning of culture has reflected and promoted changes in the ideological interpretation of individual and collective human nature.

A focus on culture as a shared set of meaning and meaningful activities inevitably emphasizes Human Agency, the power to symbolise, and the reproductive significance of ritual, potentially reducing the weight generally given to economic structure in human-geographical explanation. Culture, here, is regarded as an active force in social reproduction, capable of being deployed by minority groups in a strategy of resistance against dominant ideologies, thus subcultures. However, it has proved no more easy in human geography than in other social sciences to incorporate culture into broader social theory. However, recently attempts have been made to develop a theory of culture as a material production within an initial human geography[2].

Geographers are required to focus on both the material culture and on the social heritage of collective mental and spiritual product and forms of human conduct so that the 'cultural wholeness' in spatial perspective can be identified. Culture is the primary factor affecting the way in which individual and societies respond to the environment. Cultural pattern of a community tends to manifest the arrangement of custom, beliefs, moral practices, technology and art across a 'defined space'. These are the socially transmitted institutional aspects with spatial dimension and identification. Each human habitation is identified by its cultural pattern and man with the help of his cultural Indices creates his landscape. This is true in the case of a community which gives expression to a cultural landscape. The following discussion concentrates on the territorial specification of the Birhor cultural pattern.

The Word 'Birhor' is made from two mundari word 'Bir' means 'Jungle' and 'Ho' means 'men'. So the word 'Birhor' stands for the meaning of 'jungle men'. Birhors are divided into two groups i.e. Uthlu (the wandeing or nomadic) and Jaghis (the settled or sedentary). The Birhors who belong to the nomadic category necessarily move with bows and arrows and appear in the stage of 'prehistoric human culture'. However, the Birhors who belong to the sedentary, seem to have made some adjustments to the milieu and neccessarily depend on the sale of the Jungle products and drums and they necessarily practice some form of primitive subsistance farming.

Rai Bahadur Sarat Chander Roy, the first Indian national anthropologist who pioneered the study of tribes of Chotanagpur and started a new era in the Indian ethnography; had published a full length monograph of Birhors in 1925, entitled 'The Birhor : A little known Jungle Tribe of Chotanagpur'.

Ethinically[3], the Birhors belong to the same dark skinned (maleness), short-statured, long headed (dolicocephalic), wavy-haired (cymotrichous), and broad-nosed (platyrrhine) race to which the Mundas, the Santhals, the Bhumij, the Hos and other allied tribes belong.

Racially, they belong to the proto-Austroloid human group, and their physical characteristics resemble the Mundas. They speak the Mundari (Austro-Asiatic), but in the general conversation they use the local contact language 'sadani'[4]. According to Sir George Grierson author of the Census Report, the Birhor dialect is more closely connected with Mundari than with Santhali. S.C. Roy had mentioned that, in the dialect spoken even by the Ranchi Birhors, it is more closely connected with Mundari than with Santhali.

Dalton's descriptive 'Ethnology of Bengal' was published in 1872. There is a legend about the origin of Birhors in this descriptive Ethnology of Dalton which states- "The Birhors affirm that they and the Kharwars are of the same race descended from the sun. They came, seven brothers, to this country from Khairagarh (in the Kaimur hills); four went to the east, and three brothers remained in Ramgarh district. One day when the three brothers were going out to fight against the chiefs of the country, the headdress of one of them got entangled in a tree. He deemed it to a bad omen, and remained behind in the Jungle. His two brothers went without him and gained a victory over the Chiefs, and while returning, found their brother employed in cutting the bark of the chob. They derided him, called him the Birhor, (Birhor is Munda word for a woodman or forester) or Chob-cutter; he replied that he would rather remain a Birhor and reign in the Jungles than associate with such haughty brothers. Thus originated the Birhors, lords of the Jungles. The other two brothers became Rajahs of the country called Ramgarh.

Mukherjee and Khatua[5] have mentioned in their paper about the origin of Birhor which states. "A lady named Koltin who had two sisters. The Birhors are the descendants of the elder sister while the younger one gave birth to another community called the Mahakul. It is said that Koltin had illicit sexual relation and as a result became pregnant. When she gave birth to a male child, her parents came to know about her illicit relation and one day when she was sleeping with her baby in the hut, her parents burnt the hut with a motive to kill (the mother and child) them. Next day, in the morning, the villagers rescued the mother, the child from the debris. The boy was brought up in the village but without any process of socialization (i.e., birth purification caremoney). The child gradually grew up in cultural isolation in the village and the villager however, looked down upon him and prevented him from participating in sacred/religious ceremonies of the community. The villagers did not even hesitate to rebuke him by saying "Majha Majha Aati Hai". (Why does he come again and again) sala Manjhai. From these reproachful terms the child came to be known as Majni. He then started dwelling in the Biru hills and thus the terms 'Birhor' was originated. The clan, descended from him, which is known at present as Birhor-Majhi.

The Birhors[6] can not tell anything about their origin or history beyond the fact that they have been 'Birhors' or Jungle men, from pre-historic times. They are commonly known amongst the people of these parts as chopdars (chop string makers). They are divided into two sub-tribes, namely, Bhuliya or wanderers, and Jaghis or settlers.

Uthlu Birhors are quite nomadic and live in groups of three to ten families camping in the Jungles, remaining only for a week or two on the same spot except during the rainy season. They are moving from Jungle to Jungle on a regular round, completed in about two years. They return to the original place and start once more on a similar move along the same route.

On the other hand, Jaghis Birhors are those families, who have settled down on some hill tops or on the outskirts of a Jungle. Some of them produce maize or beans during the rainy seasons. But Majority of them are landless. In some conditions or cases, after getting ill-treatment by the landlords or neighbourers, they move to some other places or fall back to their old uthlu life.

The settlement of the Jaghis as well as the temporary encampments of the Uthlus are both known as 'Tandas'. A tanda consists of about half dozen or more huts. In a tanda of the Uthlu the huts are mere improvised leaf-sheds in the form of low triangular kumbas. Smaller kumbas are called chu-kumbas and the comparatively larger ones, ora-kumbas or ghar-kumbas. A kumba has one opening, sometimes, provided with a door which is made of branches and leaves.

The typical conical hut of the Uthlu Birhor is about five feet in height and about nine feet in diameter and only opening which serves as the doorway is not more than twenty inches wide at the bottom and about twenty-two inches in height.

In contrast to Uthlu, in Jaghis Tanda, the roofs of huts are generally made of branches covered with leaves. The huts have wall and some of them are made of branches plastered over with mud, and a few even wholly made of mud. Huts usually possess slightly raised floors. Rectangular settlement is found in Jaghis Tanda.

The Birhors of Chotanagpur are composed of two segments, the Uthlu and the Jaghis. Next, they are divided into Gotra, i.e., clan and finally come to the primary unit of the family. So their social set up is, Tribe-sub-tribe-clan-family-individual[7]. The Birhor family is highly patriachal in character which is reflective of the tribes' adaptability to the geographical milieu across the forest land.

The family among them is nuclear in character. Extended type of family is found only is exceptional cases. When all sons of the family are married, they may demand a division of their parental property. The share of each son is not proportionate but varies with the age and father keeps a small share to himself. The son-in-law, particularly, Ghar-Jamai comes next in order of preference in inheritance of the property. Daughters are not entitled to share the parental property with their brothers, but in absence of a ghar-Jamai, daughters are entitled to property. In all cases, the heir bears the funeral expenses of the parent.

Some writers have mentioned the presence of youth dormitory called 'Giti-ora'. Today it has ceased to exist. However, it has been observed that young boys build their huts close to their parents and young girls live with other sisters or, the grand-mother near the huts of their parents.

The social organization of the Birhor has two aspects-one related to the quest for food and the others to marriage and kinship. Some three to ten families constitute a group, a community for all purposes, and they live together in one settlement called Tanda. It implies a minimum lineage in comparative isloation from another tanda. Each tanda has a Naya, the spiritual and political head, and supposed to be supernaturally elected. In every Birhor tanda, the post of Naya is practically hereditary.

Kotwar or Diguar is appointed by Naya, as his assistant. The duty of Kotwar is to call people for collective hunting.Mati or ghost doctor is neither appointed nor elected, but is selfmade. The function of a mati is to suggest the sacrfice to remove misfortune.

The head of the Birhor Tanda, has two assistants,Kotwar and Mati. The Kotwar collects the people for the communal hunt and other gatherings. The mati helps people in religious and magical matters.[8] The monkey hunt[9] or Gari-sendra is conducted jointly by the adult members of an entire tanda and the game is shared by them. The Inter-tanda association is also found in hunting. Once a year, all the 'able-bodied men belonging to a number of tandas, come together for purpose of hunting. This annual hunting expedition is known as Disum Sendra (or regional hunt). Baibera ceremony is performed by Nayas of one tanda, when all the parties have arrived and intended to hunt. All the animals killed at the hunt are finally taken to the Jilu-Jayar and they are skinned dressed and chopped into pieces and shared by the tanda's members. Weddings and Panchayats are the few occassions on which representatives from a number of tandas gather together.

Birhors have no tribal organisation in the sense of an association of the different clans of the entire tribe of which every member or family is regarded as an unit.

The second form of social organization is concerned with kinship and marriage. The Kinship terminology is classificatory in nature. The Birhors are grouped into exogamous hereditary totemic clans, called gotras, which are named after some animal, plant, fruit, flower or other material object. Clan is the controlling factor in the regulation of kinship and marriage. There are 37 clans or gotras of Birhors as has been maintained by S.R. Roy, these are as follow :

(1) Andhi- (Wild cot).
(2) Bonga Sauri (a kind of wild grass),
(3) Bhat (name of a Hindu caste).
(4) Bhont or Bhuntil (a kite)
(5) Bhuiya (name of a tribe)
(6) Chauli Hembrom (Chauli = rice, Hembrom = betel Palm)
(7) Ganda Garua (a large species of vulture)
(8) Geroa (a small bird).
(9) Gidhi (Vulture)
(10) Goar (Milkman caste).
(11) Guleria or Galaoria (Pellet-bow).
(12) Gundri (a kind of bird).
(13) Hembrom (betel-palm).
(14) Here Hembrom (here = rice-husk).
(15) Induar (eel).
(16) Jegseria Latha (latha = a lake made of mohua flowers).
(17) Kauch or Horo (tortoise).
(18) Kawan Hembrom.
(19) Keoduar (a kind of fruit).
(20) Khangar (name of a sub-tribe of the Mundas).
(21) Kharea (name of a tribe (Kharia)
(22) Khudi Hembrom (Khudi = broken grains of rice).
(23) Ludamba (a kind of flower).
(24) Lunchi Jal (= lakur chata).
(25) Lupung (myrobalan) (called BeherCar in Hindi).
(26) Maghaia hembrom (Maghaia = belonging to Magha or Bihar).
(27) Mahali (name of a tribe).
(28) Modi (name of a caste or section of a tribe).
(29) Murum (nilgai or portax pictu).
(30) Nag (cobra) or Nagpuria (belonging to Chotanagapur).
(31) Sada (white).
(32) Samduar (Sadom = horse).
(33) Saunria (a kind of wild grass).
(34) Sham-Jhakoa (a composition used in whetting weapons).
(35) Singpuria (Singhara fruit or Trapa bispinosa).
(36) Suia (a kind of bird).
(37) Toriar (belonging to Pargana Tori in the Palamu district).

Nagpuria and Toriar are derived from names of localities, whereas Bhat, Goar, Bhuiya, Khangar and Mahali would appear to have been derived from names of other tribes.

The totem, the legends about their origin, are associated with necessary taboos. The members of one clan may not take cooked rice from those of other clans belonging to another tanda except in certain cases of relationship. It may be assumed that in early days, the Birhor tanda might have been an uni-clan group.

There are three main factors of Birhor kinship organization i.e. Totemism, exogamy and father-right. They are patrilineal, patrilocal and patriarchal in character. Marriage or sexual intercourse between persons of the same totemic clan is forbidden. The names of a man's younger brother's wife and of his wife's elder sister are taboos to the Birhor and the names of the husband's elder brother and of a younger sister, husbands and a younger brother's wife are taboos to a Birhor Woman.

Marriage is considered indispensable for every Birhor.[10] There is rule of adult marriage in all Birhors. The age of marriage of a boy is 20 or 21 years, and of a girl, is 16 or 17 years. There are different types of marriages valid in Birhors, they are as follow :

(a) Sadar Bapla : (marriage by negotiations). In this type of marriage the parents select a partner for their children and make all negotiations for the marriage. This type of marriage is found more among the Jaghis than among the Uthlu.

(b) Nam-Napam Bapla : This type of marriage is more prevalent among Uthlu than among the Jaghis. The girl gets permison from elders of tanda to keep her lover in her house and when the father of the girl gets bridal price, the nam-napam Bapla. marriage takes place.

(c) Udra-Udri Bapla : This type of marriage is known as 'elopement marriage'. A young man and a girl secretly leave the village together and remain in hiding as husband and wife. When they are found out, they are brought home, the customary bride-price is paid, sindur is applied and a feast is provided to relations and the tanda people to validate the marriage.

(d) Bolo Bapla : A female enters the house of a man, carrying on her head either a basket of the corolla of the mohua flower or a bundle of firewood and stays in the house. She is then recognized as a Bolo wife or a Dhukni.

(e) Sipundar Bapla : In this type of marriage, a young man, wishing to marry with a particular girl, dilutes the Sindur (vermilion) in oil and applies it on her forehead, after getting the girl alone. It is done sometimes at a market or at a fair.

(f) Sangha Bapla and Hirum Bapla : When a man having a wife living, marries another woman, the form of union is known as Hirum Bapla. Sangha Bapla is applied to the marriage of a widower to a widow or to a divorced woman.

(g) Kiring-Jawae Bapla : In this type of marriage, the expenses required for the marriage are advanced by the father-in-law and repaid in convenient isntalments by the son-in-law. It is also called brought son-in-law marriage.

(h) Golhat Bapla : (marriage by exchange) In this type of marriage bride price is not paid but bride and groom are exchanged by two families.

(i) Beng-Karhi Bapla : In this type of marriage, the bride owing to her parents, poverty, is taken to the bridegroom's house to be married.

The Birhor follows monogamy and marriage takes place only when two persons of opposite sex decide to undertake responsibility for an independent household. Pre- marital relationship is not tabooed but forbidden in the same clan. Divorce is not very frequent among them, as to secure a bride is not a very easy task. They do not follow any definite procedure for the divorce. The party seeking for divorce has either to return the bride price or to forgo it. However, Polygamy is not uncommon but it is a rare phenomenon. Widow marriage is reluctently allowed.[11]

The pregnant woman observes certain food taboo such as not eating the head of animals. The husband also observes such food taboo to protect her from evil spirits. The pregnant woman shifts to the Kumba which has been made, for the purpose. Some elderly Birhor woman serves as midwife. In some cases, Chamain or dagrin (villages midwife belonging to chamar caste) may also be called. The Thathi or first purification ceremony, celebrated on the seventh day from the date of the birth, is meant for the final purification of the other members of the tanda and the preliminary purification of the newborn child and its mother and of the other members of the particular family. Generally, on the twenty-first day after birth, the final purification ceremony is performed. This ceremony is known as the 'Chhota thhathhi.' On the morning following the Chhota thhathhi day, a name is selected for the child, and this ceremony is called the 'Saki'.

Tattooing : At the age of 12 or 13, Birhor boys burn scalds on each hand with lighted wicks. Birhor girls of ten to twelve years of age must have tattoo marks made on their arms, chest, chin, nose and the upper side of feet with an iron needle. Floral designs are commonly used.

Death : The hut in which death takes place is deemed to be infected with gehi-loton (death pollution). The dead body of children and women dying during childbirth is buried. In other cases, cremation is preferred but burial is optional and is the normal mode of disposal during the rains. Among the Birhors[12] when it is clear that the person is dying he is given a little quantity of water and his son or wife or husband comes out of the hut leaving a person alone and keeping the door open for a clear passage for the outgoing soul . Lamentatios and cries are made by the near and dear ones so that the soul could not rumble and would feel that his or her relatives are very much grieved .

Religion

Birhors' religious beliefs are centered on their feeling that they are surrounded by supernatural beings and spirits and therefore, they take life with a sense of awe and fear. Religious beliefs thus dominate the social, economic and domestic life of the Birhor. In case of nomadic Birhors their deities move with them.[13] The Birhor's iconography or the system of beliefs is basically animistic in nature.

Birhor's gods and goddesses are named after hills, ancestor and even beasts. The Singbonga is the supreme deity and is symbolised by the Sun. Singbonga is recognized as the creator of the world. Birhors regard Singbonga as Bhagwan, which is a Hindu name. Singbonga is also described as the Sakhi or witness of what man and spirits do. They pray Singbanga before going to hunting or collecting honey.

Devi Mai and Burhi Mai, the mother-goddess is generally represented by a piece of wood, daubed red with vermilion. Chandi is regarded as Hunting god. Bandar Bir and Hulmin Bir are believed to bring success in catching monkeys.[14]

Mahali chaati is said to be a wife of the spirit Lugu Pahar. (spirit of the lugu hill). She is regarded as presiding deity of smaller game like the togo (a kind of wild cat) and torhot (a species of large lizard). She is also regarded as powerful spirit.

Buru Bongas, Larankia Bhuts, Manita etc. are regarded as clan spirit.[15] Buru Bongas or Ora Bongas are believed to be the masters of sickness. Jaghis Birhors call Buru (Hill) Bongas whereas Uthlu Birhors, invariably call these spirits the Ora (house) Bongas. Buru Bongas are also credited with certain powers over nature, such as that of causing and stopping rain and storm.

Larankia Bhuts are regarded as fighting spirits. Manita spirits are to be regarded as an acquired spirit and provided with seats either in a small leaf-hut called Bonga-Ora (spirit-hut) or in special thaan or spirit-seat of the family as distinguished from the common thaan of the tanda. In case of an epidemic of cholera or small pox in the tanda, the mother-goddess Devi is generally offered one red goat and the goddess Kali Mai is offered one black goat. A vow or manita is made when the epidemic spreads and the promised sacrifices are offered by the Naya when it abates.

Haprom or ancestor spirit, Manita Baghouts, family Manita Bhuts or the acquired spirits of a family are grouped as family spirits of Birhor.[16]

The Haprom or ancestral spirits are divided into two classes-the Burha-Burhi or near ancestors of the family whose names are still remembered and the Chowrasi Haprom who are supposed to be the ancient dead of the family whose names are no longer remembered : Sacrifices are done in both the cases. In case of Burha-Burhi, a red hen is offered by the head of the family after the thathi ceremony of a new-born baby and also after a marriage in the family, while in Chowrasi Haprom, a fowl is offered by Naya or priest at the tanda on the occasion of thathi ceremony of a new-born baby in the family and at a wedding in the family.

When a member of a family is killed by a tiger, such a Baghoul spirit is represented by a stone or a lump of clay which is placed in the spirit hut. Spotted red and white fowl is offered to the spirit periodically by the head of the family to avert any mischief which this spirit may cause.

Some families have what are known as Kudra bhuts and some have Andher bhuts. These are believed to manifest themselves (lit, rise) when they feel hungry and cause sickness until they are appeased by sacrifices. Marang Buru which is a general god amongst the Mundas appears as a family god amongst some Birhor families who trace their descent from a Birhor ancestor who married a Munda wife.

Sangi Bhuts[17] or Group Spirits are spirits sacrificed by an entire tanda or food-group. This type of sacrifice is done by both Jaghis and Uthlu. Some Birhors occasionally seek the help of the Sangi-Bhuts to convert spirits of dead men or animals into Nasan bhuts to wreak vengeance on an enemy. The Sangi-Bhuts are characterized as Arhaia-Bhuts of whose order stray spirits and minor bhuts kill people or do them other harm.

There are also minor spirits or Ningchha Bhuts of Birhors. Darha is a ningchha bhut, that dwells in stones by the side of some low land or don, and is a Manita-bhut to the owner of the land. The owner of the land has to offer periodical sacrifices to the Darha who is often represented by a piece of bamboo planted by the side of the stone.

There are certain conditions in which women among the Birhors may have to offer sacrifices to certain spirits. This happens when she eats the meat of the head of an animal or fowl sacrificed to a sprit so that the spirit is there by drawn on to her and begins to cause trouble to herself and her family until she adopts the spirit as a manita to be periodically propitiated with appropriate sacrifices.[18] There are two other methods by which a female may acquire a Manita Bhut, one by accident or "Luck" and other by inheritance; so to say, from her mother.

Magic : Magic is an integral part of a religion of tribal dimension. Magician or a mati generally is born and not made. Witch- craft is rare amongst the Birhors. Witches as exist amongst them are believed to harm a person by throwing some rice in the direction of person and afflict the person with some trouble.

There are various types of magical practices[19] which exist among the Birhors that seek to control the natural phenomena, such as stopping the rain, stopping lightening, stopping storms and rain making.

Jaghis families usually perform magical rain-making ceremony which they adopted from the neighbouring Mundas. For rain the Birhors go up to the nearest hill and push down stones which produce a rumbling noise while falling to the ground, and this noise, at the same time is intensified by beating a drum so as to produce a low, heavy, continuous sound in imitation of the pattering of rain on the roofs of their huts.

Taboo : Taboo is another sacred belief which is a rather negative custom of any belief. Majumdar[20] takes the religious side of taboo as safeguard of ritual operations to protect religious persons and places of worship and prevent irreligion from spreading. There are different kinds of taboos which exist in Birhors, and which include,[21]

(i) A pregnant Birhor woman must not eat the head of the chora fish and also must not eat tiki lad. A pregnant woman must not step over a sagar or block-wheel cart and also must not step over a dog. Neither a pregnant woman nor her husbard must go to a pool or stream where people are catching fish. A pregnant woman must not eat the flesh of deer.

(ii) A woman must not step over hunting net or hunting stick or club.

(iii) Birhors youth and maidens must not eat the flesh of the Suia bird and they also must abstain from eating the brain of an animal.

(iv) A bachelor must not plant a plantain tree.

(v) A Birhor youth must not eat an egg which emits a sound when shaken.

(vi) A marriage or other auspicious ceremony must not be celebrated on a Sunday or Tuesday or a Saturday.

(vii) A Birhor must not bury the leaves or the wood of the Soso and Loa tree.

(viii) A Birhor must not throw used leaf plates into fire.

(ix) A Birhor must not sit on the central part of a Yoke.

(x) A Birhor must not sit on the earth.

(xi) A Birhor must not sit on a winnowing fan.

(xii) A Birhor must not point with the finger at the rainbow.

(xiii) A Birhor must not look back when leaving home to join a hunting expedition.

(xiv) A menstruant female is taboo to the whole community. She may not touch her husband or any other persons. She may not cook food or draw water nor even touch any food or drink, she may not touch the walls or roots of hut.

Festival and Ceremonial :

Uthlu section of Birhors cannot indulge in more elaborate religious feasts than the Jaghis section of Birhor, because Uthlu section of Birhors are usually involvaed entirely in food-gathering and at the same time they take precautions against the consequent dangers from natural and supernatural sources.On the other hand, Jaghis celebrate certain periodical festivals to ensure future good luck and avoiding bad luck in agriculture[22].

The Karama festival is celebrated on the eleventh day of the moon in the month of Bhado (September). A nubmer of families of the Latha, Chauli Hembrom, Naguria, Mahali and Gidhi clans have adopted the Karama festivals. A Karama Adina cordifolia branch is brought to the angan where it is ceremoniously planted.

The Jitia festival is celebrated annually twelve days after the Karama festival. Andi clan's family has adopted the Jitia festival. The head of family and his wife remain fasting the whole day.

The Soso Bonga[23] festival is held in the month of Asarh (July). When transplantation of the paddy seedlings is finished, the head of Jaghis family who has taken part in cultivation brings a few branches of the soso plant and performs the rest of ceremonial task.

Nawajom festival is also held in the month of Asarh (July). This is the ceremony of eating the new rice. Chiura (flattened vice) is made from upland rice (gora rice). The chiura is offered to Singbonga and ancestor-spirit (Burha-Burhi) by putting the Chiura on Soso-leaves and drink rice-bear. After this, rice is boiled and all the family members and friends take part in the feast.

The Dasai festival is celebrated in the month of Aswin. Adult family members remain on fast the whole day and night and goats are sacrificed at the family thaan.

Finally, it can be said that the Birhor religious setiment consists mainly, in a sense,of fear and in some cases, of approaching 'awe' in the presence of such powers and energies and a consequent sense of mysterious 'sacredness'. Their religious belief is full of Animism, Bongaism, Naturalism, Magic, Taboo etc.

Food Habits :

Birhors get their food through hunting of wild animals, collection of roots, fruits and honey from the forest. Fishing in their native streams and pools is also occasionally practiced to some extent.[24]

Agriculture[25] is practiced by some Jaghis. Rice is highly esteemed as food. Salt and red pepper and sometimes turmeric are used. Food is usually cooked by the women inside their huts among the Jaghis and outside their conical leaf-sheds (Kumbas) by the Uthlu. Food for men and women are cooked together. Father and sons take their meals earlier than female members of the family.

Rice-beer is the favourite drink of the Birhors. The method of preparation is the same as being done by other tribes of Chotanagpur. But there is a slight difference from others i.e.the Birhors use bamboo sieve to strain the liquor. Tobacco is commonly taken by Birhors, but ganja is rarely taken by them.

Pete sanga, arrha, dura, kundri, kukui and piska yams are the principal tubers and roots which Birhors collect from the forest and boil them to eat.

Jereng, hasa-ara, koinar, katai, mathha, munga and pui are the edible leaves which are boiled and taken as side-dishes with boiled rice or other grains.

Keond, Piar, Kadam, Bar, Piper, Koer, Kanthal or the Jack-fruit, Mangoes and Figs are wild fruits that the Birhors usually eat.

Mohua, Sakhua, Pumpkin gourds of the kohnra and laua varieties, the doro or lady's finger, the simbi or beans are boiled and eaten by the Birhors.

The Birhors eat almost anything, of animal food, that they can procure except the flesh of his totem beast, bird or reptile and the flesh of tigers, bears, Jackals, wild cats, domestic cats, snakes and frogs. The tortoise is not eaten but fishes of all varieties are relished as food.

Chop strings, knife, crude wooden cups and bowls, Kandis, samat are the domestic utensils. Net, tainis, thenga, tangis are the hunting articles. Birhor boys employ pellet bows with wooden heads to kill birds.[26]

Barter system is more in vogue among Birhors than buying and selling for cash.

Fever and Raskondra (Strangury) are the two diseases which are commonly met with by them. They use various plants and tubers for medicinal purposes. A common remedy for Raskondra is a tuber known as bans-Kohora which is pounded and mixed with sugar and eaten.

Dress and Ornament :

An adult Birhor[27] wears a bhagoa or karea which is a short narrow strip of cloth, at the time of going to town or other village. In this type of cloth, one end of which is wrapped round the waist the other end being passed between the legs and tucked in through the part which serves as the girdle. Women wear round the waist a lahanga about one and a half to two yards long and one and a half cubit wide. A portion of this cloth is allowed to pass diagonally over the upper part of the body so as to cover the breasts.

Jaghis Birhors who are well-to-do wear a short dhoti which is simply wrapped round the waist over the kaupin or sometimes the bhagoa. They also wear either a gamcha or napkin or a Pechhouri or wrapper over the shoulders. This type of Birhor dress is seen at the time of going to town or other village.

At home, the Birhors wear a kaupin or short narrow strip of cloth passed between the legs and attached to a waist-string i.e. called danda-dor and made of chop fibres.

During winter, the Birhors who are well-to-do, wear wrapper round the body and a pechouri and women wear either an unstriped cloth called thethi or a striped cloth known as paria.

At weddings and on festive occasions, the Birhors wear the best clothing they possess. As a protection against the sun, a Birhor may occasionally be seen wearing a cloth round the head as a pagri.

Children up to about five years of age usually remain naked, and after that age boys wear either kaupins or bhagoas. On the other hand, girls wear a piece of cloth called putli about 4.5 feet long and one foot wide.

Although women keep their hair long, men cut their hair short in order to avoid the hair being entangled in bamboo thickets and other trees and bushes in the Jungle. They employ no barbers, but exchange the services of each other for cutting their hair or shaving their beards, moustaches. When a baby is born in a tanda all the men in the tanda, whether belonging to the same clan or not shave their beards by way of ceremonial purification.

The only ornament which is generally worn by young men, consists of one iron bracelet (bera) on each arm and bead necklaces. Some young men may also be seen with brass rings in the lobes of their ears.[28]

On the other, hand Birhor women wear brass bracelet (beras) and anklet (bankis and andus), bead necklaces and sometimes metal necklaces and brass rings for the fingers and the toes, nose ornaments and nose - sticks are not in use. Married women smear vermilion on their forehead on festival days,on occasions of wedding and the like. Feathers are not worn on the hair.Let us examine whether or not the Birhor habitation in the study area has experienced 'landscape' evolution.

Cultural Landscape

The word cultural landscape refers to a concrete and characteristic product of the complicated interplay between a given human community, embodying certain cultural preferences and potentials, and a particular set of natural circumstances. It is a heritage of many areas of natural evolution and of many generations of human effort.[29] However, Carl Sauer[30] writes; "the cultural landscape is fashioned from the natural landscape by a culture group. Culture is the agent, the natural area is the medium, the cultural landscape is the result. Under the influence of a given culture, itself changing through time, the landscape undergoes development, passing through phases and probably reaching ultimately, the end of its cycle of development''

The cultural indices and or traits of the Birhor people do not seem to have had much impact and imprints on the landscape because their genre de vie is yet to achieve territorial specification. The Birhor habitat across the forest and mountain of the Chotanagpur region, particularly in the study area is poorly developed.

Still a section of the Birhor tribe is of wandering and nomadic category, moving from one place to another in search of food etc.Their cultural indices end traits are so weak as to have produced a 'landscape' of their own. The cultural landscape of the sedentary Birhor is poorly developed and that, too, does not manifest a spontaneous development, involving various phases of development through time. The Birhor landscape, as has been observed in the sample villages reflects a kind of 'sponsored' landscape, as the Birhor have been reluctantly colonized by the Government Agencies under different welfare schemes in the past three decades ,in the forest neighbourhoods, of the study area : Ranchi , Gumla and Hazaribagh. The genre de vie of the sedentary Birhor in the study area does not seem to reveal a 'spontaneous adaptability' to the environment. There is a wide gap between their institutional aspects of the cultural traits and their material expression on the land and also between their custom,beliefs, practices and morality.

The Birhor cultural ecology is poorly expressive and developed because they do not share a common genre de vie both material and mental/spitual because a section of them is still characterised and categorised as 'wandering'. Therefore, the relationship between the Birhor in its total aggregate and in natural environment does not appear to be in a state of balance, as a result the tribe is not properly adjustable to exploit its natural habitat in specific ways. Because of the lack of reciprocity the Birhors who have been brought to the new environment, have not transformed it actually and completely so as to fulfil their requirement. Their culture is yet to be explained in term of 'survival' strategies in their natural surroundings and environment. It is better to say that the Birhors are yet to have a well defined-cultural-landscape of their own and at the same time worth-noting that in spite of being a forest tribe, the Birhors are yet to express their territorial-environmental activity and genuineness in term of cultural ecology.

References :

1. William , R., 1976: Keywords : A Vocabulary of Culture and Society, Oxford University Press, New York.

2. Cosgrove, D., 1983 : 'Towards a Radical Cultural Geography, Problems of theory', Antipole 15-1, pp, 1-11.

3. Roy, S.C., 1925 : The Birhors : A little known Jungle Tribe of Chotanagpur, Man in India Office, Ranchi, p. 59.

4. Oraon, P.C., (ed.), 1994 : Bihar Ke Birhor, Bihar Government, Welfare Department, Bihar Tribal Welfare Research Institute Ranchi, p. 7.

5. Mukherjee, B.M. and Khatua, N., 1996 : 'The Birhor of Madhya Pradesh,' Man and Life, Vol. 22, Nos. 1-2, pp. 13-14.

6. Driver, W.H.P., 1888 : 'Journal of Asiatic Society of Bengal', Vol. VII, Pt. I, pp. 12-15.

7. Vidyarthi, L.P. and Rai, B.K., 1985: The Tribal Cultural of India, Concept Publishing, New Delhi, p.157.

8. Vidyarthi L.P. and Rai, B.K., op. cit., p. 210.

9. Roy, S.C., op. cit., p. 69.

10. Roy, S.C., op. cit., p. 143.

11. Singh, R.P. and Kumar, A. 1976 : Evolution of Man and Racial Studies (Hindi), Bihar Hindi Granth Academy, Patna, pp. 291-92.

12. Vidyarthi, L.P. and Rai, B.K., op. cit., p. 298.

13. Vidyarthi, L.P. and Rai, B.K., op. cit., p. 254.
14. Roy, S.C., op. cit., p. 298.
15. Roy, S.C., op. cit., pp. 300-302.
16. Ibid. pp. 305-12.
17. Roy, S.C., op. cit., pp. 313-20.
18. Roy, S.C., op.cit., pp. 325-26.
19. Roy, S.C., op.cit., pp. 366-70.
20. Majumdar, D.N., 1961 : Races and Culture of India, Asia, Publishing House, Bombay, pp. 357-62.
21. Roy, S.C., op.cit., pp.376-83.
22. Roy, S.C., op.cit., p.352.
23. Ibid ; p. 355
24. Roy, S.C., op. cit., p. 512.
25. Ibid ; pp. 514-15.
26. Roy, S.C., op. cit., pp . 520-22.
27. Roy, S.C., op. cit., p. 523.
28. Roy, S.C., op. cit.,p.526.
29. Wagner, P.L. and Mikeswell, M.W., (eds.), 1962 : Readings in Cultural Geography, University of Chicao Press, Chicago, pp. 8-10.
30. Sauer, C.O., 1925: The Morphology of Landscape, University of California Press, Berkeley, pp. 1-12.

7

Sample Villages

Geography is basically an empirical science because it deals with observable phenomena in spatial perspective. Or in other words, geographers tend to concentrate on identifying observable phenomena through observation and experience. However, these are examples of geographic deductive based on a priori theories. But empirical geographical theories and laws, particularly in the positivist nature of work are required to be developed on hypothesis testing and their validation and /or rejection. This necessarily encircle the empirical theoretical formation and when gets validated, it may developed in to a law and /or explanation.

In order to test the veracity of the hypothesis or statements with regard to the Birhor mentioned in first chapter, sample studies have been done through panel surveys which include periodical observation of the collection of fixed data, preparation of diagram and map on the basis of primary data. Altogether seven villages of the study area: Ranchi, Gumla and Hazaribagh have been personally visited and intensively studied for developing an empirical theoretical structure with regard to the Birhor.

Village : Beti

Beti (Revenue thana No. 25) is located in Bishunpur block of Gumla Sub-division of Gumla district. It is bounded on the north by Morawal, on

Table 7.1
Land Under Different Uses in Beti

	In Hectare (1991)	In Percentage
Forest	100.18	19.40
Culturable Waste Land	35.03	6.78
Area not available for cultivation	44.10	8.55
Agricultural Land	337.00	65.27
Total :	516.31	100.00

Source : N.I.C. Bihar State Unit , 1991

the east by North Koel River and Tithi and Solam Nawatoli Village, on the south by Chatakpur and Blatu Village, on west by Range and Langarnar villages.

Eastern part of the village is mainly highland and its slope is towards south, while western part is a low land area. Except a few patches of rugged area, entire village is basically a flat land area. Settlement pattern is linear. The soil is red and not very fertile.

It is clear from the table 7.1 that geographical area of Beti Village is 516.31 hectares of which 65.274 percent or 33.00 hectares comes under agricultural land which is spread over the entire village except northern and south-western part of the village. 19.40 percent or 100.18 hectare of land in the south-western part of the village is covered by forest where as 6.78 percent of land is culturable waste which is spread over the portion touching the northern boundary of the village [Fig. 7.1] .

According to the 1991 census, Beti's total population is 839 in which 401 are males and 438 are females. There are 174 households in Beti, out of which the number of Birhor household is 24 with a population of 121. Table 7.2 shows the main occupation of the Birhor's household. Out of 24 Bihor household of Beti main occupation of 22 household is agriculture

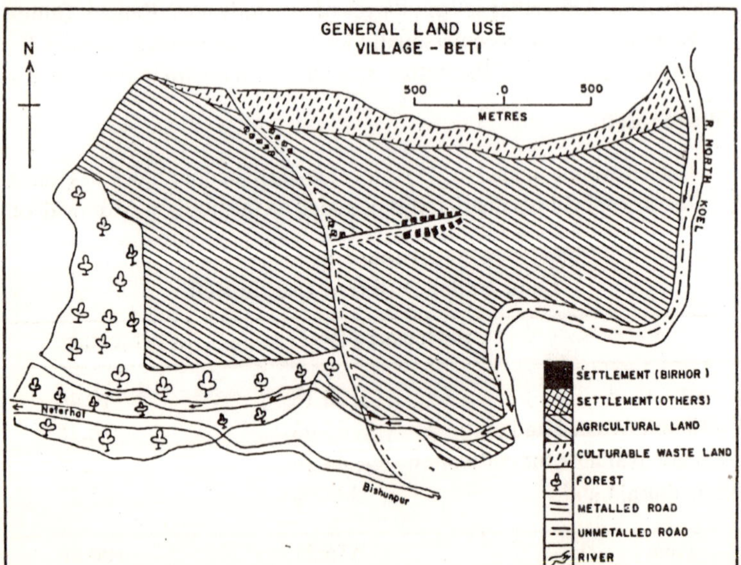

Fig. 7.1

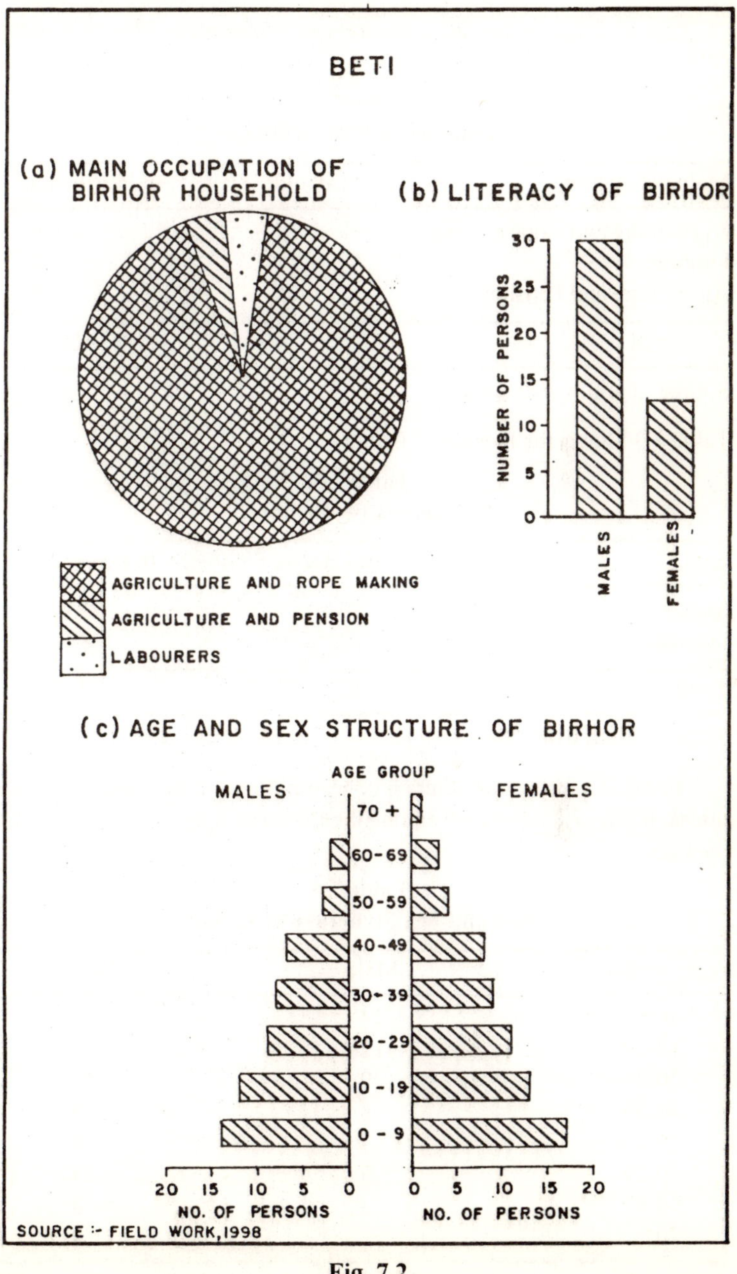
BETI
(a) MAIN OCCUPATION OF BIRHOR HOUSEHOLD
AGRICULTURE AND ROPE MAKING
AGRICULTURE AND PENSION
LABOURERS
(b) LITERACY OF BIRHOR
NUMBER OF PERSONS
0
5
10
15
20
25
30
MALES
FEMALES
(c) AGE AND SEX STRUCTURE OF BIRHOR
AGE GROUP
MALES
FEMALES
70 +
60-69
50-59
40-49
30-39
20-29
10-19
0-9
20 15 10 5 0
0 5 10 15 20
NO. OF PERSONS
NO. OF PERSONS
SOURCE :- FIELD WORK, 1998

Fig. 7.2

and rope making, the rest are Labourers and Pensioners. The main occupation of Birhor's household is indicated by means of Pie chart [Fig. 7.2a].

Table 7.2
Main Occupation of Birhor

Main occupation	No. of household	In Percentage
Agriculture and Rope making	22	92.00
Labourer	01	4 .00
Agriculture and Pension	01	4.00
Total :	24	100.00

Source : Field work - 1998

Table 7.3 Shows the literacy of Birhor

Table 7.3
Literacy of Birhor

Sex	No. of Literate	In Percentage
Male	30	71.43
Female	12	28.57
Total :	42	100.00

Source : Field work 1998

In all, 42 Birhors are literate of whom 30 are males and 12 are females. In Fig. 7.2 b Literacy among the Birhor is shown by means of Bar diagram.

Table 7.4
Age and Sex Structure of Birhor

Age - Group	Male	Female
0-9	14	17
10-19	12	13
20-29	9	11
30-39	8	9
40-49	7	8
50-59	3	4
60-69	2	3
70+	–	1

Source : Field work - 1998

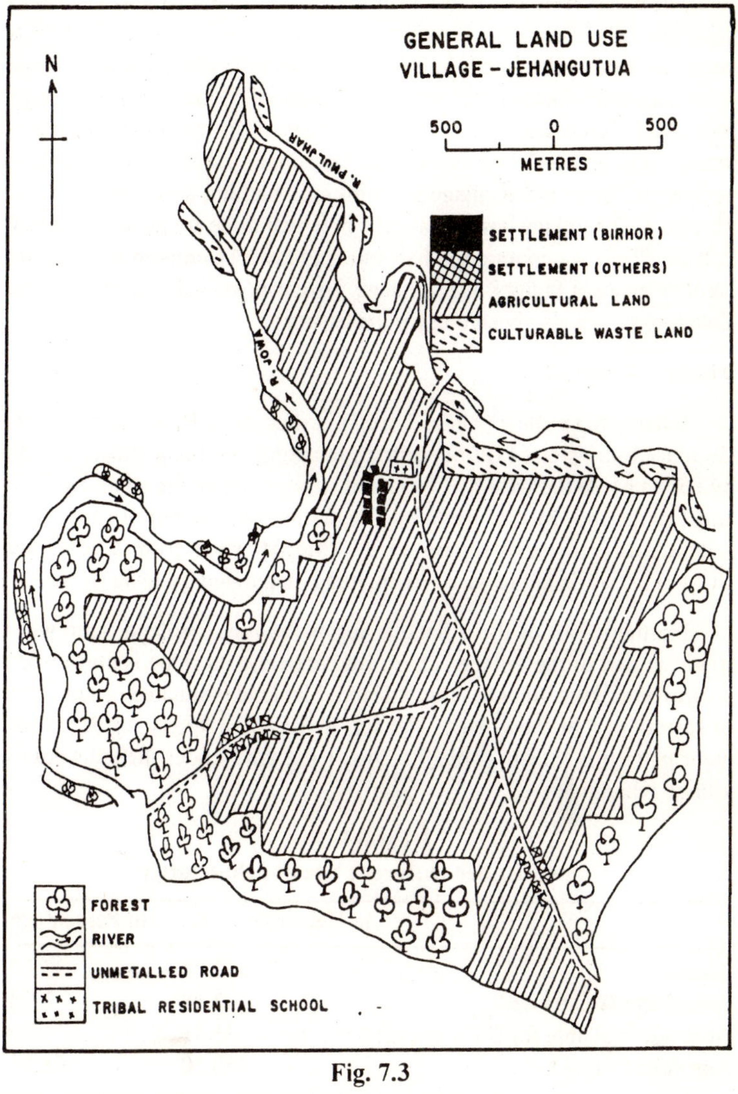

Fig. 7.3

Table 7.4 Shows the age and sex structure of Birhors. It is clear from this table that there are 66 females and 55 males out of total of 121. Age group of 0-9 represents the highest number of Birhor population . In Fig. 7.2C age and sex of Birhor is demonstrated by means of simple pyramidal diagram.

The distance of bus stand from the village is about 3 km. The Block head quarter (Bishunpur) is situated 13 km. away from Beti. The thana head quarters and high school lie at a distance of 13 km. from the village. A hospital with doctor is situated at a distance of 13 km. from the village. post office is situated at a distance of 2 km. from the village. Weekly market (Banari) is 3 km. away from the village . There are three hand pumps available in the village for drinking , bathing and also for other purposes. The village has also 4 wells in which three are pucca and one is kutcha. There is a community hall and Anganwari Centre in the Village . Neither medical facility nor drainage system is available in the village. Two tanks have also been dug for the Birhors .

Village- Jehangutua

Jehangutua village (Thana No.57) is situated in Bishunpur block of Gumla sub-division of Gumla district. Jehangutua is bounded on the east by Dipadih , on the west by Oreya and Arangloya, on the south by Helta and Longa and on the north by Chenri and Bishunpur. In the north Jehangutua Village is separated by Phuljhar river from Chenri and Bishunpur, while in the west Jehangutua is separated by Jowa river.

Northern part of the village is comparatively low land area while southern part of the village is high land area and its slope is north ward, central part of the village is rugged land. Flat land is situated in some area of eastern part of the village. The soil is red and not very fertile. Settlement pattern is linear. Table 7.5 shows the land under different use in village Jehangutua.

Table 7.5

Land Under Different Use in Jehangutua

	In Hectares (1991)	In Percentage
Forest	152.38	23.17
Culturable Waste Land	8.18	1.24
Area not available for Cultivation	46.48	7.06
Agricultural Land	450.50	68.53
Total :	657.54	100.00

Source : N.I.C. Bihar State Unit, 1991

It is clear from the table 7.5 that Jehangutua has 657.54 hectares ot total geographical areas, out of which 68.53 percent or 450.50 hectares of

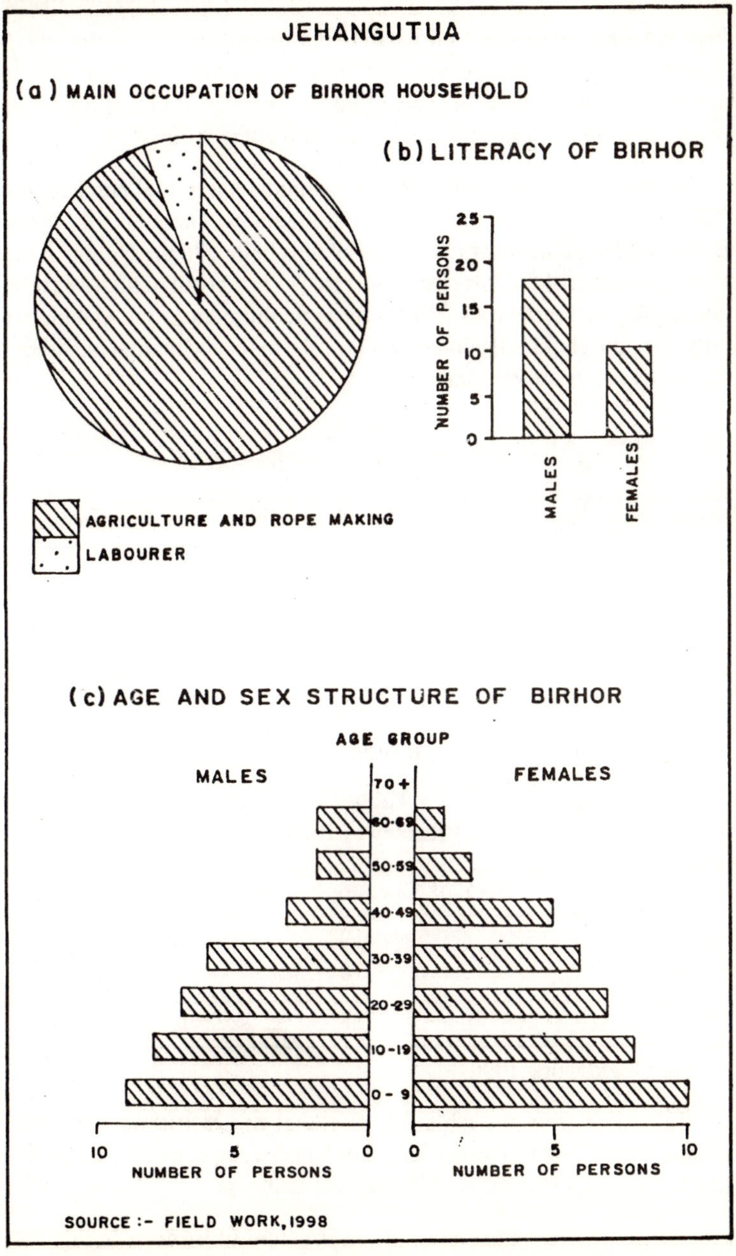
JEHANGUTUA
(a) MAIN OCCUPATION OF BIRHOR HOUSEHOLD
AGRICULTURE AND ROPE MAKING
LABOURER
(b) LITERACY OF BIRHOR
NUMBER OF PERSONS
25
20
15
10
5
0
MALES
FEMALES
(c) AGE AND SEX STRUCTURE OF BIRHOR
AGE GROUP
MALES
FEMALES
70+
60-69
50-59
40-49
30-39
20-29
10-19
0-9
10
5
0
0
5
10
NUMBER OF PERSONS
NUMBER OF PERSONS
SOURCE :- FIELD WORK, 1998

Fig. 7.4

land is under agricultural purposes which is spread over entire village except some part of the village. 152.38 hectares of land in south-western and eastern part of the village is covered by forest. Culturable waste land of 18.18 hectares forms northern part of the village [Fig. 7.3]

According to the 1991 census, Jehangutua has a total population of 787 in which 373 are males and 414 are females. There are 149 households in Jehangutua in which 18 households belong to the Birhors with a total population of 76. It is clear from table - 7.6 that out of total 18 Birhor household, 17 households depend on agriculture and rope making and only one household is labourer . In Fig. 7.4 a main occupation of Birhor is shown by means of Pie Chart.

Table 7.6
Main Occupation of Birhor

Main occupation	No. of household	In Percentage
Agriculture and Rope making	17	95.00
Labourer	01	5.00
Total :	18	100.00

Source : Field work- 1998

Table 7.7 Shows the Literacy of Birhor.

Table 7.7
Literacy of Birhor

Sex	No. of Literate	In Percentage
Male	18	64.28
Female	10	35.72
Total	28	100.00

Source : Field work-1998

It is clear from the table 7.7. that total of 28 Birhors are literate among whom 18 and 10 are males and females respectively. In Fig. 7.4b literacy among the Birhors of Jehangutua is shown.

Table 7.8 Shows the age and sex structure of Birhors. In Fig. 7.4C age and sex of Birhor is demonstrated by means of Simple Pyramidal diagram.

Table - 7.8
Age and Sex Structure of Birhor

Age - Group	Male	Female
0-9	9	10
10-19	8	8
20-29	7	7
30-39	6	6
40-49	3	5
50-59	2	2
59-69	2	1
70+	-	-

Source : Field work - 1998.

The Block head quarters is located 3 km away from the village. The Thana head quarters, a metalled road and bus stand are situated at a distance of 3km. from village. Middle school, high school , post office, weekly market, all are situated at a distance of 3km. away from Jehangutua. A Sub-health centre with a nurse is also available in the village. There is a primary school and also a Tribal Residential school in Jehangutua village.

There are two handpumps available in the village for drinking and bathing and also for other purposes. The village has only one pucca well. There is a community hall in the village. The approach to this village is by a kacha road. Nearest town is Gumla which is 57 km. away.

Village : Katiya

Katiya village (Thana No. 4) is situated in Bishunpur block of Gumla Sub-division of Gumla district. Katiya is bounded in the north by Jamti, in the south by Ghaghra, in the east by district boundary of Lohardaga and in the west Borang. Suda river passes through Katiya in its northern part.

Low land area is situated in north-west part of the village Katiya which is a flat area. On the other hand high land area or higher sites occur on the peripheries of the village. However higher site also occurs in the centre of the village. Katiya are highland areas and its slope is towards west. Entire high land is covered by forest. Settlement types is disperse where as pattern is linear. Soil is mainly red and not very fertile.

Table - 7.9 shows land under different uses :

Table 7.9
Land under different uses in Katiya

	In Hectares (1991)	In Percentage
Forest	1342.58	73.65
Culturable waste land	19.50	1.07
Area not available for Cultivation	158.26	8.77
Agricultural Land	300.66	16.51
Total	1821.00	100.00

Source : N.I.C. Bihar State Unit, 1991

It is clear from the table 7.9 that total geographical area of Katiya village is 1821.00 hectares out of which largest percentage of 73.65 or 1342.58 hectares is covered by forest. Lowest percentage of land is covered by agricultural waste land situated in the northern part of the village [Fig. 7.5.]

According to the1991 census, Katiya has 207 households with total population of 1041 (542 are males and 499 are females). 15 households

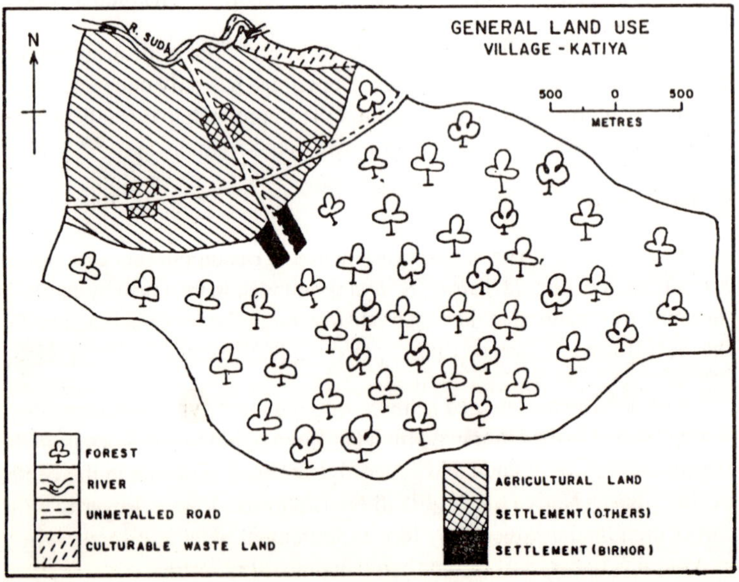

Fig. 7.5

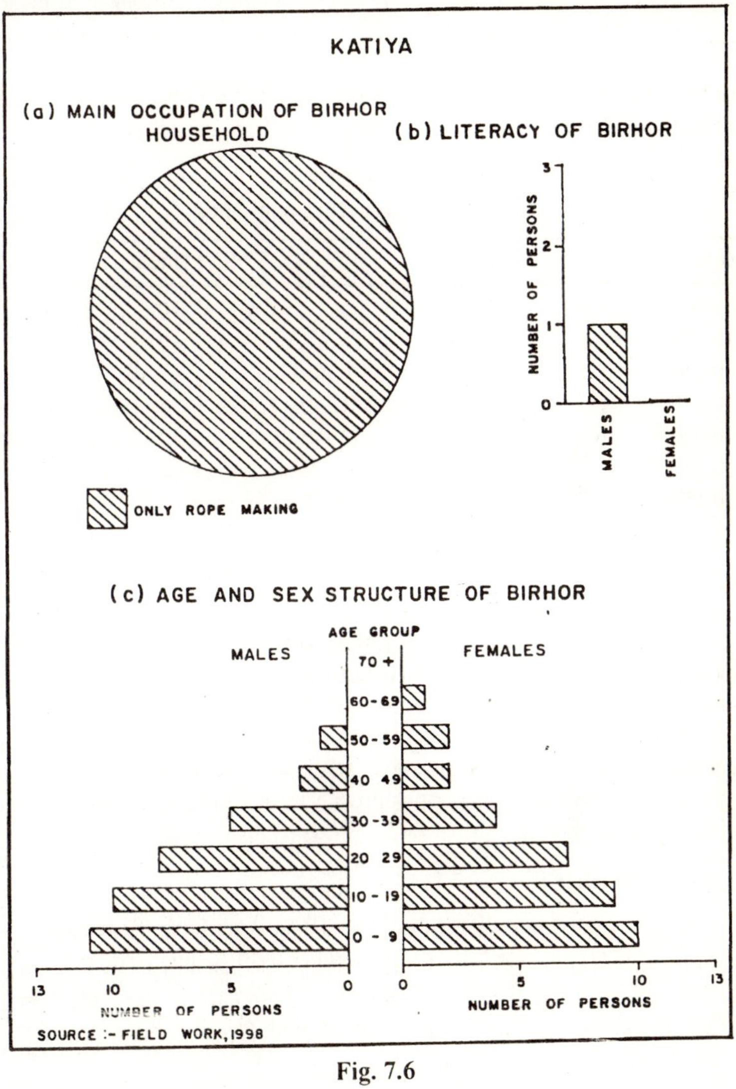

Fig. 7.6

belong to the Birhors with a total population of 72 . Main occupation of Birhor of Katiya is shown is Fig. 7.6 a. Rope making is the only occupation of all the 15 households of Birhors. This is shown by Pie chart. Fig. 7.6b shows the position of literacy among Birhors of Katiya. Only one Birhor is literate who is a male.

Table 7.10 Shows the age and sex structure of Birhors. It is clear from the table - 7.10 that there are 37 males and 35 females out of total 72 Birhors population. Age - group of 0-9 represents the highest number of Birhor population. Fig. 7.6c shows the age and sex structure of Birhor of Katiya village.

Table 7.10
Age and Sex structure of Birhor

Age - Group	Male	Femele
0 - 9	11	10
10- 19	10	9
20-29	8	7
30-39	5	4
40-49	2	2
50-59	1	2
60-69	-	1
70+	-	-

Source : Field work -1998

Katiya is situated at a distance of 31 km. from the Block and Thana head quarters. Metalled road, bus stand and post office, all are located about 8 km from the village. Hospital with a doctor is situated at a distance of 1 km. Weekly market is situated at a distance of 1 km. Health sub-centre, Anganwari centre and primary schools all are situated at a distance of 1 km. Kacha road serves as approach to this village. Latehar is the nearest town (24km.).

Village : Kairbera

Kairbera village (Thana No.8) is situated in Simdega block of Simdega sub-division of Gumla district. Kairbera is bounded on the east by Kesalpur and Rengarpani, on the west Kinbira, on the south by Sarkhutoli and Maskera, on the north by Hardibera and Raidih Revenue thana of Raidih C.D. Block

South and south-east area of Kairbera village is high land area, and its slope is towards north. Northern part of the village Kaibera is low land, while central part is less higher than the southern part and there exist some patches of rugged areas. Soil is red. Utihal river passes through the village from south to north. Settlement type is disperse where as pattern of the settlement is linear.

Table 7.11 indicates land under different uses :

Table 7.11
Land under different uses in Kairbera

	In Hectares (1991)	In Percentage
Forest	463.57	25.77
Agricultural land	970.24	53.94
Culturable waste land	329.92	18.34
Area not available for Cultivation	34.73	1.95
Total	1798.46	100.00

Source : N.I.C. Bihar State Unit. 1991

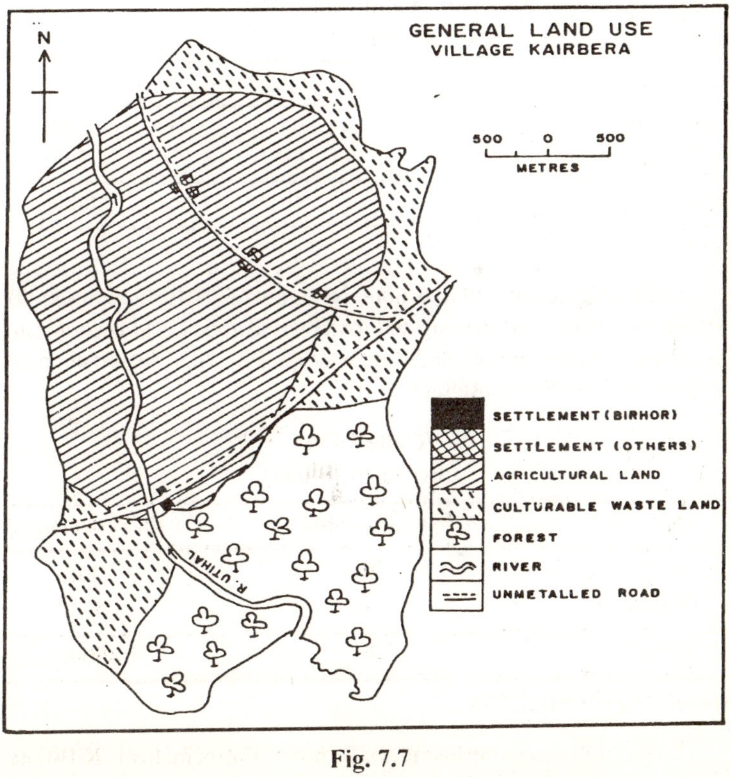

Fig. 7.7

Table - 7.11 Shows that total geographical area of this village is 1798. 46 hectares, Out of which 970.24 hectares are agricultural land , spread over west and central part of the village. 463.57 hectares are covered by forest in south and south - eastern part of the village, which constitutes 25.77 percent of the total geographical area. Culturable waste land cover 329.92 hectares in north east and south-west region of the village Kairbera [Fig.7.7].

According to the 1991 census, Kaibera has registered a total population of 1554, out of 788 are males and 766 are females. Total household number was registered as 354. Out of total population of Kairbera, the tribals are 876 in number, in which 459 are males and 417 are female. There are 65 Birhors (34 male and 31 female) living in 'DO Bhaya Birhor Colony' in Kairbera village. The number of Birhor household is 14. Table 7.12 shows the main occupation of the Birhors household :

Table 7.12
Main occupation of Birhor

Main Occupation	No. of household	In Percentage
Agriculture and Rope making	05	35.00
Rope making and forest based	09	65.00
Total :	14	100.00

Source : Field work- 1998

Table 7.12 indicates that 9 households out of 14 Birhor households depend mainly on rope making and forest based goods. 5 households are associated with agriculture and rope making. Fig. 7.8a shows the main occupation of Birhor households.

Table 7.13a
Literacy of Bihar

Sex	No. of Literate	In Percentage.
Male	20	71.42
Female	8	28.58
Total :	28	100.00

Source : Field work, 1998

Table 7.13a shows the literacy of Birhor of Kairbera. In all 28 Birhors are literate. Out of which number of males and females are 20 and 8

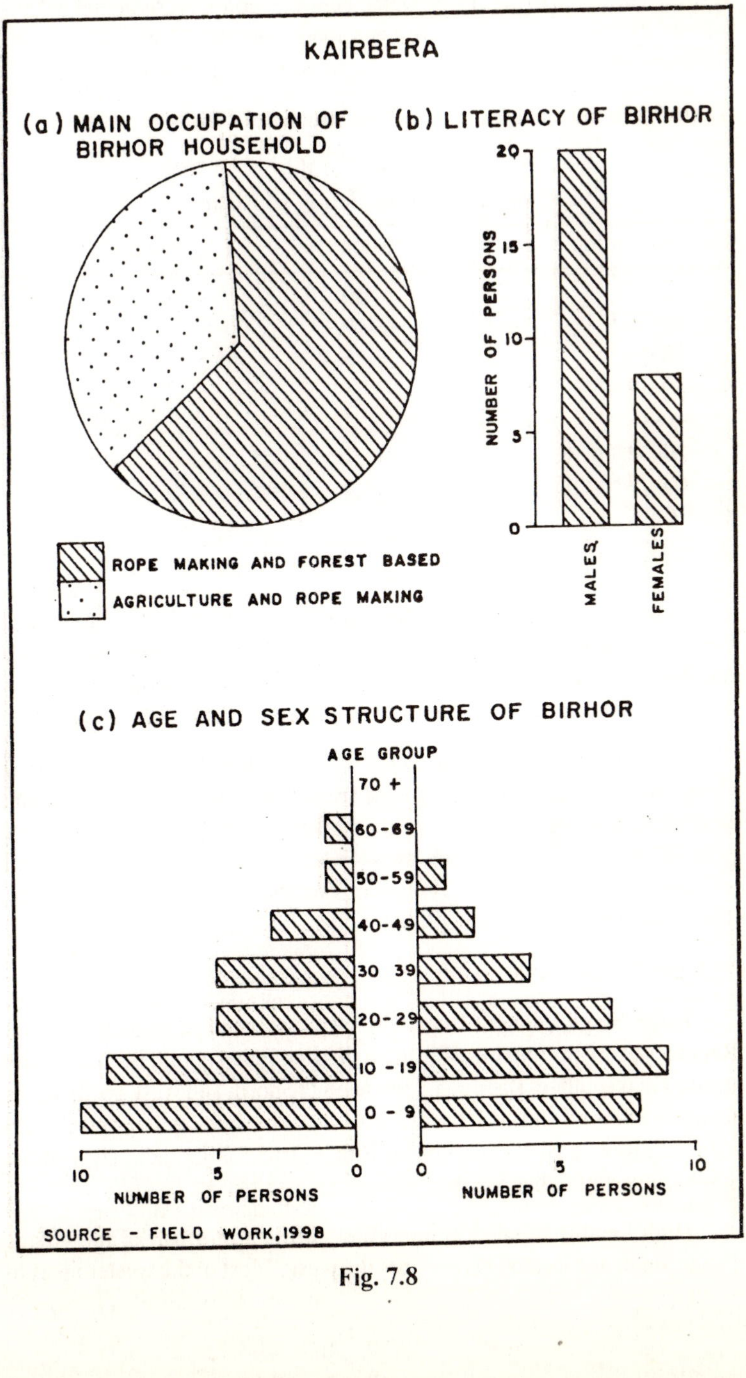
KAIRBERA
(a) MAIN OCCUPATION OF BIRHOR HOUSEHOLD
ROPE MAKING AND FOREST BASED
AGRICULTURE AND ROPE MAKING
(b) LITERACY OF BIRHOR
NUMBER OF PERSONS
0
5
10
15
20
MALES
FEMALES
(c) AGE AND SEX STRUCTURE OF BIRHOR
AGE GROUP
70 +
60-69
50-59
40-49
30 39
20-29
10 - 19
0 - 9
10
5
0
NUMBER OF PERSONS
NUMBER OF PERSONS
SOURCE - FIELD WORK, 1998

Fig. 7.8

respectively. Due to the 'Injot Dahar centre' a non-governmental organization efforts, 28 Birhors have been made literate, 37 persons are still illiterate, Fig. 7.8b shows the literacy of Birhor of Kairbera.

Table 7.13b indicates the age and sex structure of Birhor.

Table - 7.13b
Age and Sex Structure of Birhor

Age-Group	Male	Female
0-9	10	8
10-19	9	9
20-29	5	7
30-39	5	4
40-49	3	2
50-59	1	1
60-69	1	-
70+	-	-

Source: Field work - 1998

Table 7.13b indicates that there are 34 males and 31 females out of the total 65 Birhors population. Age-group of 0-9 represents the highest number of Birhor among the others age-group population of Birhors. Fig. 7.8c shows the age and sex structure of Birhors of Kairbera village.

Kairbera village is situated 24 km. from Block and thana head quarters. Hospital with doctor and high school are available at a distance of 24 km. from the village . Bus stand, weekly markets are situated at 0 km. While post office is situated at 5 km. away. Kairbera has two hand Pumps for drinking and other purpose. There is no facility of well in Kaibera village. This village has a community hall.

Village: Pahar Singh

Pahar Singh village (Thana No. 64) is situated in Angara block of Ranchi Sadar sub-division of Ranchi district. Pahar Singh is bounded on the east and south by Barwadag, while on the north and west, by Revenue thana of Silli of Silli C.D. Block . Muri- Ranchi Railway line and Ranchi - Purulia Road pass through Pahar Singh. There is Jaruadih river in the southern part of Pahar Singh.

High Land is situated in north and north-eastern part of the village Pahar Singh and its slope is towards the west . Most of the western part of the village is low land area, while south -east part of the villages is highly rugged. Soil is red. Settlement type is disperse whereas pattern is linear.

Table - 7.14 shows land under different uses :

Table 7.14
Land under different uses in Pahar Singh

	In Hectares - 1991	In Percentage
Forest	334.04	56.54
Culturable waste land	1.34	0.22
Agricultural land	206.03	34.89
Area not available for Cultivation	49.37	8.35
Total:	590.78	100.00

Source: N.I.C. Bihar State Unit - 1991

It is clear from the above table that total geographical area of this

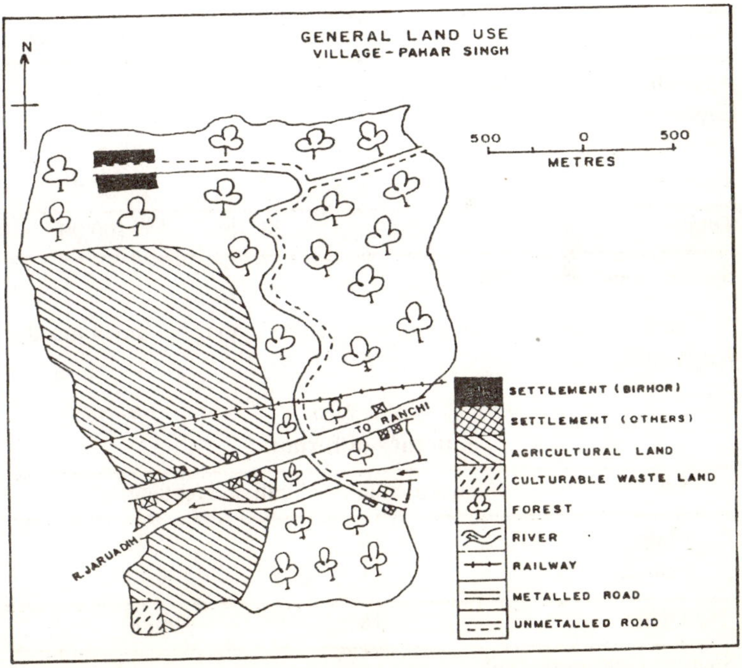

Fig. 7.9

village is 590.78 hectares. Forest area constitutes the largest percentage of 56.54 or 334.04 hectares, spread over north, east and south-eastern part of the village . Culturable waste land covers the lowest percentage of 0.22 , in the south-western region of village. 34.89 percent of total geographical area comes under agricultural land which is spread over western and south -western part of the village [Fig. 7.9].

According to 1991 census, Pahar Singh's total population is 761 with 170 households. There are 33 Birhors households in Pahar Singh with total population of 115 in which 59 are males and 56 are females.

Table 7.15 shows the main occupation of Birhor households. 15 out of 33 Birhor households are engaged in rope making and forest based activities. Agriculture and rope making are engagements of 11 Birhor households. 4 and 3 households are engaged in labour and rope making respectively. Fig. 7.10a shows the main occupation of Birhor households.

Table 7.15
Main occupation of Birhor

Main Occupation	No.of household	In Percentage
Agriculture and Rope Making	11	33.33
Labourer	04	12.12
Only Rope Making	03	9.10
Rope Making and Forest Based	15	45.45
Total :	33	100.00

Source : Field work, 1998

Table 7.16 indicates the position of literacy among the Birhor of Pahar Singh village.

Table 7.16
Literacy of Birhor

Sex	No. of Literate	In Percentage.
Male	15	93.79
Female	1	6.21
Total :	16	100.00

Source : Field work, 1998

It is clear from the above table that only 16 Birhors are literate out of

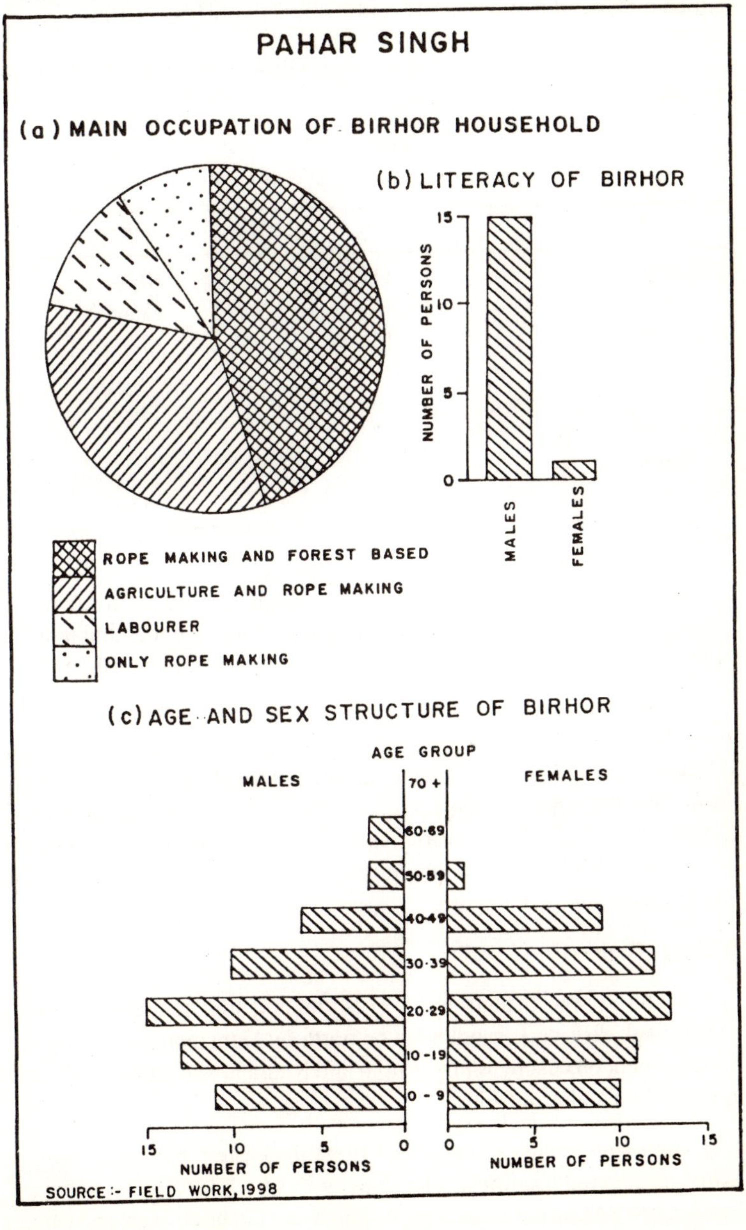
PAHAR SINGH
(a) MAIN OCCUPATION OF BIRHOR HOUSEHOLD
(b) LITERACY OF BIRHOR
NUMBER OF PERSONS
15
10
5
0
MALES
FEMALES
ROPE MAKING AND FOREST BASED
AGRICULTURE AND ROPE MAKING
LABOURER
ONLY ROPE MAKING
(c) AGE AND SEX STRUCTURE OF BIRHOR
AGE GROUP
MALES
FEMALES
70 +
60-69
50-59
40-49
30-39
20-29
10 -19
0 - 9
15 10 5 0
0 5 10 15
NUMBER OF PERSONS
NUMBER OF PERSONS
SOURCE :- FIELD WORK, 1998

Fig. 7.10

which males and females are 15 and 1 respectively [Fig. 7.10b]

Table 7.17 shows the age and sex structure of Birhors of Pahar Singh village.

Table 7.17
Age and Sex Structure of Birhor

Age - group	Male	Female
0-9	11	10
10-19	13	11
20-29	15	13
30-39	10	12
40-49	6	9
50-59	2	1
60-69	2	-
70+	-	-

Source : Field work- 1998

There are 115 Birhors in which 59 are males and 56 are females. Age-group of 20-29 represents the highest number of males and females among the other age-group of the Birhors population [Fig.7.10C]

The Block and Thana headquarters are situated at a distance of 23km. from the village. High school and weekly market are situated at a distance of 2 km. Hospital, post office and middle school all are situated at 1km. from the village. Village has a primary school. There is also a community hall in the village. The Government has constructed two tanks, one for irrigation and other for drinking purposes for animals. There is no hand pump facility in the village.

Village- Bigha

Bigha village (Thana No. 67) is situated in Chauparan block of Hazaribagh district. It is bounded on north by Domaponari, on south by Madhgopali, on east by Ranik, Rupin and Kharahuwan and Madhgopali, on west by Sanjha and Ahri.

High land area is situated mainly on the eastern part of the village which is covered by forest. The slope of this high land is towards west. Except few patches of rugged areas which exist in north-west and central part, the entire village presents a flat surface. Type of settlement is disperse where as pattern shows linear.

Table 7.18 shows the land of Bigha village under different uses.

Table - 7.18
Land under different uses in Bigha

	In Hectare 1991	In Percentage
Forest	46.18	17.66
Culturable waste land	18.74	7.11
Agricultural land	188.07	72.12
Area not available for cultivation	8.13	3.11
Total :	261.12	100.00

Source : N.I.C. Bihar state unit -1991

Bigha village has 261.12 hectares as its geographical area. 188.07 hectares of land is used for agricultural purposes, spread over entire village except eastern and west-central part of the village. While 46.18 hectares are covered by forest in eastern part of the village Bigha, agricultural waste land is to the extent of 18.74 hectares, situated in west -central part of village [Fig. 7.11]. Soil is red and not very fertile.

According to 1991 census the population of Bigha is 592 in which 301 are males and 291 are females with 104 households. There are 41 Birhors household in Bigha village. Table-7.19 shows the main occupation of Birhors households of Bigha village :

Table 7.19
Main occupation of Birhor

Main Occupation	No. of households	In Percentage
Labourer	13	31.70
Only Rope making	8	19.52
Rope making and forest based	20	48.78
Total	41	100.00

Source : Field work - 1998

It is clear from the above table 7.19 that there are 41 Birhors household in the village. Main occupation of 20 households is rope making and forest based activities. Members of 13 household are Labourer. 8 Birhor households are engaged in only rope making. Fig. 7.12a shows the main occupation of Birhor household.

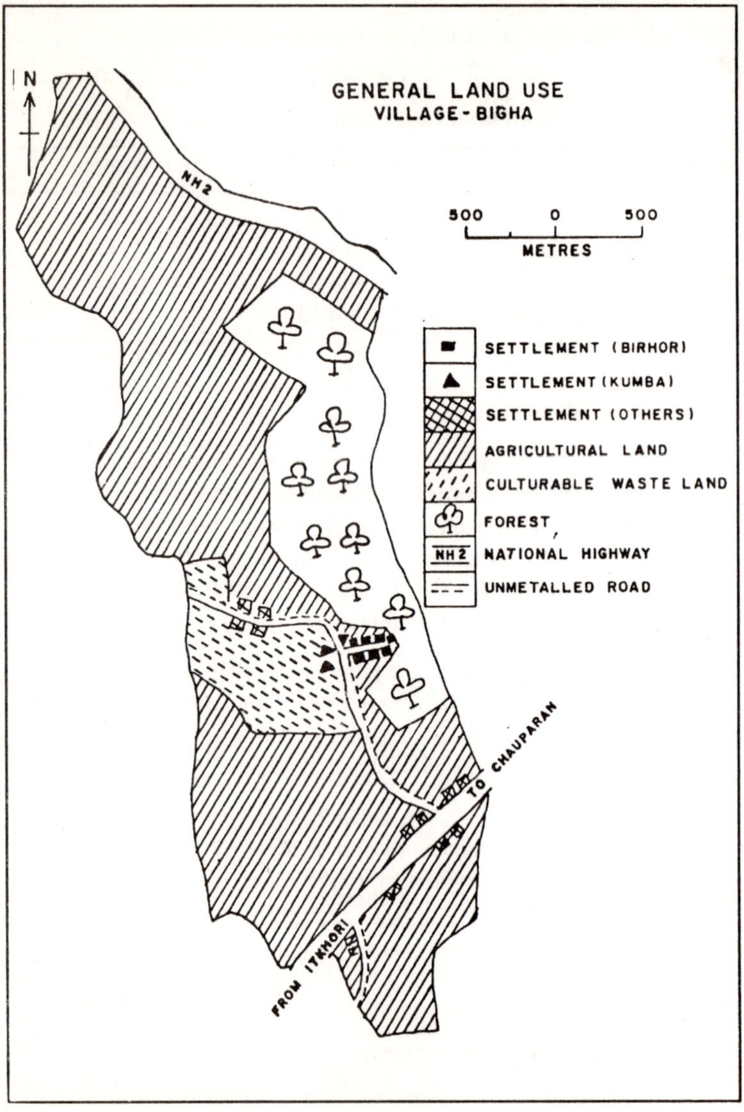

Fig. 7.11

Table-7.20 indicates the position of literacy among the Birhors of this village. In all 30 Birhors are literate among which 27 and 3 are males and female respectively. Fig. 7.12 b shows the literacy of Birhor of Bigha village.

Table 7.20
Literacy of Birhor

Sex	No. of Literate	In Percentage
Male	27	90.00
Female	3	10.00
Total :	30	100.00

Source: Field Work - 1998

Table 7.21 indicates the age and sex structure of Birhor in Bigha village. It is clear from the table 7.21 that total number of Birhors are 224, out of which 114 are males and 110 are females. Age -group of 10-19 represents the highest number of Birhor population among the all age-group of population. Age and sex structure of Birhors of this village is shown in Fig. 7.12c.

Block and Thana head quarters are situated at a distance of 3.1/2 km. from the village. Bus stand, post office and doctor all are available at a distance of 2.1/2 km. from the village. Village has a community hall. There are two hand pumps and a well in village for drinking and other purposes. Weekly market is situated in the village itself.

Table 7.21
Age and Sex Structure of Birhor

Age - Group	Male	Female
0-9	21	23
10-19	24	26
20-29	24	23
30-39	21	19
40-49	15	13
50-59	05	04
60-69	03	02
70+	01	00

Source : Field work -1998

VILLAGE : DEMBU

Dembu Village (Thana No. 245) is situated in Hazaribagh Sadar Block of Hazaribagh district. It is bounded on the north by Chapwa and Bhelwara, on the south by Morangi and Tumba, on the east by Chehla and Barasi, on

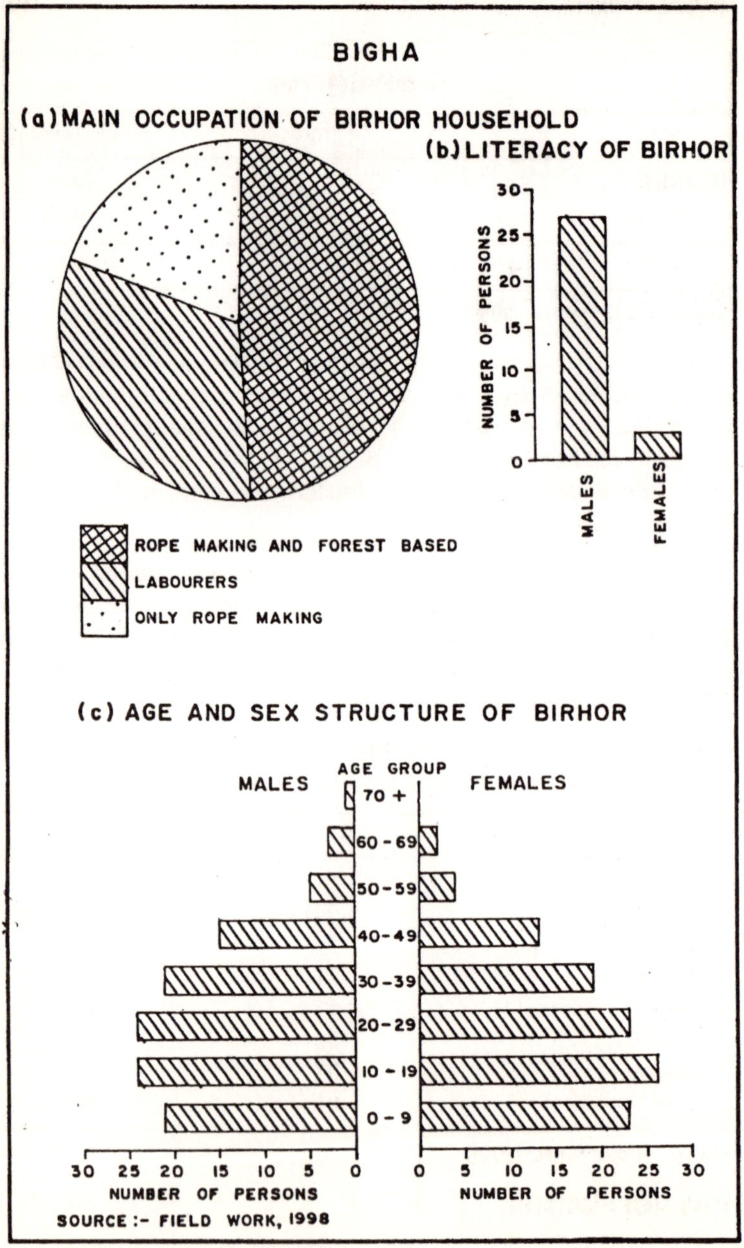
BIGHA
(a) MAIN OCCUPATION OF BIRHOR HOUSEHOLD
(b) LITERACY OF BIRHOR
NUMBER OF PERSONS
30
25
20
15
10
5
0
MALES
FEMALES
ROPE MAKING AND FOREST BASED
LABOURERS
ONLY ROPE MAKING
(c) AGE AND SEX STRUCTURE OF BIRHOR
MALES
AGE GROUP
FEMALES
70 +
60 - 69
50 - 59
40 - 49
30 - 39
20 - 29
10 - 19
0 - 9
30 25 20 15 10 5 0
0 5 10 15 20 25 30
NUMBER OF PERSONS
NUMBER OF PERSONS
SOURCE :- FIELD WORK, 1998

Fig. 7.12

the west by Hupad.

High land is situated in north and to the north -east part of the village Dembu and its slope is toward south. While low land area exists in south east of the village, central part of the village is highly rugged, western and south-western area are basically flat. Red and sandy soils are found in village Dembu. Disperse type of settlement is found in village, where as pattern is linear.

Table 7.22 shows land under different uses. It is clear from table 7.22 that, Dembu village has a total geographical area of 501.32 hectares. 34.53 percent of the area is covered by forest in eastern, south -western and in

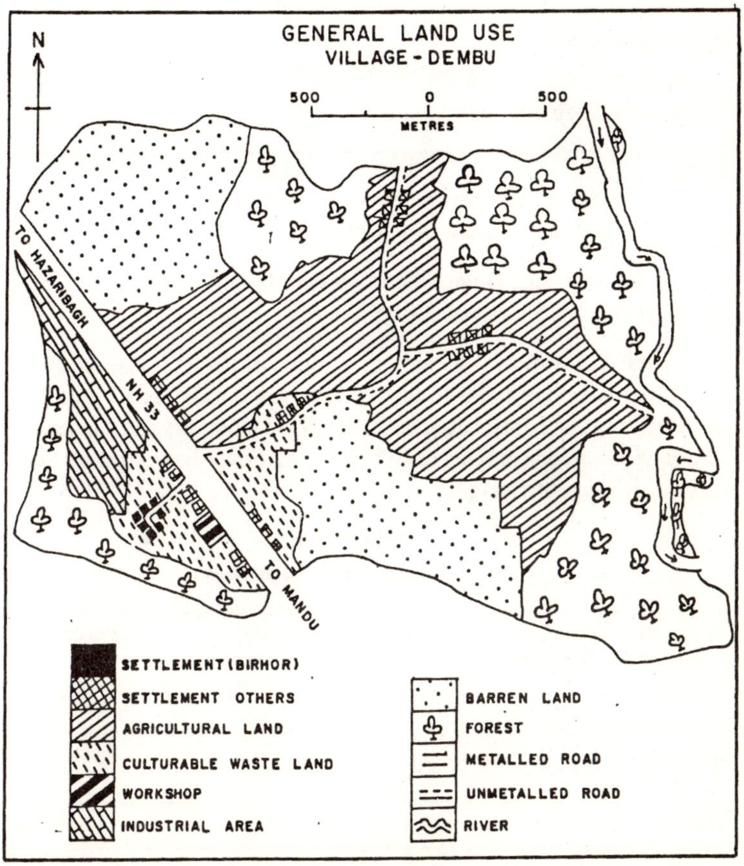

Fig. 7.13

northern part of the village. 25.12 hectares of land is classified as agricultural waste land, situated in south-western portion of the village. Agricultural land covers 145.76 hectares in central, northern and in some part of eastern portion of the village Dembu. Fig. 7.13 indicates the land use of the village.

Table 7.22
Land under different uses in Dembu

	In Hectares 1991	In Percentage
Forest	175.12	34.53
Culturable waste land	25.12	5.01
Agricultural land	145.76	29.48
Area not available for cultivation	155.32	30.98
Total :	501.32	100.00

Source : N.I.C. Bihar State Unit-1991

In 1991 census, Dumbu has total population of 1231, out of which 163 persons are S.C. and 86 are S.T.

Table 7.23a shows the main occupation of Birhor household . There are 24 Birhor households in this village. 12 households are engaged in rope making and forest based activities. 9 are labourers and 3 households are engaged in rope making only. Fig. 7.14a shows the occupational position of Birhors of Dembu.

Table 7.23a
Main Occupation of Birhor

Main occupation	No.of household	In Percentage
Labourer	9	37.50
Only Rope Making	3	12.50
Rope making and forest based	12	50.00
Total :	24	100.00

Source : Field work 1998

On literacy fronts, as Table 7.23b shows, in all, 12 Birhors are literate out

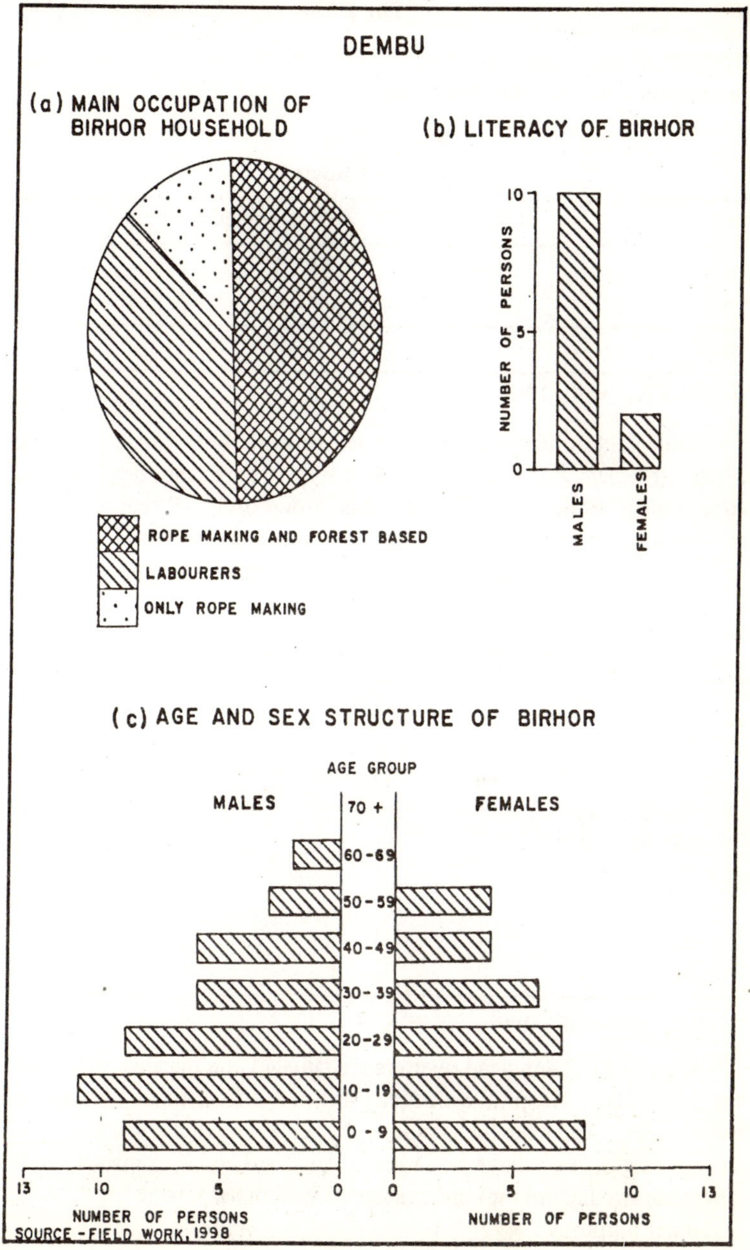
DEMBU
(a) MAIN OCCUPATION OF BIRHOR HOUSEHOLD
ROPE MAKING AND FOREST BASED
LABOURERS
ONLY ROPE MAKING
(b) LITERACY OF BIRHOR
NUMBER OF PERSONS
0
5
10
MALES
FEMALES
(c) AGE AND SEX STRUCTURE OF BIRHOR
AGE GROUP
MALES
FEMALES
70 +
60-69
50-59
40-49
30-39
20-29
10-19
0-9
13
10
5
0
0
5
10
13
NUMBER OF PERSONS
NUMBER OF PERSONS
SOURCE - FIELD WORK, 1998

Fig. 7.14

of which 10 and 2 are males and females respectively Fig. 7.14b shows the literacy of Birhor of Dembu village.

Table 7.23b
Literacy of Bihar

Sex	No.. of Literate	In Percentage
Male	10	83.33
Female	2	16.67
Total :	12	100.00

Source: Field work 1998

Table 7.24 indicates the age and sex structure of Birhors of Dembu village. It is clear from the above table that there are 82 Birhors, in which 46 are males while 36 are female . Age group of 10-19 represents the highest number among the all age-group of Birhor population. Fig. 7.14C shows the age and sex structure of Birhors of Dembu Village.

Table 7.24
Age and Sex Structure of Birhor

Age - group	Male	Female
0-9	9	8
10-19	11	7
20-29	9	7
30-39	6	6
40-49	6	4
50-59	3	4
60-69	2	-
70+	-	-

Source: Field work 1998

Block and Thana head quarters are situated at a distance of 10 km. from the village. Hospital with doctor and post office, all are available at a distance of 2 km. from the village, while weekly market is situated in the village itself . The village has a community hall and Anganwari centre There are two handpumps and one pucca well in the village for drinking and other purposes.

BIRHORS'S HOUSEHOLD INCOME GROUP

In Table 7.25 below and Fig. 7.15 Birhor household under different income group in seven surveyed villages are shown in percentage form:-

Table 7.25

Birhors Household Income Group (per month, in percentage)

Name of Sample Village	IncomeGroup Rs. 1 to 200	IncomeGroup Rs. 200 to 400	Income Group Rs. 400 to 600	IncomeGroup Rs. 600 to 800
Beti	12.50	50.00	37.50	----
Jehangutua	----	55.60	38.80	5.60
Katiya	----	20.00	26.66	53.34
Kairbera	14.30	28.60	57.10	----
Pahar Singh	12.10	24.20	36.40	27.30
Bigha	14.60	46.50	34.10	4.80
Dembu	16.60	50.00	20.50	12.90

Source : Field Work -1998

It is clear from the table -7.25 that highest percentage of income group rupees 1 to 200 is found in the village Dembu, where as the highest percentage of income group rupees 600 to 800 is found in the village Katiya. The highest and lowest percentage of income group rupees 200 to 400 is found in the village Jehangutua and Katiya respectively.

House Type

In table 7.26 below Birhor house (according to their size) in seven surveyed villages are shown in percentage form :-

Table 7.26 Size of Birhor's House

Percentage of Birhors House According to their size

Name of Sample Village	One Roomed House	Two Roomed House	Three Roomed House
Beti	45.83	50.00	4.17
Jehangutua	55.55	33.33	11.12
Katiya	80.00	20.00	00.00
Kairbera	85.72	14.28	00.00
Pahar Singh	100.00	00.00	00.00
Bigha	90.24	09.76	00.00
Dembu	91.66	08.34	00.00

Source : Field work -1998

From the above table 7.26, it appears that percentage of 'one-roomed

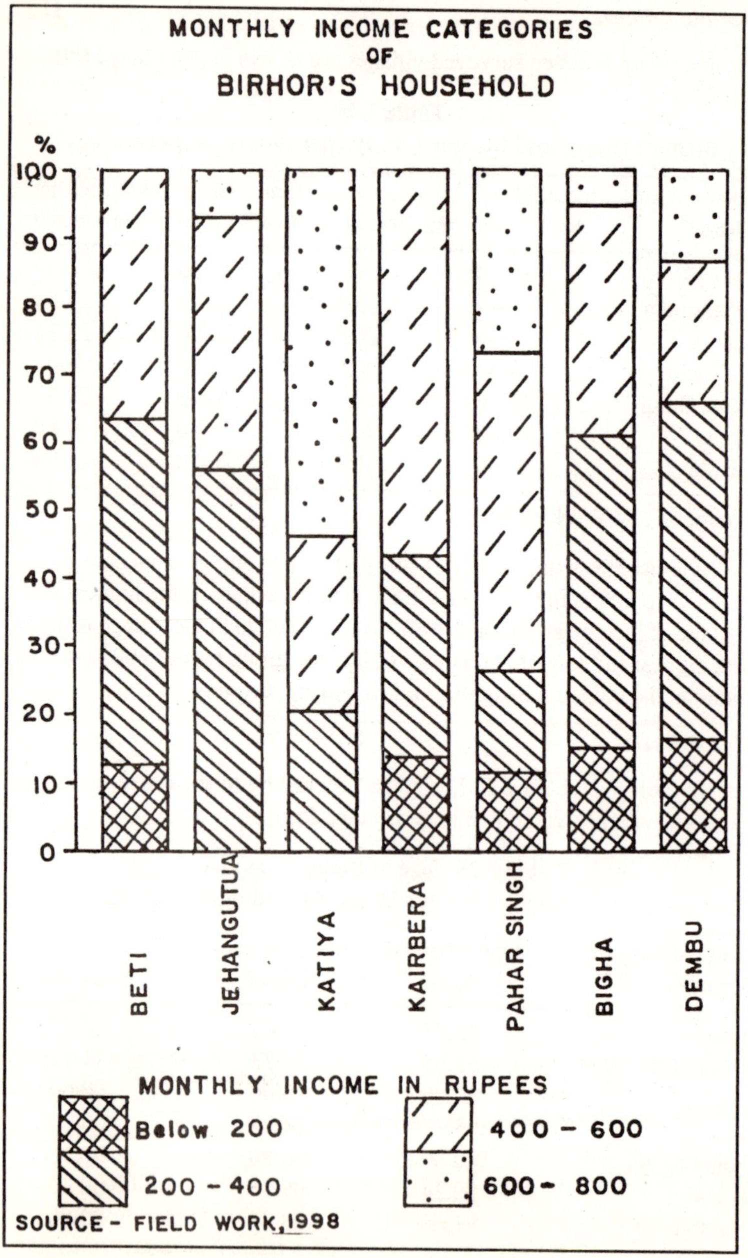
MONTHLY INCOME CATEGORIES
OF
BIRHOR'S HOUSEHOLD
%
100
90
80
70
60
50
40
30
20
10
0
BETI
JEHANGUTUA
KATIYA
KAIRBERA
PAHAR SINGH
BIGHA
DEMBU
MONTHLY INCOME IN RUPEES
Below 200
200 - 400
400 - 600
600 - 800
SOURCE - FIELD WORK, 1998

Fig. 7.15

house' is higher in all the sample villages. In Pahar Singh village percentage of 'one roomed house' is cent per cent . In this village, Pucca roofed houses have been constructed by the Government under 'Indira Awas Scheme'. The lowest percentage of such 'one roomed house' is noticed in Beti village where it is 45.84% only. Percentage of such houses in Bigha and Dembu is 90.24 and 91.66 respectively. Three -roomed houses are found in Beti and Jehangutua villages of seven sample villages shown in the above table. Three -roomed houses in Beti and Jehangutua constitute 4.17% and 11.12% respectively. In the rest five sample villages, three roomed houses are not seen. The highest percentage of two-roomed houses is found in two sample villages of Beti and Jehangutua where it is 50.00 and 33.33 respectively. In Pahar Singh sample village, two - roomed houses are not found. Percentage of two-roomed houses in Katiya and Kairbera sample villages is 20 and 14.28 respectively.In table.7.27 below, houses of Birhors (according to building material) of seven surveyed village, are shown in percentage form on the besis of building materials.

Table 7.27
Building Material of Birhor house

Name of Sample Village	Mud Wall and tiled roof	Vegetative matter	BrickWall and Cemen-ted roof	Stone Wall & Cement roof	Stone Wall & tiled roof
Beti	50.00	-	-	16.66	33.34
Jehangutua	33.33	-	-	55.55	11.12
Katiya	20.00	-	-	53.33	26.67
Kairbera	100.00	-	-	-	-
Pahar Singh	-	-	100.00	-	-
Bigha	-	26.83	-	73.17	-
Dembu	-	-	100.00	-	-

Source : Field work -1998

In Pahar Singh and Dambu Sample Villages, cent per cent houses are brick-walled and having cemented roofs. In both the villages, government has constructed houses with improved technique and design under 'Indira Awas Yojna'. In Bigha village, out of all the houses built there, 73.13% houses are stone-walled and having cemented roofs. Rest 26.83% houses are made of vegetative matters. Although Government has constructed pucca houses for the Birhors of this village, they are insufficient for their accommodation, due to increase in their population and as such, some

Birhors are residing in huts built by the side of such pucca houses. Such huts are called 'Kumba'. There are, in all, 11 Kumbas, which are about 8 feet high and its radius is about 6 feet. There is no provision of ventilation in such Kumbas. There is only one exit which is 2.5 feet in height and 2 feet wide.

Government has also constructed mud-walled houses with tiled roofs but such houses were constructed long ago. In Kairbera sample village, all the houses of Birhors are of such type. In Beti and Jehangutua villages, percentage of such houses is 50.00 and 33.33 . No such houses are found in Pahar Singh, Bigha and Dembu villages.

Except Bigha village, stone-walled and cemented roofed houses of Birhors are also found in Beti, Jehangutua, and Katiya villages where the percentage is 16.66, 55.55 and 53.33 respectively.

The highest percentage of stone-walled and tiled roofed houses of Birhors is seen in Beti villages. Such houses were also formerly constructed by the Government. Percentage of such houses in Jehangutua and Katiya villages is 11.12 and 26.67 respectively.

Government- welfare schemes

After gaining Independence, Government of India has taken various steps for the upliftment of the tribals as provided under different Articles of Indian Constitution. Huge sums have been spent under various five year plans.

In Bihar also, Government efforts towards upliftment of Tribals have been Praise- worthy. Special efforts have been made for the upliftment of Birhor Tribe, which was at vanishing stage. To inspire sense of permanent existence among them, Government of Bihar has allotted 5 acres of land for agriculture and 10 decimals of land for plantation to each family of Birhors in three villages (Beti, Jehangutua and Katiya) of Bishunpur Block of Gumla district. 90% of the land settled with these Birhors falls under category of 'Tarn Lands'.

In 1957-59, welfare department of the Govt. had constructed 15 residential houses in Jehangutua and 30 such houses in Beti village. In 1957-59 itself, primary school building was also established. Balwari Scheme was also started. Rope making centre was also opened.

In 1985-86 and 1987-88, again pucca houses were built in the above three villages under 'Indira Awas Yojana'. Birhors of Jehangutua and

Beti have been given tractors on the basis of cent percent grant by the welfare department. One community hall has been constructed in each of the three villages. Along with these facilities, hand pumps have been made available for pure drinking water. In Jehangutua and Beti, tanks have also been dug for irrigational facilities. Govt. has also made available one pair of bullocks, goats and other animals to each family of Birhors. At times fertilizers and seeds are also provided to them for agricultural purposes. In Beti village, arrangement has also been done for supply of electricity ,but unfortunately, it is not in order at present.

Birhors have been settled by constructing 'Do Bhaya Birhor colony' in Kairbera village of Simdega block of Gumla district. Govt. has constructed 15 houses in this village. Each of 5 households of this colony have been given one acre of land for agricultural purposes , but this land is less fertile. Here, one community hall has been constructed and two hand pumps have been sunk for pure drinking water. Due to active participation and initiative by a non-Govt. organisation called 'Injot Dahar Centre', 28 Birhors of Do Bhaya tola, became literate.

In Pahar Singh village of Angara Block of Ranchi district, 15 Kucha houses were built in the beginning. In 1995-96, Govt. constructed 33 pucca houses under 'Indira Awas Yojana'. Walls of these houses are of bricks and the roofs are cemented. In 1997, Govt. grants were given for rearing pigs, goats, honeybees etc. Jute was made available for rope-making. Grants were also given to purchase machines for rope-making. In 1997 itself, district welfare officer of Ranchi had distributed 70 mosquito-curtains among the Birhors. In August 1998 jute, seeds and fertilizers have been given to them by theDistrict welfare officer of Ranchi. Two tanks have been dug in Pahar Singh village by the Govt. agency. Scheme for sinking two hand pumps has not been successful so far.

In Bigha village of Chauparan Block in Hazaribagh district, Govt. has made a successful attempt to instill sense of permanent existence among the Birhors by constructing 33 pucca '2 in one' houses. This happened 20 years ago. Govt. has constructed here a community hall and also dug a well. 2 hand pumps have also been sunk for pure drinking water.

Also in Dembu village of Sadar subdivision of Hazaribagh district, Govt. has settled Birhors by constructing Birhor colony. In the beginning, Govt. had constructed 15 houses, but in 1997-98, 22 new type of houses with cemented roof have been constructed under Indira Awas Yojana. In constructing such houses, bricks, iron doors and windows have been used,

Govt. has also constructed a community hall and two hand pumps have been sunk for drinking water. Welfare department is making available jute for rope-making. At times. grants are given for basket making and rearing goats etc. Garments and medicines are also distributed by govt. agencies.

Since 1957 , even continuous Govt. attempts to improve the economic condition of Birhors have not achieved the desired results, on the contrary, mentality of Birhors is growing to thrive on Govt. grants only.

Economy and Culture

Chotanagrpur is the habitat of tribals. Thirty branches of these tribals are settled in this region. One of them is Birhor.

Birhors represent group of people whom Dr. L.P. Vidyarthi (1958) has put in the category of 'food gatherers'. This group of people lead simple life than those of 29 other tribal communities. From the point of view of cultural form and cultural way of life, Birhors are important and different from the neighbouring tribals. While living in the forest for centuries they have adopted the life style of wanderers (Nomadic). Their standard of living is confined to that level where they are content with those items of life which they can carry on their shoulder and arms. Vidyarthi drew the attention of the Government through his deep study for the upliftment of Birhors. Consequently , attempts have been made through different schemes for their upliftment. In 1956, with a view to change their way of life as 'wandering ' to the stable and permanent way of life, the Govt. constructed Birhor Residential colonies and attempts were made to get them settled.

Although, the schemes did not prove successful in the beginning , in due course, Birhors took interest and began settling in those colonies. They have begun living in those residential colonies constructed in some villages of Hazaribagh, Gumla and Ranchi districts. Population of Birhors is scattered and noticed in the districts of Ranchi, Gumla, Hazaribagh, Lohardaga, Singhbhum (East and West), Palamu, Garhwa, Giridih, Nawada and Dhanbad. Besides , their population has been recorded in the neighbouring state of Orissa and West Bengal. During last four decades, attempts to uplift them have been made by Government and non-Government agencies.

According to the recent survey undertaken by Bihar Tribal welfare Research Institute, Ranchi, in 1993 total population of Birhor has been recorded as 5017. Hence the belief that 'the Birhor population is declining' does not seem be quite relevant.

One group of Birhors which has adopted permanent way of life is called 'Jaghis' This group of Jaghis' perhaps being in contact with neighbouring communities for long, has adopted permanent way of life. However, this group is not different from Uthlus. Difference between the two in regarding their economic activities. The Jaghis have their habitation on the hills near the forest. Their kumbas resemble those of the Uthla but they are bigger in size and more durable. Their members have begun more or less cultivation works after clearing shrubs and forests for agricultural purpose. There is no confirmed knowledge as to when the 'Uthlu' associated and converted themselves into 'Jaghis' and when they assumed permanent way of life. By the way, S.C.Roy (1925) has recorded their existence. As regard agricultural activities, the Jaghis, have been able to produce maize or beans (sem). For this purpose they have adopted shifting cultivation. Majority of them have no land of their own, they are not in a position to stay at one place for longer period.

On account of govt. initiative, Uthlu Birhors have been settled in the residential colonies of Jehangutua, Katiya and Beti of Bishunpur Block of Gumla District. Birhors are also now living in the Residential colonies of Bigha, Dembu, Peta, Sultan Adara and Amnari of Hazaribagh district. Each of these newly settled Birhor families has been allotted 5acres of agricultural land, 10 decimil of plantation land, one pair of bullock, goats and hens. Residential schools have also been run for their education. We can name them 'Newly settled Birhors'. They have got not only permanent status having settled at fixed place, but their world view has also changed. The Birhors of Jehangutua as compared with Birhors of other places, have developed themselves to great extent and in course of time adopted Christianity. Being Christian there has been reform in their way of life and the living standard.

Under Govt. spornsered Birhor Resettlement scheme, in Jehangutua, Beti and Katiya of Bishunpur Block and in many Blocks of Hazaribagh and Ranchi district, pucca residential houses have been constructed. In Bishunpur Block, Birhor families have been allotted lands for agricultural purposes and they are doing cultivation in those lands. They have also begun rearing honey bees, besides keeping cow, bullock goats and hens. This has been made possible due to huge aid made available by the Govt. agencies.

Following are the categories of lands, made available by the Govt.

(i) Tanr land : This kind of land is mainly made of red sandy soil. Birhors of Jehangutua and Beti have more of Tanr land . Gora rice, Maize, Mahua, Gondiali, Jatangi, Arhar and Urad crops are raised in such kind of land.

(ii) Don land: Some Birhors have Don Land, lands which are not suitable for cultivation purpose.

(iii) Bari Land : On this category of land, which is situated near their house, Birhors mainly produce vegetables.

Cultivation is done mainly by bullocks. In Jehangutua and Beti of Bishunpur block, even tractors have been given by the Government in group, as a results, Birhors are using tractors for cultivation in these villages. Time to time, seeds and chemical fertilizers are also provided to the Birhors by the Govt. Besides this, Birhors are also using Gobar khad (Organic manure). But due to lack of proper irrigational facilities Birhors have to depend on rain. In some villages, wells and ponds have also been dug for irrigation purposes. Due to inadequate lands available to Birhors, they also depend on forest product and commodities made from forest. They also work as labourers. Their main occupation is confined to rope -making and manufacturing various kinds of goods from wood. They also get some money by selling rabbits, deer etc. which they get from forests in course of hunting.

Main occupation of Birhor of Birshunpur was hunting, rope making, collecting herbs and honey from forest. But at present, they have adopted modern way of rope- making and bee-keeping. Now, they also do agricultural work. They do every work individually. System of Gitiora has now ended.

As stated above, rope -making is the main occupation of Birhors They make ropes from many varieties of chops of forest. Now Jute is being provided by the Govt. to the Birhors of Paharsingh, Bigha and Dembu for manufacturing ropes. Birhors hunt hares, deer and peacocks, by using,' Net' and they get good income from this occupation.

Birhors are famous for collecting honey. They move for honey in the Jungle and after procuring it they sell to 'Bikash Bharti' of Bishunpur Block. They have been provided with boxes to rear honey and also the machines for extracting honey.

Birhors have adopted a kind of barter system for marketing the forest produce. A forest produce called ' Chironji, is exchanged for another necessary items being brought in the local market or elsewhere. Birhor also get substantial money by selling Kendu leaves.In the weekly market of Bishunpur, Banari, Avor, Johna (Angara), Bigha etc, Birhors make transaction of articles of daily use.

Due to being in contact with nearest neighbours, Hindus, there has been perceptible change in the form of their festival and beliefs. Due to above fact, Birhors have begun celebrating Raksha Bandhan, 'Gomha Puja', Makar Sankaranti, Saraswati puja , Holi, Dipawali and Lakshmi puja etc. Besides, they are also celebrating festivals like, Karma, Dashara, Sarhul etc. This trend indicates that they have been greatly influenced by Hindu religion.

Among the newly settled Birhors, their traditional political system of mukhiya (Naya) has ended. Being influenced by neighbouring tribals, some Birhors have been acknowledging Pahan as their religious heads (Mukhiya) . But those Birhors who are more enlightened, normally get their problems settled from Block officials and other modern panchayat functionaries.

Change has also been noticed in the use of clothes and ornaments of Birhors. While using clothes, male Birhors used to wear Bhagwa and put ' gamcha ' on their shoulder . But at present, male Birhors wear pants and shirts, kurta Dhoti, shoes and chappal and lungi etc. while female Birhors are wearing sarees, blouse, peticoat and the girls are using skirts, blouse , Salwar and kurta etc. In the past, only one saree was worn by females and they used to cover their bodies with the small saree. They used 'Kekana' as ear-ring which was made of Palm tree leaves. Modern ornaments are lesser in use.

In the past, Birhors were using earthen utensils, but in due course, they have been using utensils made of .aluminium, brass, bronze and even steel. In some households, articles made of even glass are found. .During course of visit of Jehangutua the author found Television set in the house of Chchtrapal Birhor. There is a change in the dietary habits of Birhors. They are using rice, wheat , maize , marua, mahua, and gondali. etc. Being in contact with the Christian missioneries, use of wine is almost matter of past. This is the view of Chchatrapal and Bijay Birhor of Jehangutua and Ashani Kumari of Do Bhaya of Kairbera village of Simdega.

Influence of Christianity has been noticed in the Birhor colonies of Jehangutua , Beti and Katiya of Bishunpur block and Do Bhaya of Kairbera

(Simdega). Birhors of these places have adopted Penticostal Mission Holiness Church branch of Christianity. The followers of this branch do not take wine of any variety. It is found that before starting any work, they pray to God, the Jesus Christ. They also celebrate the Baradin of Christian festivals.

Among the non/Govt. organizations, Christain missionaries are actively working in Bishunpur and Simdega Block. Bikas - Bharti of Bishunpur is also active in upliftment of Birhors' way of life.

There has also been a change in the constitution of family of Birhors. Joint family system has been substituted by single family. In Birhor tribal family, community system has changed and in its place sense of being individualist has developed. There has also been comprehensive change in their social status. In the past, economic condition was the main base of their social status, but now change in social status is based on individual strength and ability.

Besides depending on herbal plants to cure their diseases , they also go to doctor and hospitals. For their safety of life and other facilities many govt. and private health centres have been opened in Birhor areas. On the one hand there is Govt. hospital in Netarhat and Bishunpur, on the other hand there is a private hospital run by missionary in Banari.

In old days, Birhors were living in huts made of grass and leaves. Those structures were known as 'Kumba', but now most of them live in houses made of tiles, bricks and cement. Their roofs are also pukka . Such houses have been made available under govt. scheme of Indira Awas Yojana. But in Bigha village of Chauparan Block of Hazaribagh district some Birhor families are living in traditional kumbas (height 8 - 10 feet) due to increase in their numbers and non-provision of housing facilities by Govt. At present, in almost every area, Govt. has established Birhor colony for their benefit and welfare. At some places, where pukka houses have been constructed, two or three Pukka toilets have also been constructed, but Birhors seldom make use of them.

On the social front, for the Birhor tribal residing in Bishunpura block, marriageable age of the Birhors couple is 20-21 year. Among the Birhors of this place, according to Christianity, some instances of marriage in church are also noticed . As stated by Phagua Birhor of Beti, marriage is arranged by the parents of the couple. His marriage was also arranged by his parent. Phagua Birhor stated that there is no custom of paying Bridal price. Shani Birhor of Jehangutua also stated in detail that parents of respective couples arranged their marriage and every function was done according to their arrangement.

Borha Birhor of Jehangutua stated that even then some Birhors did come to the residence of bride's father with Barati and Bridal fee was actually paid by the bride - groom's side. Ashani kumari of Do Bhaya Birhor colony of Kairbera stated that at the time of marriage barati used to come to the residence of bride and Bridal fee was either paid in kind or in cash. This custom was also confirmed by Budha Ram Birhor of Pahar Singh settled areas of Angara Blcok of Ranchi district.

Usually, marriage is performed out of Gotras. Marriage among same patriarchal and matriarchal relatives is prohibited. Many kinds of marriags are prevalent among the Birhors but all acceptable kind of marriage is that of Sadar Bapla . In such kind of marriage, fathers of bride and bride/ groom arrange marriage. Also prevalent are the kinds of Nam Mapm Bapla, Udra Udri Bapla and Bolo Bapla.

Family of Birhor is patriarchal one. Generally, Birhors have nuclear family of which husband wife and unmarried children are the members. Beside this, there are some joint families also which consist of father, mother, married son and daughters. In Birhor tribe, generally male is the head of the family and power of taking every decision is vested in him. The female partner is merely a partner.

Statistical Analysis

The present study follows statistical analysis for the Birhor population compared with tribal population in Chotanagpur region. The author of the present work takes into account the seven sample villages namely- Beti , Jehangutua, Katiya, Kairbera, Pahar Singh, Bigha and Dembu and intrinsically considers the Birhor population of each village . The consideration relating to statistical analysis comes into the mind of the author due to the existence of variation in case of Birhor population corresponding to the variation in each village. It, therefore, requires to apply the statistical technique for finding the accuracy of the sample observation of the Birhor groups. Since the variation takes place with different numerical evidence, therefore the object of the statistical analysis is perceived by various statistical tools for classified data, as given in Table - 7.28 to 7.37 . Therefore it could be known whether sample observations are more consistence with the statement relating to proportion on the sample value significant or not. In addition, the author is keenly interested to find out the intensity between two sets of sample observations such as age and sex structure, and the educational attainment of Birhor population when the constraints of sex is being applied there.

In view of examined statistical evidences the following measure are being considered for analysis of procure data —

(1) Tests of proportion for two sets of observation in given sample;
(2) Association between two sets of sample observations; and
(3) Consistence of Data .

(1) Tests of proportion for two sets of observation in the given sample

To analyse the data relating to Birhor population to the tribal population, the application of Tests of proportion is being considered and formulated as follows under the assumption of equivalency of two proportions i.e.

[H.O.: $p_1 = p_2$] Where p_1 and p_2 are denoted for proportion of Birhor and tribal population in two given sample values.

Under the assumption of normality of last sample test the required formula is given:

$$|Z| = \frac{|p_1 - p_2|}{\left(\frac{p_1 Q_1}{n_1} - \frac{p_2 Q_2}{n_2}\right)^{1/2}} \sim N(0,1),$$

.............[I]

that is, p_1 p_2= respective proportion for Birhor and tribal population respectively.

n_1 n_2 = Value of observation considered two tests of observation.

$|Z|$ = the statistical, which is normally distributed with mean Zero and variance unity, under assumption of normality.

Since (HO: $p_1 = p_2$)

Using given formula of [I] the required interpretation follows that if $|Z| \leq 1.96$ then ,their is no evidence to reject the Null Hypothesis HO. That means to say that there is equivalence in the two proportion which is being accepted . If |Z| > 1.96, then, Null Hypothesis is refuted ,and that follows the difference of the proportion between two tests of observation.

Based on above formula (I) the author seeks to obtain following values Z's corrésponded to each of seven sample village (Table 7.28) to make Justification of acceptance or rejection of Null-Hypothesis for mentioning to condition of the referred tests of significance.

Table 7.28
General Population of Sample Villages

Village Name	1	2	3	4	5	6	7	8	9
Beti	174	839	156	779	24	121	14.42	15.53	15.36
Jehangutua	149	787	142	711	18	76	9.65	10.68	12.67
Katiya	207	1041	205	1026	15	72	6.92	7.01	7.31
Kairbera	316	1555	175	876	14	65	4.18	7.42	8.00
Pahar Singh	170	761	101	506	33	115	11.55	15.11	32.67
Bigha	104	592	41	224	41	224	37.83	100.00	100.00
Dembu	225	1231	25	86	24	82	6.66	95.34	96.00
Total	1345	6806	845	4208	169	755	11.38	17.94	20.00

1. Total Household
2. Total Population
3. Tribal Household
4. Tribal Population
5. Total Birhor's Household
6. Total Birhor's Population
7. % of Birhor's Population to Total Population
8. % of Birhor's Population toTribal Population
9. % of Birhor's Household to Tribal Households.

Sample Village	|Z|
Beti	19.96> 1.96
Jehangutua	20.23> 1.96
Katiya	2.778> 1.96
Kairbera	98.18 > 1.96
Pahar Singh	55.62 > 1.96
Bigha	986.82> 1.96
Dembu	1140.52> 1.96

Interpretation

From obtained value of |Z|'s there might be assumed that the proportions between Birhor and tribal population followed significant values.

(2) Association between two sets of sample observation:

The table 7.29 of the present research work seeks to provide observations concerning with the literacy of Birhor population (male and female) of all seven surveyed villages. In visual inspection recorded observations followed more variation in attainment of literacy of both sexes: males and females- residing in sample villages. In fact, with regard to such variation the author makes an attempt to concentrate on association of literacy between two observational texts of values that indicates variation in literacy among the Birhor population. To find associations or relationship between observational values in following product moment, co-rrelation co-efficient formula of Carl Spearman's is being used to obtain measure of correlation of all surveyed villages. So that association of literacy might be tested out to subject: male and female.

Table 7.29

Percentage of literate male & female to the total no. of literate Birhor

Name of the	Male		Female		Total		Child 1-12 years	
Village	No	%	No.	%	No.	%	No.	%
Beti	30	71.43	12	28.57	42	100.00	10	23.80
Jehangutua	18	64.28	10	35.72	28	100.00	6	21.42
Katiya	01	100.00	—	——	01	100.00	—	—
Kairbera	20	71.43	08	28.57	28	100.00	7	25.00
Pahar Singh	15	93.75	01	6.25	16	100.00	3	18.75
Bigha	27	90.00	03	10.00	30	100.00	8	26.66
Dembu	10	83.33	02	16.67	12	100.00	2	16.66
Total	121	77.07	41	22.93	157	100.00	36	22.92

Source : Field work, 1998

The required mathematical formula to measure of co-rrelation has been contributed as-

$$r = \frac{COV(x,y)}{\sqrt{V(x)V(y)}} \text{...........II}$$

The numerator of two denoted co-variation between two sets of observational values specifying the present case as literacy of male and female of Birhor population of all surveyed villages. This quotient has important characteristic concerning the sign of the measure of co-efficient 'r' that depends upon sign of co-variation between sets of variable, that is-

If, COV follows negative values 10, then measure would be negative, if COV provides positive sign, then 'r' would give positive values.

If COV xy = O, then r = o, hence concluding about the limits of measure of correlation are entirely depend on co-variation between two sets of observation, particularly the literacy attained by males and females of Birhor population.

The denominator placed in definition II tends to provide some of squared variation of the variables from mean of the distribution which always gives positive sign.

In order to find such characteristics of given measure, the author is keenly interested to make concentration on the attainment of the literacy of males and females of Birhor population of extended form of literacy to males and females of such specified population. Though the required limit to measure the co- efficient ranges between - 1 to + 1.

In order to make assertion of such limits of r, the author is very interested in the following issues;

(a) Whether the literacy prevailing between Birhor male and female gets negative association or negatively related, that is, whether the spread of literacy to any of the both sexes in positive dimension, while the other sex in negative dimension?

Explaining such statement, if it has to be inferred whether the literacy does have any relation between the attainment of Birhor male and female ?

(b) Whether the literacy attained by males and females of such specific population follows in the same dimension and

(c) Whether the literacy to both Birhor males and females is independently distributed ?

Keeping in view of the dimension concerning literacy attainment by Birhors males and females, the following figures corresponding to the

Table 7.30
Birhor - Age & Sex Structure of surveyed villages -1998 [in no. of persons]

Age group	Beti		Jehangutua		Kairbera		Pahar Singh		Katiya		Bigha		Dembu	
	M	F	M	F	M	F	M	F	M	F	M	F	M	F
0-9	14	17	9	10	10	8	11	10	11	10	21	23	9	8
10-19	12	13	8	8	9	9	13	11	10	9	24	26	11	7
20-29	9	11	7	7	5	7	15	13	8	7	24	23	9	7
30-39	8	9	6	6	5	4	10	12	5	4	21	19	6	6
40-49	7	8	3	5	3	2	6	9	2	2	15	13	6	4
50-59	3	4	2	2	1	1	2	1	1	2	5	4	3	4
60-69	2	3	2	1	1	—	2	—	—	1	3	2	2	-
70+	-	1	-	-	-	-	-	-	-	-	1	-	-	

[Source - Field work, 1998]

literacy of males and females of the observed villages are obtained by r = (0.6839 ≤ 1)

The above statistical result shows a positive association between males and females literacy of Birhor population. Though in the present situation, the result would not achieve the positive association in respect of males and female literacy of such specific population that means they do not make any indication of positive relationship in respect of their literacy.

Further the author intends to point out the relationship for age component of males and females of Birhors population based on collected information for same seven surveyed villages (table 7.30). The purpose of this statistical study is mainly related with the demographic study stressing on the age component of the two sexes due to variation in the age component. Because some time the age component of persons of any population indicates variation in males and females particularly in case of matrimonial performance.

Keeping such concept in mind, the author makes and endeavours to compute measure of correlation as being formulated by mathematical formula contributed by Carl Spearman's as is expressed in equation II. Using this formula, the following values provide measure of correlation corresponding to each surveyed village. Further the author is more interested to visualise the age component in associated form between male and female of surveyed villages. That means which of the surveyed villages follows more association in case of age component of Birhor population.

Considering such assumptions with regard to the following figures that provide the result for measure of coefficient as being shown below-

Village	*r*
Beti	0.9948.
Jehangutua	0.9709.
Katiya	0.9928.
Kairbera	0.9378.
Pahar Singh	0.9220.
Bigha	0.9901.
Dumbu	0.8753.

From above result, it is clear that Birhor population in each surveyed village provides more association between age of male and females. But in personal observation of such association in each village, the author has

Table 7.31

Birhor-General Population of Sample Villages

Sample Village	Total Birhor Population			Birhor Surveyed Population			Total Birhor Children of 1-12 years		Surveyed Birhor Children of 1-12 years	
	Popualation	Male	Female	Population	Male	Female	Male	Female	Male	Female
Beti	121	55	66	121	55	66	17	21	17	21
Jehangutua	76	37	39	76	37	39	12	12	12	12
Katiya	72	37	35	72	37	35	14	13	14	13
Kairbera	65	34	31	65	34	31	13	11	13	11
Pahar Singh	115	59	56	115	59	56	16	13	16	13
Bigha	224	114	110	112	57	55	28	32	13	14
Dembu	82	46	36	41	23	18	12	11	7	6
Total	755	382	373	602	302	300	112	113	92	90

[Field Work 1998]

obtained the result for village Beti (0.9948) that follows more association in the age components of males and females of this villages and next comes Katiya , where as village Dembu provides the value of r = 0.8753.

Thus, in this way, it can be concluded that the village Beti is more considerable and deserving for the demographic study out of six other surveyed villages.

(3) Consistence of Data

For given study, one of the statistical measures known as coefficient of measure that describes 100 percent measure of dispersions in observational values. The table 7.31 of the present study provides some variation that raised two villages of surveyed Birhor population to total Birhor population for measure of males and females. The same situation exists in the case of children in the 1-12 of age group having found existence of variation in the two villages between Birhors surveyed and total Birhor population. Even in the case of children of the 1-12 age group, the measures of coefficient of variation would be attained for both males and females in raised situation.

The following formula has been explained for coeffecient of variation as a measure of statistic , is given by-

$$\text{Coefficeint of Variation} = \frac{\text{Standard deviation}}{\text{mean}} \times 100 \qquad \text{............ III}$$

Based on given formula the following result for C.V. have been obtained for both male and female—

C.V.

Total Birhor population		Total surveyed Birhor population	
Male	Female	Male	Female
47.31%	48.72%	29.69%	36.26%

Explanation

Since two villages Bigha and Dembu provide variation between accorded data of surveyed village and total Birhor population. therefore

Table -7.32
Birhor Total no. of rooms in different sizes

Name of the Village	Total rooms	8' x 8'	10' x 8'	12' x 10'	10' x 10'	'6' radius x 8' height	15' x 20'	12'x12'
Beti	26	1	12	-	11	-	01	1
Jehangutua	24	2	16	02	1	-	01	2
Katiya	15	3	12	-	-	-	-	-
Kairbera	17	2	01	-	12	-	02	-
Pahar Singh	38	-	01	33	-	-	02	2
Bigha	42	-	30	01	-	11	-	-
Dembu	25	-	02	01	22	-	-	-
Total	187	8	74	37	46	11	06	5

Source: Field work - 1998.

the statistic coefficient of variation (C.V.) has been obtained as shown above to the population. The C.V.'s of surveyed Birhor population to both male and female are obtained less than C.V.'s of the total Birhor population as being found expressed above. Therefore it might be assumed that statistical data procured for surveyed villages are more consistent.

C.V

Total Birhor Children 1-12 age group		Total surveyed Birhor Children 1-12 age - group	
Male	Female	Male	Female
32.55%	44.73%	23.07%	32.06%

Explanation

Since two villages Bigha and Dembu provided variation between accorded data of surveyed Birhor children of 1-12 age - group and total Birhor children of 1-12 age- group, therefore the statistics coeffecient of variation (C.V.) has been obtained as shown above to the population. The C.V.'s of surveyed Birhor children of 1-12 age group to both male and female are obtained less than C.V.' s of the total Birhor children of 1-12 age group as being expressed above. Therefore it might be assumed that statistical data procured for surveyed villages were more consistent.

Table 7.32 deals with living condition in different rooms measured in terms of feet to the Birhor population for surveyed villages which provides variation in number of rooms to the different size . Now the problem arises here that the variation is less due to liking or disliking or deserving or not deserv to the population . In this situation the author makes an effort to classify procure data with respect to different size of rooms. Therefore using the formula, coefficient of variation has been obtained as follows-

	8x8'	10x8'	12x10'	10x10'	6' radius x 8' height	15'x20'	12'x12'
C.V.(%)	80.70	92.43	205.49	99.84	216.56	62.35	74.64

From the above result it is clear that rooms constructed in the size 15' x 20' by following less value of coefficient of variation than others. C.V.'s for different measures of rooms. This result shows that the sample observation of the population like 15'x20' rooms, is found more consistent than others measures.

Table 7.33
Birhor - House Types

Village Name	According to Size Rooms 1	2	3	According to Material					Height of Structure 8' to 10'	11' to 12'	13' & above	Ventilated Yes	No
1	2	3	4	5	6	7	8	9	10	11	12	13	14
Beti	11	12	1	12	-	4	8	-	17	5	2	24	-
Jehangutua	10	6	2	6	-	10	2	-	16	2	-	18	-
Katiya	12	3	-	3	-	8	4	-	14	1	-	15	-
Kairbera	12	2	-	14	-	-	-	-	12	2	-	14	
Pahar Singh	33	-	-	-	33	-	-	-	33	-	-	33	-
Bigha	37	4	-	-	-	30	-	11	40	1	-	30	11
Dembu	22	2	-	-	24	-	-	-	22	2	-	24	-
Total	137	29	3	35	57	51	14	11	154	13	2	156	11

Column No. 5 - Mud Wall and Tiled Roof.
Column No. 6 - Brick Wall and Cemented Roof.
Column No. 7 - Stone wall and Cemented Roof.
Column No. 8 - Stone Wall and Tiled Roof.
Column No. 9 - Vegetative Matter.

Dealing with table 7.33 the collected data followed different characteristic such as number of rooms, rooms made by different materials, height of structure and ventilation. On the basis of these characterised factors the following results for coefficient of variation have been obtained.

Number of rooms

Rooms	C.V.(%)
1	53.60
2	79.95
3	88.09

From the obtained result, room 1 provides consistency in sampled observation than result obtained from other number of rooms. This is concluded that such value is found more consistent with the tribal population and further inference might be drawn that the whole population of the tribe possesses only one room.

Rooms constructed by different materials

Materials -	C.V.(%)
Mud wall and tiled Roof	87.80
Brick wall and cemented Roof	137.71
Stone wall and Cement Roof	121.42
Stone wall and tiled Roof	119.50
Vegetative Matter	216.56

The above result merely reveals that room made of mud - wall and tiled roofs of the Birhor in the surveyed village is more consistent . It has been observed that most of the Birhor population is living in such condition for their residential purposes.

Height of the structure

In continuation of the above study 'Height of structure' has been taken by considerable height such as 8-10, 11-12' and 13' and above. Given below is the C.V. results of different heights of house structure of the Birhor.

Height	C.V.(%)
8-10'	44.45
11-12'	66.56
13' and above	132.40

In observation C.V. for 8-10' is found to be more consistent in respect of height of the structure for Birhor population. By such result an assertion might be made that the Birhor population is found usually living in structure of 8-10' height due to various reasons as finances , facilities and untoward attitude of government administration in respect of their living condition.

Ventilation

Following miserable condition of the Birhor population, the author makes an enquiry about condition of ventilation or non -ventilation living. The required figure followed these two cases-

Ventilation	C.V.(%)
Ventilated	30.55
Non-Ventilated	216.56.

These two results show that the persons of the Birhor population have been living in ventilated house type (Open spaced areas). From such result it is clear that they cannot afford money for construction of houses in case of non-ventilated and at the same time it is also clear that the authority does not seem to be looking into living conditions.

Table 7.34
Percentage of Houses According to their Size

Sample Village	One Roomed Houses	Two Roomed Houses	Three Roomed Houses
Beti	45.83	50.00	4.17
Jehangutua	55.55	33.33	11.12
Katiya	80.00	20.00	-
Kairbera	85.72	14.28	-
Pahar Singh	100.00	-	-
Bigha	90.24	9.76	-
Dembu	91.66	8.34	-

Source : Field Work -1998

Table 7.34 is prepared for percentage of houses according to their size for all seven sample villages. The observation has confirmed variation in different numbers of rooms, in house in each village of all seven surveyed villages. So, in this situation the following figures provide coefficient of variation to the sought consistency of data corresponding to different rooms houses.

House	C.V.(%)
1. Roomed	23.70
2. Roomed	81.68
3. Roomed	179.81

From above result the figures show that one roomed house is found to be more consistent than other cases.

Table 7.35. In light of observing statistical interpretations, Birhors population (living condition, materials of house etc.), numerically stated as below :

Table 7.35
Percentage of Houses According to Building Materials.

Sample Villages	Mud Wall and tiled roof	Vegetative matter	Brick Wall and Cemented roof	Stone Wall and Cemented roof	Stone Wall and tiled roof
Beti	50.00	-	-	16.00	33.34
Jehangutua	33.33	-	-	55.55	11.12
Katiya	20.00	-	-	53.33	26. 67
Kairbera	100.00	-	-	-	-
Pahar Singh	-	-	100.00	-	-
Bigha	-	26.83	-	73.17	-
Dembu	-	-	100.00	-	-

Source : Field Work -1998

Village	C.V.(%)
Beti	73.75
Jehangutua	87.15
Katiya	76.05
Kaibera	178.85
Pahar Singh	178.85
Bigha	119.85
Dembu	178.88

From the above result the surveyed village Beti is found more consistent than other surveyed village.

Table 7.36 - The given table has been prepared for an important study of Birhor population - income of the population. The observation has confirmed that there exists variation in the surveyed villages. Income is assumed in terms of rupees. The following C.Vs. have been obtained to know as consistent in procured data :

Table 7.36
Birhor's Household income Per month (In No. of Household)

Sample Village	Income Group Rs. 100-200 per month	Income Group Rs. 200-400 per month	Income Group Rs. 400-600 per month	Income Group Rs. 600-800 per month
Beti	3	12	9	-
Jehangutua	-	10	7	1
Katiya	-	3	4	8
Kairbera	2	4	8	-
Pahar Singh	4	8	12	9
Bigha	6	19	14	2
Dembu	4	12	5	3

Source: Field Work-1998.

Income (Per months)	C.V.(%)
Beti	61.16
Jehangutua	77.55
Katiya	57.60
Kaibera	68.00
Pahar Singh	34.66
Bigha	64.78
Dembu	71.09

The village Pahar Singh is found to be more consistent than other villages.

Table 7.37

Birhor's Household Main Occupation. (In Number of Household).

Sample Village	Agriculture and Rope making	Labourer	Agriculture and Pension	Only Rope Making	Rope Making and For--est Based
Beti	22	1	1	-	-
Jehangutua	17	1	-	-	-
Katiya	-	-	-	15	-
Kairbera	5	-	-	-	9
Pahar Singh	11	4	-	3	15
Bigha	-	13	-	8	20
Dembu	-	9	-	3	12

Source: Field Work-1998.

Table 7.37. The occupation of population has been classified by different profession such as (a) Agriculture and Rope making, (b) Labourer, (c) Agriculture and pension (d) Rope making only and (e) Rope making and forest based occupation. For these classified occupations of the Birhor population, the following C..V. has been obtained for all seven surveyed villages and the following results show an indication of consistency of data for all the villages. :-

Village	C.V.(%)
Beti	166.72
Jehangutua	168.72
Katiya	128.66
Kairbera	105.00
Pahar Singh	70.91
Bigha	69. 39
Dembu	79.37

The above result shows that two villages Bigha and Pahar Singh are found to possess consistence of data when the entire data are however classified in to different occupations of said population. In addition the village Bigha is found to be more consistent in respect of occupation of the population.

Thus it can be concluded from table -7.37 that the village Bigha follows consistency in procured data.

8

Conclusion

On the basis of available literature on the Birhor, particularly by the sociologists and anthropologists and also on the basis of the personal observation, it can be said with certainty that the sedentary Birhors or Jaghis Birhors live in significant number in Hazaribagh district along with Ranchi, Gumla and other districts of the Chotanagpur region. The habitable limit of the wandering or Uthlu Birhor is geographically confined to the forested area of Hazaribagh, Ranchi, and Gumla districts. It can be said with certainty that since Uthlu still believes in what is called animism , they practice nomadism . Except for the Jaghis Birhor, particularly those who are brought to be colonized in different villages of Hazaribagh, Ranchi and Gumla ,rest of the Birhors, irrespective of whether they are sedentary or migratory, are a little known Jungle tribe, of Chotanagpur region.

There is no doubt that relief necessarily controls Birhors settlement. This is simply a fact that their habitation occurs in the rugged undulating and plateau surfaces of Hazaribagh , Ranchi and Gumla districts which are forested as well. The settlement which sprang after they were colonized by the Govt. agencies, reflects the control of relief features on the nature of their settlement to some extent. The settlement types of the Jaghis Birhor range from semi-compact on the plateau to semi- sprinkled and sprinkled in area of rugged topography of the settled villages, where as the settlement which the Uthlu Birhors temporarily build up conical in shape and which are known as 'kumba' necessarily are isolated hamleted type. These are very transient in nature.There are differences between the settlement of colonized Birhors and non -colonized wandering Birhors. The settlement of the colonized Birhors is to an extent planned because these settlements have been developed under Govt. Welfare programme in the past three decades. The kumbas which are more transient in nature, show influence of the physical features, including relief and forest.Birhors settlement in most of the cases across the Chotanagpur region in general, in the Study area in particular, is rectangular and hollow rectangular though in some cases elongated and circular settlement also occur.

The colonized or the sedentary Birhors do have social organization with patriarchal organization .Their culture does not seem to be more rooted in the territorial specification of the territory of the habitation. This is simply because of the fact that the Birhor territoriality vis-a-vis the cultural landscape is not developed to the extent as has developed what is called landscape in true sense. Nonetheless, the Birhors' cultural life in colonized villages is gaining momentum in terms of family structure, in terms of belief and iconography and in terms of co-habitation. The sedentary Birhors mostly believe in the Hindu way of life and celebrate all important Hindu festivals. In spite of the fact, they also celebrate some of their traditional festival and ceremony. Their areas of habitation have experienced christion missionary activities for long. The Uthlu Birhos have a rudimentary social organization because of their nomadic nature. The concept of youth dormitory is not found at present in the Birhors' society. However, the marriage system more or less resembles the system of other tribes. The marriage between close relatives barring siblings is practiced in the Birhor family. Tatooing was common in past but at present it is not in vogue.

The genre de vie of the Jaghis Birhor necessarily a colonized structure in the sense that they were brought to be colonized order under different Govt. welfare schemes and were settled in villages where other local in habitat thrives with their specific life style to influence the Birhor genre de vie . However their life style to an extent, shows variation in major districts of their concentration, particularly in Hazaribagh, Ranchi and Gumla.

Though the Birhor economy is primitive subsistence features, but in the sample villages their economy is found to be quiet different and distinguishable. In the colonized villages they practice agriculture, in the traditional way but what is distinguishable is their occupation related to rope making. The Govt. provides raw materials i.e. jute free of cost for rope making. The Birhors also collect certain forest based materials, which to a greater extent, sustain their life. In recent years, a significant number of Birhors have been working as labourers in the neighbourhood area and villages. Some Birhors also work in the mines. It can be said with certaintly that their modes of production is now showing certain structural changes- a kind of transformation . This is not like 'economy' being practiced by Uthlu Birhors, it is simply a nomadic activity coupled with hunting and forest gathering.

Although the Birhor population particularly the colonized Birhor population during 30 years, has experienced an increasing trend because of various Govt. welfare schemes, their death rate has declined. The total population of Birhor, according to a study conducted by Bihar Tribal welfare research institute, Ranchi is 5017. This number is recorded by a Sampling done by the Institute in the year 1993. The population in 1961 was 2438, in 1971, 3464 and in 1981, 4377. However the growth of Population during 1961-81 was 1939 and during 1981-1993 was 640. The projected population of Birhor for 2001 and 2011 is 6315 and 7284 respectively. Though the Birhor population has witnessed an increasing trend in the last 30 years, yet the rate of growth is not as fast and rapid as in the case of other tribes in the region. Previously the Birhors were used to be called a vanishing tribe, but with their colonization in villages and Govt. aids, they no longer remain to be called so.

APPENDIX No. - I

The Birhor : Household Schedule

Serial No. of Questionnaire — Date of survey
Name of Village — Thana No.

1. General
   (i) Name of Informant:
   (ii) Religion : Hindu/Christian/Animist.
   (iii) Type of family : Nuclear/Extended/Compound/Others.

II. Family composition.

Sl. No.	Name of Relation with head	Marital Status M/Un. W/S/D	Age	Sex	Edu-cation	Occ-upation Principal	Sub-sidiary
1.							
2.							
3.							
4.							
5.							
6.							

III. Vital statistics.	Year	Male/Female	Relation to Head
Birth in family			
Death in family.			
Age at death of above			

IV. Marriage	Cash	Kind
(i) Bridal fee paid for marriage (give details)		
(ii) Kind of marriage (give details) - Purchase/Exchange/Service/Adoption/Others.		

V. Agricultural Tenure.

(i) Area of raiyati land
(ii) Area of homestead land
(iii) Land mortgages,
(iv) Land leased out
(v) Land leased in,

(vi) Any other land.
(vii) Size of operational holding
(viii) Area of irrigated land
  (a) Perennial
  (b) Seasonal.
(ix) Plough Cultivation area.
(x) Shifting cultivation area,

VI. Agricultural Inputs .

		kg.	Value.
(i)	Seeds		
(ii)	Fertilizers		
(iii)	Insecticides.		
(iv)	Drought animals: Type and No.		
(v)	Implement : Type and No.		

VII. Crops- cultivated in a year

Sl.No.	Name of Crop including vegetable	Area in acres	Seeds used in kg.	production in kg.	Production value in Rs.
1.					
2.					
3.					
4.					
5.					

VIII. Crops Disposal in Kg.

Sl.No.	Name of crop including vegetable	Given to Mahajan against debt.	Sold in market	Kept for seed	Paid in kind to	House consump-tion
1.						
2.						
3.						
4.						
5.						

IX. Live Stock and Poultry owned.

(i) Lows
(ii) Oxen
(iii) She-buffaloes
(iv) He-buffaloes
(v) She-Got
(vi) He-Goat
(vii) Pigs
(viii) Hens.
(ix) Other.

X. Other occupations

		cross annual income	Net annual income
(i)	Service holder: Nature of Service (Charwaha etc.)		
(ii)	Livestock produce		
(iii)	Hunting produce		
(iv)	Sale of forest produce (wood. Fruit grass etc.) Specify.		
(v)	Fishing produce.		
(vi)	Industry- Wearing , Tikkar Koela for Hukka, Basket making, rope making etc. (Specify)		
(vii)	Labourer; Type of employment		
(viii)	Mahua wine making, Quantity		
(ix)	Business - nature of ware		
(x)	Any other		
(xi)	Source of Raw Material and value.		

XI. Marketing :

(i) Frequency to visit and Distance

(ii) Articles sold Type quality per month Value in Rs.

(a)
(b)
(c)

(iii) Article purchased Type Quantity Value in Rs.

per month

(a)
(b)
(c)
(d)

(iv) Number of customers contact per visit;
(v) Any other purpose of visit - visit to mahajan/to Govt.

XII. Consumption pattern.

		Quantity House	Consumed Grown	Monthly Purchased		Total.	
		Kg.	Rs.	Kg.	Rs.	Kg.	Rs.
(i)	Rice						
(ii)	Wheat						
(iii)	Maize						
(iv)	Other cereals						
(v)	Pulses (Name)						
(vi)	Potatoes						
(vii)	Other vegetable (name)						
(viii)	Fish						
(ix)	Meat						
(x)	Eggs.						
(xi)	Milk						
(xii)	Other animals product						
(xiii)	Mustard oil						
(xiv)	Salt.						
(xv)	Species						
(xvi)	Other food items						
(xvii)	Coal						
(xviii)	Firewood/cow dung						
(xix)	Kerosene Oil						
(xx)	Dhotis						
(xxi)	Sarees						
(xxii)	Blankets						
(xxiii)	Chadar						
(xxiv)	Other clothes						
(xxv)	Medicines						
(xxvi)	Bidi/Cigarettes						
(xxvii)	Country wine						
(xxviii)	Other intoxicants.						

XIII Miscellaneous Expenditure

	Monthly	Last year
1. Metal utensils		
2. Earthen Utensils		
3. Furniture		
4. Ornaments (Gold/Silver)		
5. Education		
6. House repair and maintenance		
7. Maintenance of Cattle		
8. Maintenance of other Livestock /Poultry		
9. Religious activities		
10. Marriage		
11. Litigation (Specify)		
12. Transport (Specify)		
13. Other expenses (Specify)		

XIV Indebtedness

	Kind	Last year Cash	Rate of Interest
(i) Loan taken from			
(a) Mahajan			
(b) Grain Gola			
(c) Government			
(d) Others (Specify)			
(ii) Loan repaid			
(iii) Loan out standing			
(iv) Loan given to (Specify)			
(v) Loan realised			
(vi) Loan due to be realised			

(xv) Legal Relations during last year :

Any family member charged by forest department give (reason) Judgment. Acquitted/Fined /jailed.

XV. House Type

a. Height of Structure
b. Material of wall
c. Material of Roof
d. Whether separated cattle shed

e. Number and size of rooms
f. Number and types of windows
g. Number and types of doors
h. Ventilation
i. Utensils (Metal/ Earthen)
j. Agriculture Tools
k. Hunting Implements
l. Dress
   (a) Male
   (b) Female
   (c) Child male
   (d) Child female
m. Ornaments

XVI Government assistance received last year

	Puropse	Type	Amount	Interest
1.	Land Reclamation			
2.	Agricultural Inputs			
3.	House Construction			
4.	Irrigation scheme			
5.	Well construction			
6.	Medicine			
7.	Education			
8.	Industry (Specify)			
9.	Clothes (Specify)			
10.	Any other			

APPENDIX No. II
The Birhor : Village Schedule

Serial Number of Questionnaire	Name of Village	Date Survey
Thana No.	Anchal	
Total Area	Total Tribals	
Total households	Total Tribal Households.	
Total Population	Total Birhor	
Total Workers	Total Birhor households.	

A. Distance of the village (in Km.) from .

(i) Block H.Q.	(vii) Middle School
(ii) Panchayat H.Q.	(viii) High School
(iii) Thana H.Q	(ix) Hospital /Dispensary
(iv) Metalled Road	(x) Doctor/Vaidya
(v) Bus Stand	(xi) Post office
(vi) Electric power line	(xii) Weekly Market

B. Physical Characteristics of Village -

(i) Relief	(a) Area of Upland
	(b) Area of Lowland
(ii) Drainage	
(iii) Soil	(a) Texture
	(b) Fertility
(iv) Land Classification	

C. Village Facilities.

(I) No. of wells	(a) Pucca	(b) Kutcha
(ii) Irrigation facilities	(a) Seasonal	(b) Perennial
(iii) Store House (Size and No.	(a) Pucca	(b) Kutcha,

(iv) Character of village roads: Width/Straight/Twisting.
(v) Character of Drains (describe)
(vi) Community hall (Area and construction)
(vii) Any other local facility (Educational/medical/others)

(viii) No. of total students going to	(a) Primary School
	(b) Middle School
	(c) High School
(ix) No. of Birhor student going to	(a) Primary School
	(b) Middle School
	(c) High School
	(d) Other institutions

D. Settlement Character of Birhor

(i) Settlement type (a) Scattered

(b) Hamleted

(c) Cluster and hamleted

(d) Nucleated

(e) others

(ii) Draw a sketch of settlements and Roads on separate sheet

(iii) Type of house (Predominating types)
- (a) Material of wall
- (b) Material of roof
- (c) Type of windows
- (d) Type of door
- (e) Height of house
- (f) Height of door

(iv) Draw sketch of type house types, plan and elevation

(v) House decoration and painting

E. Total Area under different land uses (year)

- (i) Forest
- (ii) Waste Land (barren)
- (iii) Waste Land (Culturable)
- (iv) Trees and orchards.
- (v) Pastures and grazing land
- (vi) Old fallows
- (vii) Current fallows
- (viii)Net Area Sown,
- (ix) Area Sown more than once
- (x) Types of Irrigation

F. Demographic Data	In total Population		In Birhor	
	Male	Female	Male	Female
(i) No. of live births				
(ii) No. of still births				
(iii) No. of deaths				
(iv) Demographic data of Birhor				

Persons	Male	Female	Child
M + F			1-12 years

(a) No. of household
(b) Total persons
(c) Total workers in

Agricultural labourers
Hunting /fishing/Milkmen, etc.
Mining/Quarrying
Households industry/Large Industry
Construction
Trade/Commerce
Transport/Communication
Other service

(d) Literate Birhor

G. Economic Data

(i) Household income per month — No. of household

Rs. 1 to 200
Rs. 200 to 400
Rs. 400 to 600
Rs. 600 to 800

Over Rs. 800

(ii) Total land owned by Birhor
Household land
Cultivated land
Others.

H. Village needs (Give details)

(1) Education
(2) Health
(3) Road
(4) Posts and Telegraph
(5) Market
(6) Live Stock
(7) Poultry
(8) Grazing
(9) Forest use (fire wood, grass (cutting)
(10) Irrigation.
(11) Agriculture (tools seeds etc.)
(12) Loans
(13) Water supply
(14) Any other supply

I. Government Aid provided (give name of scheme and type)

Welfare scheme	Amount benefited	Household benefited	Persons
(i)			
(ii)			
Relief scheme			
(i)			
(ii)			

J. Material culture of Birhor

(i) Religious rites
- (a) In house construction
- (b) At pregnancy
- (c) At birth
- (d) At puberty
- (e) At marriage
- (f) At death
- (g) Before sowing
- (h) At harvesting.
- (i) Any other.

(ii) Religious beliefs;
- (a) Place of ancestor
- (b) Role of priest

(iii) Agricultural rituals and officials who preside.

(iv) Sacrifice

(v) Place of women in religious rituals

(vi) Bachelors dormitory - role land rituals

(vii) Inheritance and right of property

(viii) Village political organization
- (a) Officials and powers
- (b) Village councils

(ix) Place of women in village society/politics

(x) Divorce procedures and price

(xi) Ornaments

(xii) Tattooing

(xiii) Personal hygiene
- (a) Bath
- (b) Cloth cleaning
- (c) Teeth cleaning

(d) Sweeping
(e) Tobacco

(xiv) Dress of

(a) Male
(b) Female
(c) Male Child
(d) Female Child

K. Changes is culture of Birhors taking place.
(i) In dress (Men/Women)
(ii) In ornaments/tattooing
(iii) In religious ceremonies (birth/puberty /death)
(iv) In bachelor dormitories
(v) In marriage customs and bridal price
(vi) In village council powers
(vii) In religious headman powers
(viii) In place of women in society
(ix) In sacrifice /feast/rituals
(x) In agricultural rituals
(xi) In type of agriculture
(a) Shifting (Kurwa)
(b) Plough (Bagri)
(c) Paddy
(d) Sabai grass
(xii) In marketing practice,
(xiii) In Subsidiary occupations
(xiv) Change due to role of Government officials
(xv) Changes due to transport development
(xvi) Changes due to urban market
(xvii) Change due to education
(xviii) Any other changes

NOTE: Enlarge outline map of village from census hand book, and draw a rough land use map on it showing:
(a) Settlement
(b) Upland fields
(c) Low land fields
(d) Water bodies
(e) Transport line
(f) Forests
(g) Waste land
(h) Any other predominant use.

APPENDIX—III
Concentration of Birhor

	District	Block	Village
1.	Hazaribagh	Sadar	Hupad/Dembu
			Barwar
		Church	Nagadi
			Dasokhanpi
			Balsagraro
		Ichak	Sijhua
			Tilra
			Jarga
		Katkumsori	Telgo
			Telgo
			Degodu
			Kansaro
		Barkagaon	Sathahiya
			Lokuro
			Lokuro
			Chopakalan
			Patango
		Bishungarh	Budhodch
			Bilandi
			Khamwa
			Chalanga
		Barhi	Baratho
			Kewal
		Kevedari	Pagar
		Barkatha	Pagar
			Badohi
			Bangawn
			Jamsati
			Sijursota
			Bariyawan
		Jainagar	Masudho
			Gondil
		Stagawan	Kataia
			Lembo
			Saosdih
		Markacho	Biryandih

		Tilyamon
	Chauparan	Bigha
		Duragadha
		Kathamba
		Jamunia Tandhi
	Patratu	Hetal
		Dahidih
	Kodarma	Jharna kund
		Jiyoradih
		Natwa
		Kantgar
		Phuldariya
		Lokai
		Jamunia Tanr
		Chitarpur
		Papara Tanr
	Ramgarh	Dohakatta
	Mandu	Chainpur
		Sugiro
		Durhasmor
		Gobindpur
		Baladohar
		Masurdih
2. Gumla	Bishunpur	Beti
		Jehangutua
		Katiya
	Chainpur	
	Dumari	
	Raidih	
	Palkot	
	Kamdara	
	Simdega	
3. Ranchi	Tamar	Jargobapukocha
		Budhadih
		Chipi Bandir
		Arhango
	Aranki	Telengadih
	Bundu	Aman Buru
	Silli	Lodhup
	Angara	Pahar Singh

4. Lohardaga	Chanho	
	Senha	
	Kisko	Kharcha
5. Palamu	Balumath	
6. Garhwa	Meral	
	Mandariya	
	Ranka	
7. East Singhbhum	Chandil	
	Patmda	
	Ghatshila	
8. West Singhbhum	Tonto	
	Sonuh	
	Bandgaon	
	Khirchu	
9. Giridih	Gomiyan	Tulbun
		Khan khonda
		Chotki Sinduari
	Dumri	
	Bagodar	Kali Chattan
		Amnari Tanr
		Mand rami
		Piparadih
10. Nawada		
11. Dhanbad		

Source : Oraon, P.C., (ed.), 1994 : Bihar Ke Birhor; Bihar Govt. Welfare Department, Bihar Tribal Welfare Research Institute, Ranchi, pp. 3-6.

Bibliography

Adhikary , A. K.,1984 : Society and world view of the Birhor, A Nomadic Hunting and Gathering community of Orissa, Anthropological Survey of India, Calcutta.

Adhikary, A.K., 1991: 'The tribal world view: Changing perspective' in Baidyanath Saraswati (ed)., 'Tribal thought and Culture, Concept publishing Company, New Delhi.

Ahmad, E., 1965 : Bihar - A physical, Economic and Regional Geography, Catholic press for Ranchi University, Ranchi.

Ashley - Montagu, M.F., 1957 : Anthropology and Human Nature, Porter Sargent Publisher, Boston.

Barclay, G.W., 1958 : Techniques of Population Analysis, John Wiley and Sons, New York.

Bogue , D.J., 1969 : Priniciples of Demography, John Wiley and Sons, New York.

Bichhieri, M.G. , (ed.), 1972: Hunters and Gatherers Today, A Socio-Economic Study of Eleven such cultures in the Twentieth Century, Holt. Rinehart and Washington Inc., New York.

Banton, M.(ed.), 1966: The Social Anthropology of Complex Societies, Tavistock Publication, London.

Baines, A, 1976: Ethnography, Castes and Tribes, Concept Publishing Company, New Delhi.

Barnes, J.A., 1971: Three Style in the study of kinship, Tavistock Publication, London.

Berreman, G.D., 1981: The Politics of Truth, South Asian Publishers Pvt. Ltd., New Delhi.

Bose , N.K., 1972: Anthropology and Some Indian Problems, Institute of

Social Research and Applied Anthropology, Calcutta University, Calcutta.

De La Blache, P.V., 1922 : Principles of Human Geography, New York.

Burman, B.K.R., 1994: Tribes in Perspective, Mittal Publication, New Delhi.

Carter, G.F., 1964: Man and the Land- A Cultural Geography, Holt Rinechart and Winston, Inc., New York.

Chakravorty, B.C., 1981: British Relation with the hill Tribes of Assam Since 1958, Firma KLM Private Ltd., Calcutta.

Choudhary, R.P.C., 1957: Hazaribagh, Bihar District Gazetteers, Secretariat Press, Patna.

Choudhary, G. 1965: Life and Culture of Birhor Tanda, M.A. Thesis, Ranchi University , Ranchi.

Chatterjee, S.P., (Director), 1968: Selected maps from the planning Atlas of the Damodar Valley Region, Explanatory notes, Map.7.

Dalton, E.T., 1872: Descriptive Ethnology of Bengal, Superintendent of Government Printing Press, Calcutta.

Das, T.S., 1987: Life Style Indian Tribes, Vol. I, Gian Publishing House, New York.

Fortes, M., 1969: Kinship and the social order, Roputledge and Kegan Paul, London.

- (ed.), 1962: Marriage in Tribal Societies, Cambridge University Press, Great Britain.

Fox, G.R., 1971: Kin, Clan, Raja and Rule, University of California Press, Bombay, Oxford University.

Fried, H.M.,(ed.), 1973: Exploration in Anthropology, Readings in Culture, Man and Nature, Thomas. Y. Crowell Company, New York.

Furer- Haimendorf, V.C., 1989: Tribes of India, Oxford University Press, New Delhi.

Goody, J., (ed.), 1966: The Development of Cycle in Domestic Groups, Cambridge University Press , Great Britain.

Husain, M., 1996: Systematic Agricultural Geography, Rawat Publication, New Delhi.

Harvey, David, (1969/Ind. Ed.1984): Explanation in Geography, Arnold-Heinemahn, London.

Hagget, Ptter, (1986/2nd. Ed.): 'Human Geography', in R.J.Johnshon, etal; The dictionary of Human Geography, Black Well reference, Oxford.

Kumar, Alok, 1986: Tribal Culture and Economy, Inter-India Publications ,New Delhi.

Keesing, M.F., 1965: Cultural Anthropology, The Science of Custom, Holt. Rinehart and Winston, New York.

Leach, R.E., (ed.), 1968: Dialectic in Practical Religion, Cambridge University Press, Great Britain.

Moore, A., 1978: Cultural Anthropology, Harper and Row, Publishers, New York.

Mair, L., 1983: An Introduction to Social Anthropology, Oxford University Press, London.

Malltiar, K.K., 1991: 'Geology', in Ram, L.N. , (ed.), A Systematic Geography of Bihar, Geographical Society, Department of Geography, Patna University, Patna.

Mandal, R.B., 1979: Introduction to Rural settlement, Concept Publishing Company, New Delhi.

Majumdar, D.N., 1961: Races and Culture of India, Asia Publishing House, Bombay.

Majumdar, D.N. and Madan, T.N., 1986: An Introduction to Social Anthropology, National Publishing House, New Delhi.

Mehra, T.D., 1977: The World View of Indian Tribes, in S.C. Dube, (ed.) , Tribal Heritage of India, Vol. 1, Vikas Publishing House Private Ltd. New Delhi.

Narayan, S., 1988: Tribe in Transition, Inter-India Publication, New Delhi.

Nag, D.S., 1958: Tribal Economy: An Economic study of Baiga, Bhartiya Admijati Sevak Sangh, New Delhi.

Notestein, F.W., 1945: 'Population : the Long View ,' in Sehultz, T. W.(ed.), Food for the world, Chicago University Press, Chicago.

Oraon, Karma , 1988: The Spectrum of Tribal Religion in Bihar, Kishor Vidya Niketan, Varanasi.

Oraon, P.C., (ed.), 1994: Bihar Ke Birhor, Bihar Govt. Welfare Deptt. Bihar Tribal Welfare Research Institute, Ranchi.

Prasad, R., 1988: Tribes : A Study in Cultural Ecology and Tribal Dynamics, Amar Prakashan, Delhi.

Prasad,N., (et al.) , 1961: Land and People of Bihar , Bihar Tribal Research Institute, Ranchi.

Rai, B.K., 1966: Nature and Man : A Study of Interaction Between Man and Forest in Chotanagpur, Ph.D. Thesis, Ranchi University, Ranchi.

Roy, S.C., 1925: The Birhor: A Little Known Jungle Tribe of Chotanagpur, Man in India Office , Ranchi.

Roy, Choudhary, P.C., 1957: District Gazetteer of Hazaribagh, Superintendent of Printing Press, Govt. of Bihar, Patna.

Roy, B.C. , 1989: Tribals of Orissa, The Changing Socio- Economic Profiel, Gain Publishing House, New Delhi.

Roy, Deb.H.L.,1981: A Tribe in Transition, The Jaintias of Meghalaya, Cosmo Publication, New Delhi.

Spencer, Robert, F., (ed.), 1954: Method and Perspective in Anthropology, Oxford University Press, London.

Saxena, R.P., 1964: Tribal Economy in Central India, Firm, K.L. Mukhopadhya, Calcutta.

Saha, S.B., 1986: Tribes of Tripura: A Historical Survey, Rupali Book Store, Agartala.

Sinha, V.N.P.,1976: Chotanagpur Plateau :Astudy in settlement Geography, K.B. Publication , New Delhi.

Singh, R.P., and Kumar,A.,1976: Evolution of Man and Racial study (Hindi), Bihar Hindi Granth Academy, Patna.

Srivastava, H.C., (et al.), 1989: Dependency and Common Property Resources of Tribal and Rural Poor, Commonwealth Publishers, New Delhi.

Saraswati, B., (ed.), 1991: Tribal Thought and Culture, Concept Publishing Company, New Delhi.

Sauer, C.O.,1925: The Morphology of Landscape , University of California Press, Berkeley.

Smith, D.M., 1975: Patterns in Human Geography, Penguin Book Ltd., London.

Singh, K.S., 1985: Tribal Society in India, An Anthropo- Historical Perspective, Manohar Publication, New Delhi.

Singh, K.A. , 1982: Tribal Festivals of Bihar: A Functional Analysis, Concept Publication Company, New Delhi.

Sachchidananda, 1992: Tribal India- Past and Present, Institute of Social Research and Applied Anthropology, Calcutta.

Singh, R.P., 1970 : Geomorphological Evolution of Chotanagpur Highland, NGSI Varanasi.

Shankar,U.,1991: 'The Chotanagpur Plateau', in Ram, L.N,(ed.): A Systematic Geography of Bihar, Geographical Society, Dept. of Gegoraphy, Patna University,Patna.

Singh, R.P. & Kumar, A. ,1970: Monograph of Bihar, Bharati Bhawan, Patna.

Singh, R.L., (ed.), 1989, (Reprint) : India: A Regional Gegoraphy, National Geographical Society, Varanasi.

Sharma, R.K., 1991: 'Vegetation', in Ram, L.N., (ed.),:A Systematic Geography of Bihar, Geographical Society, Department of Geography, P.U., Patna.

Singh, J. & Dhillon, S.S., 1994: Agricultural Geography,Tata Me -Graw Hill Publishing Co. Ltd., New Delhi.

Singh, R.L., and Singh, K.N., (ed.), 1975: Readings in Rural Settlement Geography, National Geographical Soceity, Varanasi.

Singh , R.L., 1975: Meaning and Objectives and Scope of Settlement Geography, in Singh, R.L., and Singh, K.N., (ed.), Readings in Rural Settlement Geography.

Singh, R.B., 1975: Rural Settlement Types and their Distribution: Examples from Varanasi District, India, In Singh, R.L. and Singh, K.N.(eds), Reading in Rural Settlement Geography, National Geographical Society, Varanasi.

Singh, L.R., 1965: Terai Region of U.P., Study in Human Geography, Allahabad.

Trewartha, G.T., (et al.) 1967: Elements of Geography, Physical and Cultural, Mc-Graw Hill Co., London..

Troisi, J., 1979: Tribal Religion, Manohar Publication, New Delhi.

Verma, M.Y., 1986: Problems of Tribal India, Classical Publishing Company, New Delhi.

Verma, K.K., 1977: Culture, Ecology and Population, National Publishing House, New Delhi.

Vidyarthi, L.P.,(ed.), 1959: Anthropology and Tribal Welfare in India, Council of Social and Cultural Research, Bihar.

- 1963: The Maler: A Case study in Nature- Man- Spirit Complex of a Hill Tribe in Bihar, Bookland, Calcutta.

- 1964: Cultural Contours of Tribal Bihar, Punthi Pustak, Cacultta.

- (ed.), 1967: Leadership in Inida, Asia Publication House, Bombay.

- 1969: Cultural Configuration of Ranchi, Bookland, Calcutta.

- 1969: Socio- Cultural Implication of Industrialisation in India : A Case Study of Bihar , Council of Social and Cultural Rescarch , Bihar, Department of Anthropology, Ranchi University, Ranchi.

Vidyarthi, L.P., and Roy, B.K., 1976/ 1985: The Tribal Culture of India, Concept Publishing Corporation, New Delhi.

William, R.,1976: Keywords :A vocabulary of culture and society, Oxford University Press, New York.

Wagner, P.L. and Mikeswell, M. W.,(eds.), 1962: Readings in Cultural Geography, University of Chicago Press. Chicago.

JOURNALS

Adhikary, A.K.,1978: 'Status and Role of Woman among the Birhor: A Nomadic Hunting and Gathering Community of Eastern India,' In Tribal Women in India, Indian Anthropological Society, Calcutta, Publication No. 4, pp.39-44.

Adhikary, Ashim Kumar, 1993: 'The Birhor and their Univese: A Study on Perception and Classification of Objects and Phenomena in a Oral tradition,' Man and Life, Vol.19, No. 1 and 2.

Ahmad, E., 1942: 'Rural Settlement Types in U.P.,' Annals of the Asssociation of American Geographers, Vol. XLII, p. 223-46.

- 1962: ' Indian Village Patterns,'Geographical Outlook, Vol. III, p.11.

Bhattachariya, A., 1953: 'An Account of the Birhor of Palamau,' Bulletin of the Department of Anthropology, Vol. 11, No.2, July, pp. 1-10.

Bose, N.K., 1956: 'Some observation of Nomadic Castes of India', Man in India, Vol.36, pp. 93-98.

Babu, B.V. and Naidu, J.M., 1994: 'Marriage Pattern and Distance among the two Sub-Tribes of Mali of Andhra Pradesh,' South Asian Anthropologist, Vol. 5, Nos. 1-2, pp. 51-53.

Behera, D.K., and Parida ,M., 1990: ' Problems and Treatments of the Aged Among the Plain - Bhuiyans of Orissa,' Journal of Social Research, Vol. 32-33, Nos.1-2, pp. 166-79.

Chib, S.C. ,1995: 'Demographic Dynamics in the Trans Himalayan Tribal Region of Kinnaur H.P.: Perspective on Socio- Economic Implication,' Geographical Review of India, Vol. 57,No.1, pp. 20-28.

Choubey,K.,1994: 'Allopathic and Tradition Health Care Services to Tribal Population of Baster (M.P.), Geographical Review of India , Vol. 56, No.2, pp. 69-76.

Devan, P.K., 1997: 'Tribal Wynad- Past and Present,' Man and Life, Vol, 23, No. 1-2, pp.37-44.

Driver ,W.H.P., 1888: ' Birhors', Journal of Asiatic Society of Bengal, Vol. 57.

DasGupta, S. , 1995: 'Impact of Changing Economy on the Social Life of

Birjia: A Primitive Tribal Group', Man and life, Vol. 22, Nos. 1-2, pp.49-54.

Das Grpta, S., 1992: 'Role of forest on the Socio- Cultural Life of theBirijia, Some Observation ,' Journal of the Indian Anthropological Society, Vol, 27, No.1.pp. 1-6.

Francis, J.V. ,1957: 'Wandering of Uthlu Birhor', Bulletin of Deptt. of Anthropology, Bihar University, pp. 58-65.

Gupta ,S.O., 1962: 'Physique and Nutrition of Tribal People with Special Reference to Tribal Bihar,' Bulletin of Bihar Tribal Research Institute, Vol. 4(1).

Georg, P., 1993: 'Kharia Totemisim,' Journal of the Indian Anthropological Society, Vol. 28, No.3, pp. 221-27.

George,T.C.,1997: 'Descent Organisation and Corporate action among the Mudugas of Kerala', Man and Life , Vol.23, No.1and 2.

Gupta , R.B. and Tiwary, R.S., 1993: 'Haemothological and Clinical Profile in Sickle Cell disease and Beta Thalassaemia of Central India,' Journal of the Indian Anthropological Society, Vol.28, No.2, pp. 151-156.

Ghose, N. C., (et al.), 1996: 'Flow strtigraphy of selected sections of the Rajmahal basalts, Easter India', Journals of South East Earth Science, Vol.13, No.2, pp. 83-93.

Haldar, A.K., 1990: 'Aging Among the Bedia of Ramgarh Hill Range,' Journal of Social Research, Vol. 32-33 No. 1-2, pp. 105-109.

Jana, Lakshma, etal : 1997: 'Dispossession of the Tribal People from their Agricultrual Land: A Case Study of Koras in Midnapore', Man and Life., Vol. 23, Nos.1-2, pp. 85-89.

Kar, R.K.,1993: 'Health Behaviour among the tribes of North- East India', Journal of Indian Anthropological Society, Vol.28,No.2, pp.157-63.

Mukherjee, B.M., and Khatua, N., 1996: 'The Birhor of Madhya Pradesh,' Man and Life, Vol. 22, Nos. 1-2, pp. 13-24.

Mukherjee, S.,1980: 'The Birhor of Bihar and W. Bengal,'Geographical Review of India, Vol. 4, No.2, pp. 48-54.

Munshi, Indira, 1995: 'Tribal Communities in their Natural Environment

: The Changing Context in Western India,' Social Action, Vol.45, No.2, pp. 217-23.

Mathur, Mita, 1995: 'Angami Nagas: Ritural and Environment', Man and Life, Vol.22, No.s 1-2, pp. 33-42.

Malik, Nitin, 1995: 'Loping with Disturbed Physical Environment: A Study on Primitive Tribal Group the Kamars (M.P.),' Man and Life, Vol, 22, Nos. 1-2, pp. 43-47.

Mishra, Miss, Jaya, 1997: ' Nature of food with Reference to Jharkhand Region, Man and Life, Vol. 23, Nos. 1-2, pp. 77-84.

Mishra, P.K., 1969: 'Numadism in India,' Journal of the Indian Anthropological, Vol.4, No. 1 and 2, pp. 79-88.

Mathew, Areepurampil, 1994: 'Tribal stiuation in Singhbhum:A Critique,'Social Change, Vol. 24, Nos. 1-2, pp. 56-59.

Mukhopadhyay, K. 1994: 'Dynamics of Ethinic Identity Maintenance among the Khasi of North - East India,' Journal of the Indian Anthropological Society, Vol.29, No.3, pp. 209-19.

Malhotra, S.B., 1963: 'Kinship Organisation among the Birhors,' Bulletin of the Bihar Tribal Research Institute, Vol. 5, (2)

Naskar, S.K., 1995: 'The Gotul And Its Utility Among the Muria,' Man and Life, Vol.21, Nos. 1-2, p. 19.

Oraon, P.C., (ed.)., 1997: Bulletin of Bihar Tribal Welfare Research Institute , Ranchi, Vol. XXXVI.

- 1994: 'Governemnt Strategies for Tribal development,' Bulletin of Bihar Tribal Welfare Research Institute, Ranchi, Vol.XXXIV, No.1, pp. 1-18.

Prasad, M.,1977: 'Tribal Geography : A Enquiry in to its progress and scope', Geographical outlook, Vol.VIII, p.42.

Rao, M.V.K., (et al.), 1995: 'Ethno medicines of Tribes of Andhra Pradesh', Man and Life, Vol., -21, Nos. 1-2, pp. 1,

Roy, Subhasri, (et al.), 1994: 'Age of Marriage and fertility among kissan Women of Orissa', South Asian Anthropologist, Vol.5, Nos. 1-2, pp. 55-59.

Rizvi, S.H.M., 1988: 'Frequency of Colour Blindness Among Kotwalias A small primitive Tribal Group of S. Gujarat,' Tribe, VolXX, Nos. 1-4, pp.37-41.

Raha, M.K., 1964: 'Demography of the Birhor of West Bengal,' Vanyajati, Vol.12(2).

Roy, S.C., 1917: 'A. Genneral Account of the Birhors,' Journal of Bihar and Orissa, Research Soceity, Vol. 2(2).

Sengupta, S.K., 1992: 'From the Forest to the Market: The mens of subsistence of the Juang,' Journal of the Indian Anthropological Society, Vol. 27, Nos. 1, pp.7-19.

Sen, B.K., and J. Sen, 1955: 'Notes on the Birhors', Man in India, Vol, 35, No. 3, pp.169-75.

Sen, J.,1965: 'Ethnographic Notes on the Birhor,' Bulletin of the Anthropological Survey of India, Vol. 14,pp. 45-58.

Sinha, D.P., 1958 : 'Cultural Ecology of the Birhor:A Methodological Illustration,' Journal of Social Research, Vol, 1, pp. 86-96.

— 1959: 'The Birhor and their World View,' Adibasi , Vol. III, Nos.3-4 pp.17-25.

— 1959: 'Portrait of Birhor Chief,' Jounal of Social Research, Vol. 2, No.1-2,

Sachchidananda, 1965: 'Directed Change among the Birhor,' The Eastern Anthropologist, Vol. 9(1).

Singh, R., 1963: 'Reproductive Life of Birhor Women,' Bulletin of Bihar Tribal Research Institute, Vol. 4, No. 1, pp. 125-42.

Sharma, K.H., 1958: 'How the Uthlu Birhor Make their Living,' Vanyajati, Vol.6(4)

Sen, Soumen, 1994: 'The Seng Khasi experiment' Journal of the Indian Anthropological Society, Vol. 29, No. 3, pp. 203-208.

Saxena, N.C.,1994: 'Impact of Industrialization on the Tribes of Jharkhand,'Social Change, Vol. 24, Nos. 1-2, PP. 85-89.

Singh, S.P., (et al.), 1997: 'Geology of Bihar- An Overview', Souvenir,

Department of Geology, Patna University, Patna, p. 22.

Sinha, V.N.P., 1969 : 'House and house types of the Chotanagpur Plateau,' Geographical Knowledge, Vol. 2, p.91.

Thompson, W.S.,1929: 'Population,' American Journal of Sociology, Vol.34, pp. 959-75.

Toppo , Sita, 1990: 'Aging and the aged in the tribal cultural variances', Journal of Social Research, Vol. 32-33, Nos. 1-2, pp. 123-30.

Vidyarthi, L.P.,1958: 'Cultural Types of Tribal Birhor' Journal of Social Research, Vol.1, p. 77.

—, 1960: 'The Birhor: A Study in Ecology, Economy, and Wandering,' In Selected Paper of the Fifth International Congress of Anthropological and Ethnological Science, Philadelphia.

Glossary

Birhor's Word	**Meaning.**
Apu	Father.
Bau	Husband's elder brother.
Bhakar	Male Monkey.
Buru	Hill.
Binti	To beseech.
Bhegna-Kimin	Sister's son's wife
Bhegni	younger brother's daughter.
Bhagni-Jawai	Sister's daughter's son.
Beti or Kurihon	Daughter.
Bir	Jungle.
Bhusri	Mosquto.
Birhor	Men of Jungle.
Bilar	Cat.
Bapla	Marriage.
Balpos	Adopted child.
Chauli	Rice.
Chura	Flattened rice.
Didi	Elder sister.
Dada	Great-grandfather.
Da	Water.
Era	Wife.
Enga bhakor	Female monkey.
Era	Adult Female.
Gungu	Father's elder brother.
Gara	River/ Stream.
Gapa	To-morrow.
Gahna-Guria	Ornaments.
Herel	Husband.
Hatom	Farther's sister.
Hopon	Son.
Haga	Brother.
Haga Kimin	younger brother's wife.
Haku	Fish.
Harta	Leather.

Hasa-Sunul	Kerosin oil.
Jawai	Daughter's husband.
Jhali	Net.
Jilu	Flesh
Jo	Fruit.
Kaka	Father's younger brother.
Kunya	Well.
Mae	Mother.
Mosi	Mother's younger sister.
Meram	Goat.
Nriyal	Coconut.
Nana	Mother's father.
Pokhara	Tank.
Sing Bonga	Sun - God.
Tanda	Band.
Uthlu	Nomadic

Plate 1 : Birhor Colony, Beti

Plate 2 : Birhor Women, Beti

Plate 3 : Different Age Group of Birhor, Beti

Plate 4 : Church in Birhor Colony, Beti

Plate 5 : Hand Pump in Birhor Colony, Beti

Plate 6 : Tank in Birhor Colony, Beti

Plate 7 : Well in Birhor Colony, Beti

Plate 8 : Tanr Land, Jehangutua

Plate 9 : Birhor Women in Rural Market, Bishunpur

Plate 10 : Don Land, Jehangutua

Plate 11 : Tribal Residential School, Jehangutua

Plate 12 : Old Borha Birhor with net, Jehangutua

Plate 13 : Chehtrapal Birhor and Family, Jehangutua

Plate 14 : Poor House, Katiya

Plate 15 : Birhor's Utensil, Katiya

Plate 16 : Do Bhaya Birhor Colony, Kairbera

Plate 17 : Community Hall, Kairbera

Plate 18 : Newly constructed Birhor's Houses, Pahar Singh

Plate 19 : Community Hall, Pahar Singh

Plate 20 : Birhor's in Rural Market Jonha Angara, Ranchi

Plate 21 : Birhor Colony, Bigha

Plate 22 : Traditional Birhor's Kumba, Bigha

Plate 23 : Newly Constructed Birhor's Houses, Demu

Plate 24 : Old Community Hall, Birhor Colony, Demu